Fundamentals
of
Digital
Machine
Computing

Fundamentals of Digital Machine Computing

GUENTHER HINTZE

Director, Computer Directorate

White Sands Missile Range, N. Mex.

Lecturer in Engineering

Texas Western College

1966

Springer Science+Business Media, LLC

ISBN 978-3-662-39160-0   ISBN 978-3-662-40151-4 (eBook)
DOI 10.1007/978-3-662-40151-4

© by Springer Science+Business Media New York 1966
Originally published by Springer-Verlag New York Inc. in 1966.
Softcover reprint of the hardcover 1st edition 1966

Library of Congress Card Number 66–20377

Title No. 1368

Preface

The first industrial revolution was concerned with the machine solely as an alternative to human muscle. It displaced man and animal as a source of power, without appreciably affecting other human functions. The development of automation which can handle problems of programming on an automatic basis will, to a large extent, condition the entire social and technical life of the future. The picture of the automatic age will be quite different from the picture of any other period. The technical revolution of automation will bring deeper and more incisive changes to man's life than did the first industrial revolution.

The digital computer is the universal machine which has already revolutionized modern technology and which will be the main instrument to render factories and business places automatic. The digital computer has brought increased impetus and new direction to the whole field of applied mathematics and to the description of problems in precisely defined and solvable relations. Since the arrival of digital computers, applied mathematics takes a place of importance at least equal to abstract mathematics. Modern engineers and scientists have become more conscious of the powerful tool of mathematical analysis through the use of computers. Two of the greatest pioneers of digital computers, Norbert Wiener and John von Neumann, have provided not only fundamental ideas for the design of computing devices but also the new concepts of cybernetics and the theory of games, for the formulation and machine solution of problems never fully studied before. The concepts of linear and dynamic programming open the way for compensation and optimization studies hitherto not done in the systematic and conclusive manner possible with modern computers.

The rigorous and exact solution of many problems eluded men before the advent of computers, because the computational work was prohibitive with regard to time and effort.

There was no stimulus to develop mathematical concepts too complicated for paper and pencil calculation. The understanding of complex scientific phenomena, previously not even considered worthy of study, now comes within the grasp of a progressive society. As with other inventions and their consequences, it will take a certain, though short, time to comprehend the full implications and the effect of computers on mankind. One particularly far-reaching consequence is already in full swing, namely the wide-spread efforts to find precise and logical descriptions of hitherto unexplored phenomena and situations, no matter how complicated these descriptions may be, because the machine is there to carry out the mental drudge-work more rapidly and accurately than any person can do.

The discovery and exploitation of new ways for the utilization of computers is spurred by the remarkable advances of the machines and by a closer contact between computer and user. The interest in the digital computer and its astonishing capabilities has penetrated into many professional fields, and the familiarization with computer performance is desired by many people.

This book is a modest attempt to help in this endeavor. It is the outgrowth of class notes developed over several years for a basic course on digital computers, with emphasis on the function rather than the design of the machines. In the rapid procession of digital computer developments, great advances are achieved year after year with regard to electronic components and circuits. The latest concepts of yesterday are often outdated a short time later. The features of computers will continue to change, but it appears that the basic principles underlying the machine operation are not subject to the same drastic variations as specific design characteristics and circuits.

The operating characteristics of digital computers are a fascinating combination of simple logical concepts and the manner in which they are made to perform different functions. The understanding of the actual machine operation in performing these functions should be of interest to the computer user, though he communicates with the machine eventually only through his program. Therefore, the book presents the basic concepts of both the usage and the working of the machine.

Chapter 1 describes, in an introductory way, the universal

role of digital computers and the principal attributes which enable the computer to play this role. Also, the typical systems configuration is presented for the computer as general data processor, and the computer family tree is sketched to give some orientation in the variety of computer developments.

Chapter 2 contains a brief discussion of binary numbers and codes and their representation in the machine. The calculus in the octal number system, as bridge between decimal and binary, and the rules for number conversion are introduced. Since the machine operates with binary numbers and codes, the prospective computer user cannot be spared this brief discussion.

Chapter 3 starts with a discourse about the applicability of logical principles to computers and the logical description of the basic computer elements, leading systematically into the logical synthesis of circuits of increasing complexity. The symbolic logic of Boolean algebra is introduced to the extent required for the discussed computer elements and circuits.

Chapter 4 explains some common arrangements for the arithmetic operations in the machine, using previously introduced logical concepts. Basic considerations for the automatic handling of arithmetic operations are emphasized more than the possible variety of arrangements, though the difference of the operation on binary numbers and codes is shown.

Chapter 5 provides the basis for the further discussion of the usage of the computer, the instruction code of the machine. General remarks about instruction formats and codes precede the introduction of a set of basic instructions for internal operations which are characteristic of many machines. The form of these instructions may vary slightly for different machines, but they are quite universal as to their function, and they refer to real and not hypothetical machines.

Chapter 6 brings the initiation to computer usage proper. Here the reader is shown how elegantly the computer handles practical mathematical problems with that reasonable degree of complexity and looping which make automatic machine computation attractive and worthwhile. First, some programming mechanics (flow charting and coding) are explained, and then realistic programs are discussed in detail for some very common mathematical relations which are used in the solution of many problems. The fact that these programs are now mostly available as subroutines only enhances their wide use-

fulness. Computer utilization and mathematics are insepara-
ble, and the idea of excluding the latter from an introduction
to computer usage is not fair to the future user.

Chapter 7 concludes the book with a glimpse into the fast
advancing field of automatic programming which is concerned
with the development of machine-independent programming
languages and the design of compilers as link between problem-oriented and machine languages. As example for a machine-independent language, the structure of ALGOL is presented. Two of the most essential compiler functions, the
listing and the decomposition process, are explained in detail,
because they will attain great importance also in future computer applications to heuristic and learning processes.

This brief description of the contents of the chapters gives
the reader and the teacher some indication of subjects on
which to concentrate, according to personal or class interest.
When emphais is placed on the usage of the computer, the
study of the arithmetic circuits in Chapter 4 may be omitted,
while the basic discussion of the application of logical principles to computer components and circuits in Chapter 3
should be of general interest. When the introduction is planned
to cover computer workings and usage, Chapter 7, on automatic programming, may be left for extra study. The chapters,
to some extent, are made self-explanatory, with the exception
that Chapter 4 requires the preceding study of Chapter 3, and
Chapter 6 the preceding study of Chapter 5. Chapter 2, on binary numbers and codes, should be perused in any case. Representative problems for the practice and test of students are
added.

The cited references, which provided the main source of information for the basic computer course and this book, contain
the original work of outstanding computer pioneers and ex-
perts to whom the highest acknowledgment and the expression
of sincere gratitude is directed. It is also my pleasant duty to
acknowledge the substantial help and encouragement I have
always had from my colleagues and students, who, by their
challenging questions, helped to clarify presentation and to
concentrate on essentials.

Guenther Hintze
May, 1966

Contents

Chapter 4

Arithmetic Operations of the Machine   74

Chapter 5

The Instruction Code of the Computer   110

Chapter 6

Principles and Examples of Programming   131

Chapter 7

Automatic Programming 177

CHAPTER 1

The Role and
Principal Attributes
of Digital Computers

1-1. THE UNIVERSALITY OF DIGITAL COMPUTERS

Digital computers are, possibly more than any other machines, in a general way responsible for the astonishing technological advances and changes of our time. Other great inventions have produced breakthroughs in special fields, as the wheel, the screw or propeller, and jet propulsion has revolutionized man's movement on land, water or air, and in space. However, the varied capabilities of digital computers ranging from routine filing and ordering to complicated computations and decision making effect and influence development and changes not only in a special field but over a broad range of human endeavors from simple clerical to highly complex engineering and scientific efforts. The forthcoming age of automation is primarily ushered in by the advent of the digital computers which have become of general interest to everyone who recognizes the vital importance of adequately processed and utilized information for efficient work and progress.

To work effectively is to work with adequate information. People, equipped with up-to-date and factual information, always have the advantage over people without this information. But useful information does not come by itself. It is normally imbedded in raw data or messages which are the primeval elements of communication. The content of useful information in messages depends on the organization of the messages. In general, the more probable a message, the less organized it is, and the task of ordering and organizing the content of messages into useful information is, in most cases, not simple. It requires either the processing of large amounts of raw data, or sophisticated schemes for the ordering of messages, or the combination of both.

The broad usefulness of digital computers is based on their capability to transform a collection of data or words into meaningful information, even if the expressions which relate information to data are very complex. The relations to be solved are to a large extent mathematical in nature. The original development of digital computers primarily as computing devices makes them well suited for the solution of mathematical relations. The additional capability for handling large amounts of data, such as listing, ordering, selecting or updating, is gradually being improved. Computers become in a more general way Data Processors with the original computational capability retained but as part of a larger process.

The first precise and very systematic treatment of design specifications for a general purpose digital computer was given by A. W. Burks, H. H. Goldstine, and J. von Neumann[1]. These specifications laid the foundation and gave guidance to the development of machines, intended for the rapid solution of large-scale mathematical problems. It was recognized that the automatic solution of mathematical problems by machines is feasible, if these problems can be translated into the performance of a sequence of logical steps. The same applies to the solution of any other problem which can be defined as a logical sequence of choices and actions.

Therefore, digital computers can basically handle all problems which are logical definable. The first large-scale computers were built to support scientific computations for nuclear research, weapon developments, and other research endeavors requiring the solution of large sets of mathematical equations. Next came computers or data processors for automatic stock and record keeping. At present, electronic data processing equipment is used or planned wherever the fast and systematic extraction of pertinent information from many inputs is required for control or decision making purposes. Manufacturing control, market forecasting, traffic studies and control, airline reservations, computer-aided medical diagnosis, weather prediction, information retrieval in libraries, wargaming, economic or social studies are typical examples.

The use of computers for the solution of such problems is generally not limited by machine capabilities but by the difficulty in formulating a clearly defined mathematical or logical procedure for machine solution. Problems must be reduced to the resolution of equations or analytic algorithms, describing physical processes or, in general, multiple-variable situations in form of mathematical models. In some cases the construction of these models requires a great deal of ingenuity, and one of the most remarkable uses of computers may prove to be the development of algorithms by the computer for the computer.

The power and versatility of modern large-scale digital computing equipment is based on many useful characteristics, among which the logical capability of sequencing operations and making decisions, and the large memory capacity stand out as two principal attributes. It is mainly these attributes that stimulate the contemplations concerning the similarity between the automated digital data processing and the deductive reasoning process of man. Other important attributes are the computational rapidity and the tireless and reliable performance of computers which outclass human capabilities.

1-2. DIGITAL COMPUTERS AS LOGICAL MACHINES

The fundamental idea in the design of digital computers is the concept of an all-or-none machine. Everything, that is to be processed by the machine, must be expressed by one of two symbols, 0 or 1, or by an ordered sequence of these symbols. In the machine the two symbols are recognized by either one of the two possible states of bi-stable elements. The two-state concept characterizes digital computers as logical machines.

In logic, different propositions are confronted with one another and consequences are drawn in the affirmative or negative. A machine with the "on" and "off" or "Yes" and "No" concept permits the drawing of conclusions as simple binary choices. Such machines are able to handle the logical task of channeling orders either in a predetermined sequence or according to actual contingencies developing during the performance of the machine. The series of orders, called the program consists of the logical steps for the operations, notably mathematical operations, and the links between operations.

The all important logical capability of sequencing orders based on binary choices presupposes the two-state concept. As it happened, bi-stable electronic elements appeared also to be the ideal choice for the hardware components, used as building blocks for the computer. Long before the large-scale developments of digital computers got started, a great variety of reliable bi-stable devices had already been built and made available for many technical applications. Computer requirements brought additional impetus to the improvement and perfection of two state elements. The phenomenal advances of digital computers were not thinkable without these elements. For multi-state or even three state elements, comparable high performance characteristics and reliability have not been attained.

The design of digital computers as logical machines with the two-state concept postulates the binary number notation in the machine, with the two symbols, 0 and 1, expressing all numbers. The cumbersome length of numbers in the binary system, requiring about 3.3 times as many digits for the representation of numbers as the decimal notation, must be accepted as a small price for the unique advantages which the two-state logical concept provides with regard to both the problem-solving capability and the physical realization of the machines.

1-3.   LARGE MEMORY CAPACITY

The execution and control of any information developing process depend not only on present data as inputs, but also on data of past experience. Sufficient memory capacity for the storage of such data is of prime importance.

The data handling capability of digital computers has lead to the assignment of new and bigger tasks to the machines, requiring large memories for the storage of increasing amounts of data.

The solution of problems associated with fully understood phenomona allows simplifying approximations and adjustment to given machine capabilities and limitations. The situation is different when problems or phenomona never previously studied are to be explored with the aid of the machine. In this case, every bit of available data must be stored, manipulated and utilized. The computer can provide the basic capability to handle unfamiliar situations which are characteristic of great classes of realistic and important multi-variable processes. The principal barrier to the realization of this basic capability is a limitation on the number of randomly addressable storage cells. Modern computer technology permits this barrier to be overcome by making possible memories of practically any desired size.

The size of memories is generally expressed by the number of computer words that can be stored. Computer words are data words and instruction words. Memory sizes are also stated in terms of characters or bytes which are parts of words. Adjustment to a common reference is required when memories are compared.

All modern computer installations have storage devices internal and external to the machine. The internal memory contains the data on which the computer works and the set of instructions which direct the operation. The external memory stores jobs waiting for execution and bulk quantities of data as files and records from which selected sets are loaded into the computer for processing.

In order to make the speed for memory access and processing circuits compatible, the internal memory shall provide fast access to the individual, randomly addressable storage locations. The major breakthrough for internal computer memories came with the development of tiny ferrite magnetic cores with a nearly rectangular hysteresis loop which can be magnetized in opposite directions and reversed from one direction to the other very fast due to their small size. From these cores randomly addressable memory arrays can be built up for any desired size; arrays for the storage of 4,000, 8,000, and 32,000 words are standard units. The assembly of huge internal memories up to one quarter or one-half million words is being announced for the latest computer models.

The external memory, usually one or several orders of magnitude in size above the internal memory, provides a fast transfer rate of data into the machine and the quick locating of a desired record in the vast arrangement of files. Devices for external memory are magnetic tapes and disks, and magnetic drums, which are finding new usefulness as external memories after having served in the early computers as internal memories.

The capacity of external memory devices depends on physical dimensions of individual units—length of tape, size of disk, diameter of drum—and the number of individual units.

The desire for a short search time sets a limit to the physical dimensions and larger memories are usually arranged by a larger number of units.

Disk storage has the advantage that several disks are easily packed into storage modules while each tape requires its own drive. Disk storage units are built with as few as six operating disks up to models with 25 disks or. 50 disk surfaces. The storage capacity of one disk is determined by the number of tracks and words per track. Typical figures are 500 tracks for each disk and densities of 466 or 974 36-bit words per track.

In addition to the efficiency of packaging, disk storage has the important merit of a low average access time. Access times are between 100 and 200 milliseconds, depending on the motion of the arm to the correct track and the rotation of the desired track sector into the position to read or write the first record called for. In comparison, the locating of records in tape files requires much longer search periods; the random access time for tapes is of the order of a few minutes.

The transfer rate of data from external memory into the machine is normally stated in characters or bytes per second. Characters consist of six bits and bytes of eight bits of information, allowing the packing of two decimal digits in one byte. Typical binary computer words are made up of either six characters or four bytes. The effective transfer rate for tapes depends on the density of characters or bytes per inch, the tape speed, and the unfilled gaps between records. Practical figures are for the density 200, 556 or 800 characters or bytes per inch, for the speed 75, 100 or 112.5 inches per second, and for record gaps .75 and .6 inches. A maximum transfer rate for highest density and speed without record gaps would be 90,000 characters or bytes per second.

This figure is compatible with the transfer rate of disks with low density, which is in the order of 90,000 characters per second or 70,000 bytes per second. On disk tracks, bits are arranged serially resulting in different transfer rates for bytes and characters, while the bits of one character or byte are entered on tape across the width of the tape and subsequently processed in parallel. Disks with higher density have approximately twice the transfer rate. Corresponding tracks of each surface are physically aligned one above the other, forming cylinders of data tracks, which are immediately available with only electronic switching between read-write heads required. Using the cylinder arrangement also, the transfer rate can be multiplied with several read-write heads operating in parallel.

Magnetic drums have the same transfer rate as disks with high density and they are the external memory device, which has by far the lowest access time in the order of a few milliseconds, depending only on the rotational delay to a specific record.

Tapes may be conveniently stored in tape libraries and files for the retention of information. Removable disks are just beginning to come into use. On-line disk and drum units must be loaded from tapes and the information which shall be saved must be removed and placed on tapes. Therefore, magnetic tapes represent still the largest amount of storage applications.

1-4. COMPUTATIONAL RAPIDITY

The speed of computers is primarily a function of the operational characteristics of the hardware components which are used in the realization of computer circuits, as well as of the manner in which these components are inter-connected and controlled. In computer literature, normally three figures related to computer speed are stated: The basic clock pulse repetition rate, the time required for arithmetic operations, and the access time to the memory which is defined as the waiting time between the demand for a word and its transmission from memory.

The basic pulse repetition rate, of particular importance in synchronous machines, has been increased from 125 kilocycles/sec in earlier machines to one megacycle/sec in modern computers in accordance with the faster response of newly developed circuit elements. This increase permits a faster sequence of arithmetic and logical operations.

Figures for arithmetic operations are often quoted with different values for otherwise comparable machines. For example, for the add operation, they may include the processing of both operands, their addition, and the storing of the result, or just the addition of the addend to the already available augend. This simplest add operation required in older vacuum tube computers 12 microseconds and with the access time to the memory for the obtaining of the add instruction from memory a total time of 24 microseconds. Hence, the overall time depends on both the speed of the computing circuits and access time to memory.

The determination of the speed requires for each individual operation the counting of machine cycles for its execution, the intentionally introduced delays to allow for propagation of signals or completion of actions and the number of times information has either to be obtained from or to be placed into memory. For simple operations with short execution time, the exchange with the memory will add relatively more to the total time than for more complicated operations such as multiplication where a series of operations is performed on the operands and where the total time is predominately determined by the speed of the computing circuits.

Computers are sometimes classified according to their speed. Present large-scale vacuum tube computers, called first generation computers, have a memory cycle of about 12 microseconds and an add time of 24 microseconds. So-called second generation, transistorized computers offer a speed advantage due to smaller sizes of the memory cores and more compact circuits throughout; they have about two microsecond memories and an add time of slightly over four microseconds.

The newest or third generation of computers uses microelectronic circuits. Instead of conventional discrete components, the computers utilize circuits with passive elements deposited as thin layers on a ceramic wafer and extremely small active elements made separately and soldered to the wafer. The micro-circuits allow ultra-highspeed switching. Response times for switching circuits for memory access and processing are in the nanosecond region. This increase in speed combined with larger memories makes computers ever more powerful tools for the solution of problems which could not be handled before.

1-5.   GENERAL SYSTEMS CONFIGURATION

In a very general way, digital computers can be considered as highly sophisticated sequential switching devices, which develop numerical outputs Z_i from numerical inputs X_i and according to previously set internal states Y_{i-1} of the device. The internal states and the outputs are functions of a sequence of inputs, consisting of both, the data to be processed and numerically coded instructions which cause the changes of the internal states required for the processing. As a consequence, operations are executed by the computer basically in sequence, and the remarkable processing speed of computers has been obtained by the shortening of the time for individual operations. First generation computers performed 40,000 operations per second, second generation computers 200,000 and more operations per second, and for third generation computers this number is expected to go up to approximately one million.

The internal processing speed of computers is so high that the fast transfer of data to and from the machine has become the major problem for the efficient utilization of computers. The increasing data handling capabilities of computers brought new applications with voluminous amounts of data and the idea of time-sharing the computer by several jobs, placing more and more emphasis on the improvement of the input-output capabilities.

The ultimate measure for the utilization of computers is the overall through-put of data including both the internal processing and the moving of data into and out of the machine. The problem to be overcome is the non-compatibility in speed of the two processes. The internal processing uses exclusively high-speed electronic switching, while the data transmission of input and output devices involves mechanical motion. The arrangement of data channels, which can be considered as some sort of pre-processors, help to alleviate this situation, and the systems configuration, as depicted in Figure 1-1, is now quite common.

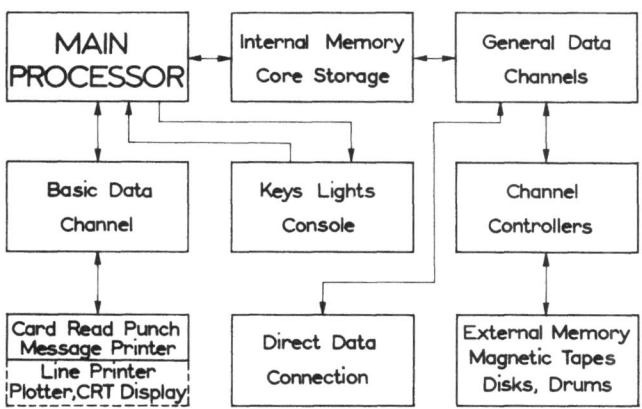

Fig. 1-1. General Systems Configuration

The main processor with its registers for control and operational purposes will be described later when the logical design and the arithmetic operations of the computer are discussed.

The internal memory, which has the extremely fast random access time of a few microseconds, is the place where the demand and supply of data meet. In general, the data channels and the main processor will compete for access cycles to the internal memory. Advanced designs provide control circuits which protect assigned memory areas for simultaneous loading of data into one area and extraction of data for processing from another.

The general data channels transmit information from channel controllers to the machine, rearranging or formatting the information, if necessary, for example from serial transfer to parallel presentation to the memory. Substantial computing time is saved for the main processor, if the data channel handles the assembly of computer words, instruction or data words, which come from input devices by bits or characters, and the disassembly of words to output devices. Processing is then delayed only while data are being moved in or out of core storage. The channel informs the processor of errors in the data transmission and the termination of transfer operations. In advanced machines, data channels may have processing capabilities under the control of a program independent of the activities of the main processor.

Each channel controller has assigned a number of input-output units. The controller selects a satellite unit and relays orders to it, such as rewind, read forward, position access mechanism to a given address. After selection of a unit, the controller transmits data from the unit to the channel which is served by the controller, and relays conditions, such as unit busy or end of record, to the machine through the channel.

A basic data channel is normally provided as input path for prime information, punched on cards, and as output path for messages concerning the computer activity as to job identification, time, completion, etc., which are printed serially by characters on a typewriter. Channel command words, placed in registers of the channel, determine the type of operation and the number of words or characters to be moved; however, the channel is integrated with the processing and control functions of the main processor, and does not operate simultaneously with it, as the general data channels do. Line printers, plotters, and cathode-ray tube displays may be connected to the channel through appropriate interfaces.

Direct data entries and exits for real-time applications are provided through one of the general data channels with the capability to assemble and disassemble words.

On the operator's console, banks of keys make possible the manual entry of data and instruction words into the computer. The contents of main processor registers are displayed in lights on the console.

The arrangement of physical devices according to Fig. 1-1 requires a hierarchy of system programs for the coordination and execution of several operations. An executive system, loaded into internal memory, consists of system programs, such as the interruption supervisor, the main processor scheduler, and program loader. The interruption supervisor coordinates transfer of control between programs after an interruption. The processing scheduler schedules the execution of programs in storage according to control information in the programs. Input-output operations of the general data channels are initiated by the main processor and executed concurrently with other activities of the main processor.

As computer installations are being built up with a growing number of highly developed hardware units, their efficient utilization as an integrated processing facility becomes increasingly dependent on well-designed system programs, which direct the traffic of data through the system and supervise the execution of individual programs.

1-6. THE COMPUTER FAMILY TREE

The family tree of computers, Fig. 1-2, shall provide some orientation in the variety of computers, past and present, and illustrate some typical development trends. The tree shows electronic computers which started families and excludes the early mechanical or electromechanical machines which have no successors.

The first electronic general purpose digital computer, called ENIAC for Electronic Numerical Integrator and Computer, was designed and built by the Moore School of Electrical Engineering of the University of Pennsylvania and placed in operation at the Ballistic Research Laboratories, Aberdeen Proving Ground, Maryland, in January 1947. Since then, the development and production of large-scale, general-purpose

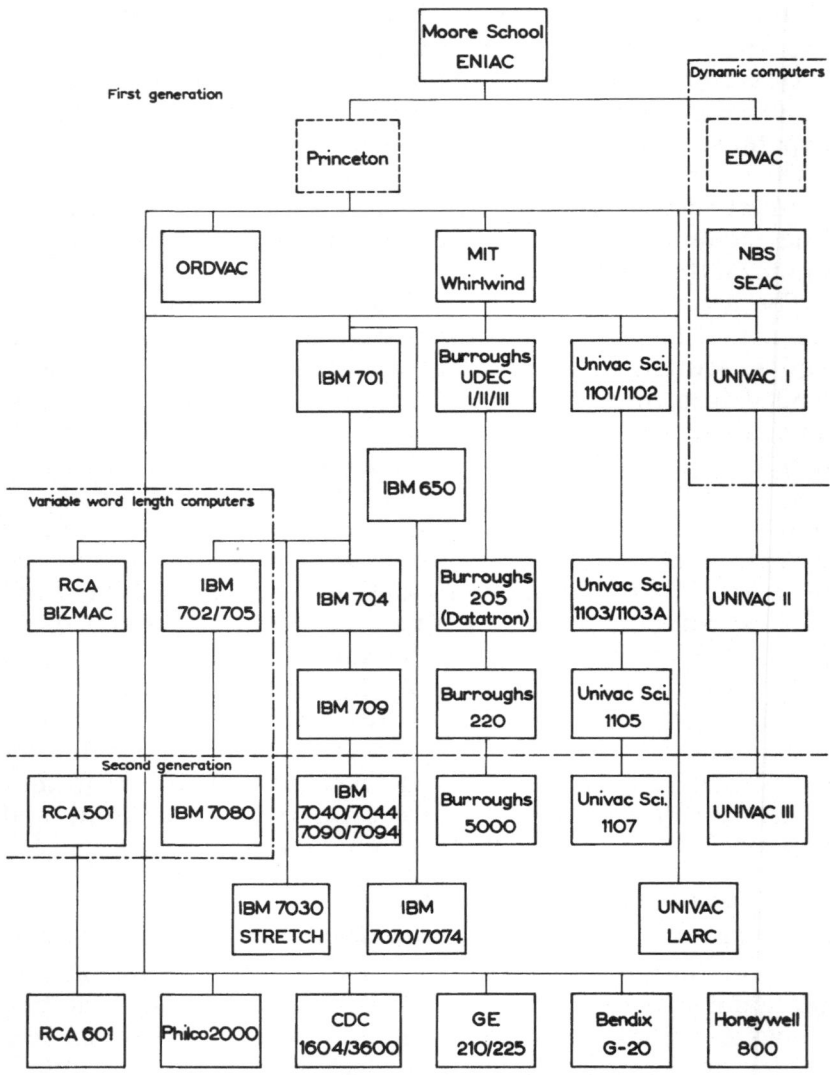

Fig. 1-2. The Computer Family Tree

computers expanded rapidly. Under the sponsorship of the Government, basic design concepts were developed and some early machines were manufactured at educational institutions such as the University of Pennsylvania, the Institute for Advanced Study at Princeton, MIT and Harvard. This work laid the foundation and formed the pattern for present-day scientific computers. Parallel research, performed by industry, added improvements, particularly with regard to the increased input-output requirements for business machines, and in the 1950's digital computers became commercially available in a great variety for scientific and business applications.

The ENIAC used static synchronous types of circuitry which are also employed in the majority of the presently constructed computers. Dynamic circuitry with circulating or dynamic type of storage has been used only in a few machines. The same group which built the ENIAC, proposed later for an Electronic Discrete Variable Automatic Calculator, the EDVAC, dynamic circuits; since this machine was delayed, the credit for the perfection of dynamic circuit concepts in the first large dynamic computer, the SEAC, is given to the National Bureau of Standards. The few dynamic computers were mostly built as one model of a type, with the exception of UNIVAC I, built by the planners of the EDVAC. The UNIVAC I, a dynamic synchronous machine, was built in a larger quantity than other big computers at this time. But its successor, the UNIVAC II, already uses magnetic core storage and is designed as a static machine. It has retained, from the UNIVAC I, the serial processing mode of information bits, which is mostly used in business type machines.

The treatise by Burks, Goldstine, and von Neumann on the design of an electronic computing instrument (Ref. 1) produced a great impact on all subsequent computer developments and led to the "Princeton-type" computer class, which stresses computational efficiency and speed by its logic and the parallel processing mode for the bits of one word. The original design, which was then realized in the ORDVAC by the University of Illinois, called for an asynchronous control with the timing effected by the actual execution time of processes, but the majority of computers which followed the Princeton-type logic, storage and arithmetic arrangement adopted synchronous or clock pulse control from the Whirlwind I, developed by MIT.

Many Princeton and Whirlwind concepts were adopted, particularly by scientific computers represented mainly by the IBM 700 Series and the Remington Rand UNIVAC Scientific 1100 Series. From the IBM 700-line, evolved the business computers 702 and 705, which are serial machines and have variable word and record length, as has the BIZMAC by RCA, a feature that gives these machines increased speed during operation on short words. In line with the demand for increased input-output capabilities for business type machines, both data processors, the IBM 705 and UNIVAC II, have buffers to allow simultaneous input-output and computation. Also, for scientific computers, the trend toward improved input-output operations is pronounced as evidenced by the IBM 709 and the UNIVAC Scientific 1105; the 1105 is a completely buffered version of the 1103A, and the IBM 709 has several synchronized data channels for input and output which are not available with the IBM 704.

Below the dotted line in Fig. 1-2, the so-called second generation or solid-state computers are shown. All existing computer series are gradually being superceeded by an advanced solid-state version. Two giant computers, the IBM Stretch and the Remington Rand LARC, have appeared, and the field of large-scale computers is now being entered by many additional companies. The prevailing trends in the operational modes continue for scientific computers and business data processors to be the same for transistorized machines as they had been for vacuum tube machines. Most of the machines listed in the bottom row may eventually start computer families of their own.

Fig. 1-2 uses computers developed in the USA to indicate typical development trends. The great variety of computers in this country is a good illustration of these trends. However, it must be emphasized that the development of modern high-speed digital computers is a major technical endeavor also in many other countries. In England large computers are being built and developed, for example, by Ferranti Ltd. in cooperation with the Manchester University, leading up to the giant Atlas Computer. For the work in Russia, where the emphasis is being placed on scientific computers, a comprehensive report[2] up to the year 1959 is available. In the common market area in Western Europe, the leader in general purpose computers is the Compaguie des Machines Bull in Paris, which has also entered the field of giant machines with the Gamma 60, while in Germany, besides scientific computer developments at universities, great emphasis is being given commercially to computers for industrial control. In the Far East, where the world's first digital counting and computing device, the famous abacus originated, Japan and China are both forging ahead energetically and successfully with the development of modern digital computers.

CHAPTER 2

Binary Numbers and Codes and Their Machine Representation

2-1. THE BINARY NUMBER SYSTEM

The binary number system is a member of the family of positional number systems, which are constructed according to common principles, and which are distinguished only by the number of digit symbols they use. This number is called the base, or radix of the number system.

The all important common property of positional number systems is the principle of place value, by which each digit symbol, though the symbol is not changed, assumes different values according to the place where it stands. The value of a digit written within a number corresponds to the symbol of this digit multiplied with the position designating power of the base. With the positional concept, a number N to the base b is expressed in the following general form:

$$N = a_n b^n + a_{n-1} b^{n-1} + \ldots + a_1 b^1 + a_0 b^0 + a_{-1} b^{-1} + \ldots + a_{-m} b^{-m} \quad (2\text{-}1)$$

Where the coefficient a_n represents the digit symbol in the n'th digit position of the number N, a_{-1} represents the digit in the first place behind the radical point, etc.

The structure of positional number systems is simple and systematic with the convention that any number raised to the zero power equals one. It sounds strange when in computations a number set zero times as factor results in one, but considering the overall structure of the positional number representation, this convention appears natural and logical.

Table 2-1 shows the numbers 0 through 24 expressed in number systems with different bases. The base number, which may be any integer greater than one, is for each system 10 or the first two digit number, when the base is expressed in the notation of the respective system. For example, the base number of the binary system is $(10)_2$ expressed in the binary system or $(2)_{10}$ expressed in the decimal system.

TABLE 2-1.

THE FIRST 24 NUMBERS IN DIFFERENT NUMBER SYSTEMS

Base $(2)_{10}$ Binary	Base $(3)_{10}$ Ternary	Base $(5)_{10}$ Quinary	Base $(8)_{10}$ Octal	Base 10 Decimal	Base $(12)_{10}$ Duo-decimal
0	0	0	0	0	0
1	1	1	1	1	0
[10]	2	2	2	2	2
11	[10]	3	3	3	3
100	11	4	4	4	4
101	12	[10]	5	5	5
110	20	11	6	6	6
111	21	12	7	7	7
1000	22	13	[10]	8	8
1001	100	14	11	9	9
1010	101	20	12	[10]	a
1011	102	21	13	11	b
1100	110	22	14	12	[10]
1101	111	23	15	13	11
1110	112	24	16	14	12
1111	120	30	17	15	13
10000	121	31	20	16	14
10001	122	32	21	17	15
10010	200	33	22	18	16
10011	201	34	23	19	17
10100	202	40	24	20	18
10101	210	41	25	21	19
10110	211	42	26	22	1a
10111	212	43	27	23	1b
11000	220	44	30	24	20

The distinguishing feature of the systems is, as mentioned before, the quantity of digit symbols with which they operate; this quantity is equal to the value of the base number. Considering base values smaller than 10, the symbols introduced for the decimal system are sufficient to build up other systems. For systems with base values larger than 10, additional symbols are required. In Table 2-1, the additional symbols a and b were used for the duo-decimal system just for simplicity reasons. If this system were ever to come into general use, it would be advisable to devise special symbols for the additional digits in order to avoid confusion between letters and numbers.

The systems are all developed according to the systematic scheme that a digit position to the left is added when all possible combinations to form numbers with the previously given number of digit positions and the available digit symbols is exhausted. For example, in the quinary system, the number 44 is the highest two-digit number which can be formed and the quinary number corresponding to the decimal number 25 would be 100.

At various times in history, systems with the base 5, 20, or others were used. A system with the base 12, which is divisible by 2, 3, 4 and 6, would have advantages for coinage, scales, and weights. Actually, time measurements, such as the division of the day and watch dials, and circular measurements refer to 12 rather than to 10. Yet, the decimal system, though the base number 10 is only divisible by 2 and 5, became the accepted system for hand calculations. But possibly the most remarkable of all number systems is the binary system which can do even the most sophisticated arithmetic operations with just two digit symbols.

The binary system is at the same time the most primitive, and that possessing the highest potential. It is being used by primitive tribes which have not yet reached the stage of finger counting and it opens at the other end of the scale calculational possibilities which could hardly have been visualized a generation ago. The great mathematician and universal genius Leibnitz remarked on the simple and powerful elegance of the binary system that: *"It suffices to draw all out of nothing."*

The binary notation requires but two symbols, 0 and 1, to express all numbers and, as a consequence, permits the performance of arithmetic operations with extreme simplicity. Considering the commutative law, only the following addition and multiplication tables have to be remembered.

The number of binary digits, which are called "bits", increases by one every time the corresponding decimal number reaches the next power of two. In this way, the length of

TABLE 2-2

BINARY ADDITION AND MULTIPLICATION TABLE

$$0 + 0 = 0 \qquad\qquad 0 \times 0 = 0$$

$$0 + 1 = 1 + 0 = 1 \qquad 0 \times 1 = 1 \times 0 = 0$$

$$1 + 1 = 10 \qquad\qquad 1 \times 1 = 1$$

binary numbers increases rapidly, which makes them impractical for hand calculations. However, due to the fact that all numbers can be expressed and all arithmetic operations can be performed using but two symbols, requiring only two states of physical devices, the binary number system became the natural choice for computing machines.

2-2. THE OCTAL SYSTEM AS BRIDGE BETWEEN DECIMAL AND BINARY

All number systems which have a power of two as base can be simply related to the binary system by the grouping of the binary digits. This is particularly of practical interest for the octal system. Due to its closeness to the decimal system, it is conveniently being used to express lengthy binary numbers in a more compact notation which is similarly comprehensible as the decimal. Every octal digit corresponds to a triad of binary digits, as can be seen from the following table.

TABLE 2-3

RELATION OF BINARY AND OCTAL NUMBERS

Binary	Octal
000	0
001	1
010	2
011	3
100	4
101	5
110	6
111	7

From the above table, it is evident that the relation between binary and octal numbers is so simple that no special rules or computations for their conversion are required.

The usefulness of the octal code in computer programming and operation can be best illustrated by a few examples. Since eventually the moving of information through the computer, the activation of circuits, the selection of storage location are all done in binary form by a long sequence of 1's and 0's, represented by pulse or no pulse or two different voltage levels, the octal code is the compact means to write computer instructions or to recognize what is in the computer in a numerical language suited for communication with computer circuits. If a computer has, for example, a storage for 4096 words, it will have storage locations 0 to 4095, corresponding to octal locations 0000−7777. The selected location $(6347)_8$ will be located in the machine by the pulse or potential grouping of (110 011 100 111). A jump instruction expressed in the octal code 41 will be executed by signals in the binary grouping (100 001). If the content of some register in the machine is displayed on the console in binary form, the operator recognizes the octal value for each group of three binary digits. In these and many other ways the octal system is used in the communication with the computer. For computer users the familiarity with both the binary and octal system is important and calculations in the octal system are briefly explained.

In deriving the octal addition and multiplication tables, it must be remembered that the octal system has single digit numbers only from 0 to 7 and that decimal 8, 9, 10 become in the octal system 10, 11, and 12.

TABLE 2-4

OCTAL ADDITION

Augend

	0	1	2	3	4	5	6	7	10	11	12
0	0	1	2	3	4	5	6	7	10	11	12
1	1	2	3	4	5	6	7	10	11	12	13
2	2	3	4	5	6	7	10	11	12	13	14
3	3	4	5	6	7	10	11	12	13	14	15
4	4	5	6	7	10	11	12	13	14	15	16
5	5	6	7	10	11	12	13	14	15	16	17
6	6	7	10	11	12	13	14	15	16	17	20
7	7	10	11	12	13	14	15	16	17	20	21
10	10	11	12	13	14	15	16	17	20	21	22
11	11	12	13	14	15	16	17	20	21	22	23
12	12	13	14	15	16	17	20	21	22	23	24

Addend

TABLE 2-5

OCTAL MULTIPLICATION

Multiplicand

		0	1	2	3	4	5	6	7	10	11	12
	0	0	0	0	0	0	0	0	0	0	0	0
	1	0	1	2	3	4	5	6	7	10	11	12
	2	0	2	4	6	10	12	14	16	20	22	24
Multiplier	3	0	3	6	11	14	17	22	25	30	33	36
	4	0	4	10	14	20	24	30	34	40	44	50
	5	0	5	12	17	24	31	36	43	50	55	62
	6	0	6	14	22	30	36	44	52	60	66	74
	7	0	7	16	25	34	43	52	61	70	77	106
	10	0	10	20	30	40	50	60	70	100	110	120
	11	0	11	22	33	44	55	66	77	110	121	132
	12	0	12	24	36	50	62	74	106	120	132	144

As it is the experience with someone who learns a new language, first thinking in his native language and then translating to the new language before he starts to think in the new language, so it is with the beginner in octal calculus; he will first calculate in decimal and then translate into octal. In this translation, two has to be added to the decimal numbers 8 through 15 in order to obtain the octal number, and then multiples of 2 to the numbers which contain multiples of 8. This means that 4 must be added to 16 through 23, the number 6 to 24 through 31, etc.; when 80 is reached 20 has to be added. In this process, it may become necessary to make two additions before the final octal number is obtained. As examples: 5 x 12 = 62 in octal is derived from 5 x 10 in decimal and adding 6 x 2 because 50 contains 8 six times; or 12 x 7 = 106 in octal is obtained from 10 x 7 in decimal and addition of 8 x 2 because 8 goes eight times in 70 and further addition of 20 because 80 was passed after the first addition. Octal results which are the same as in decimal are easily remembered, but they may be derived in the same systematic way. For example, 12 x 12 = 144 octal is obtained from 10 x 10 in decimal plus 12 x 2 because 8 goes in 100 twelve times and plus 20 because 80 has been passed.

When in octal calculus subtractions are performed with the digit of the subtrahend larger than the corresponding digit of the minuend, borrow and use the following octal Subtraction Table:

TABLE 2-6

OCTAL SUBTRACTION

Minuend

	1	2	3	4	5	6	7
7	2	3	4	5	6	7	0
6	3	4	5	6	7	0	
5	4	5	6	7	0		
4	5	6	7	0			
3	6	7	0				
2	7	0					
1	0						

Subtrahend (left column)

A one borrowed from any column becomes 10_8 or 8_{10} when added to the digit of the minuend in the next column to the right.

As an example, the octal subtraction 2 minus 5 shall be performed. If the one borrowed from the preceding column is taken in decimal as 8_{10} then the calculation in decimal gives $(2 + 8) - 5 = 5$; if the borrow is taken in octal as 10_8 and the calculation done in octal: $(2 + 10) - 5 = 5$; checking with the octal addition table, we see that $5_8 + 5_8 = 12_8$.

2-3. NUMBER CONVERSION

The computer user is often required to convert by hand decimal numbers into octal or binary when going to the machine, and back to decimal for the interpretation of results. The conversion rules for integers differ from those for fractions. The derivation of these rules will explain the reason for the difference.

If a number N represents an integer it can be expressed in positional number systems with the different bases b and d by relation:

$$N = \sum_{i=0}^{m} a_i b^i = \sum_{j=0}^{n} c_j d^j \tag{2-2}$$

where $a_i = 0, \ldots, b - 1$ and $c_j = 0, \ldots, d - 1$ are the elements occurring in the digit positions of the base b and the base d system respectively.

The number N is given in one, say the base b system, and the problem of converting from the base b system to the base d system is the problem of determining the c_j given the a_i, b and d. Writing the number N for the system to which conversion shall be made in polynomial form, we obtain:

$$N = c_n d^n + c_{n-1} d^{n-1} + \ldots + c_1 d + c_0 \qquad (2\text{-}3)$$

If both the left and right member of this equality (2-3) are divided by the base d, an integer part and a remainder are obtained. Every term of the right member divides by the base d with the exception of the term c_0 which is the remainder of the right member. The numerical value of c_0 corresponds to the value of the remainder resulting from the division of the left member N by the base d. After the first division, the integer part of the right member is: $c_n d^{n-1} + \ldots + c_2 d + c_1$, which has the numerical value equal to the integer part obtained in dividing the left member N by the base d. If this integer part is again divided by the base d, a new integer part $c_n d^{n-2} + \ldots + c_2$ and the remainder c_1 are obtained with the numerical values according to the values which result for the integer part and the remainder from the second division of the left member, which is now the quotient of the first division by the base d. In this way, consecutive divisions by the base d yield the coefficients c_0, c_1, c_2, etc., of the number in the d base representation. In this process the division of the number N by the base d has to be performed in the number system in which N is represented.

Therefore, the basic rule for the conversion of integers can be stated as follows: Conversion of integers is obtained by successive division of the number to be converted by the base of the system to which conversion shall be made; in this process the base must be expressed and the calculation must be performed according to the number system from which the conversion is being made. With each successive division the coefficients of the number in the new base system are obtained for the digit positions in the order of increasing significance; after the first division the remainder yields the value of the least significant digit; the remainder of the next division gives the value of the next to the least significant digit, etc. The successive divisions are continued until only a fraction remains. The numerator of this fraction is the value of the most significant digit.

Example 2-1.

Convert the decimal number 896_{10} to octal.

$$8\overline{)896_{10}}$$

$$8\overline{)112} \quad R = 0$$

$$8\overline{)\ 14} \quad R = 0$$

$$8\overline{)\ \ 1} \quad R = 6$$

$$\overline{\quad 0} \quad R = 1 \qquad \text{Result: } 896_{10} = 1600_8$$

The conversion according to the above rule presents no problem for converting from decimal with the calculation performed in decimal calculus. However, the conversion from octal or binary to decimal, using the above rule, is a different problem, because octal or binary calculus is required. The octal calculus was introduced in the preceding section and its application is illustrated in the following example.

Example 2-2.

Convert the octal number $56,361_8$ to decimal; note that the base 10 to which conversion shall be made is 12 in octal.

4513	355	27	2	0
12)56361	12)4513	12)355	12)27	12)2
50	36	24	24	0
63	71	115	R = 3	R = 2
62	62	106		
16	73	R = 7		
12	62			
41	R = 11 in octal, or		Result:	
36	R = 9 in decimal		$56,361_8 = 23,793_{10}$	
R = 3				

An alternate conversion method, avoiding the calculus in an unfamiliar system, is the evaluation as a polynomial, whereby calculation is done according to the number system to which conversion is made. This method is generally preferred when going to decimal, resulting in the following simple conversion.

$$56{,}361_8 = 5(8)^4 + 6(8)^3 + 3(8)^2 + 6(8)^1 + 1(8)^0$$
$$= 5(4096) + 6(512) + 3(64) + 6(8) + 1(1)$$
$$\doteq 20480 + 3072 + 192 + 48 + 1 = 23{,}793_{10}$$

For a fraction F, expressed in two different number systems with the bases b and d, the relation exists:

$$F = \sum_{i=1}^{m} a_{-i}b^{-i} = \sum_{j=1}^{n} c_{-j}d^{-j} \qquad (2\text{-}4)$$

When F is given in the base d system and has to be converted to the base b system, then the coefficients c_{-j} and the bases d and b are known and the elements a_{-i} occurring in the digit positions of the base b system have to be determined. The fraction F, written as polynomial in the system to which conversion shall be made, is:

$$F = a_{-1}b^{-1} + a_{-2}b^{-2} + \ldots + a_{-m}b^{-m} \qquad (2\text{-}5)$$

Multiplying equation (2-5) with the base b we obtain an integer part a_{-1} as a number in the position to the left of the radical point and the fractional part $a_{-2}b^{-1} + \ldots + a_{-m}b^{-m+1}$ to the right of the radical point. In this way the coefficients a_{-1}, a_{-2}, etc., are obtained by consecutive multiplication with the base b. The process is continued until the fractional part becomes zero or, if it does not become zero, until the converted fraction is developed for the required number of digits which give the desired accuracy. Here again, the calculation has to be performed in the number system in which the fraction F is represented.

Example 2-3.
     Convert the decimal fraction $.372_{10}$ to octal to 4 places.

$$.372 \times 8 = 2.976$$
$$.976 \times 8 = 7.808$$
$$.808 \times 8 = 6.464$$
$$.464 \times 8 = 3.712$$
$$\text{Result:} \quad .372_{10} = .2763_8$$

The conversion from octal and binary to decimal is done for fractions, as for the integers, by the evaluation as a polynomial with the calculation performed according to the system to which conversion is made.

Example 2-4.

Convert the binary fraction $.101100_2$ to decimal.

$$.1011 = \frac{1}{2} + \frac{1}{8} + \frac{1}{16}$$

$$= \frac{11}{16} = 0.6875$$

Result: $.1011_2 = .6875_{10}$

The conversion of mixed numbers is done separately for the integral and fractional part applying the rules outlined above. After the conversion, the two parts are combined to form the converted mixed number.

2-4.   BINARY CODES

The straight conversion from decimal to binary yields lengthy binary numbers whose values are not readily identifiable in terms of the decimal notation. When this identification must be preserved, the binary encoding of decimal numbers is applied, whereby each decimal digit is represented by a group of binary digits and the original and coded values are directly correlated digit by digit. Machines which work with these encoded decimal numbers are called decimal machines, while machines which handle numbers in their straight binary representation are called binary machines.

In order to represent ten decimal digits at least four binary digits are required. Since with four bits sixteen numbers can be represented of which only ten are used, the Binary Coded Decimal (BCD) representation is somewhat wasteful with regard to the available combinations of bits. Also, the ratio of 1 to 4 for the required digits in decimal versus BCD representation is less favorable than the 1 to 3.33 ratio for decimal to straight binary which bears out the larger equipment requirement for BCD data handling.

From the many possible encoding schemes, some of the four bit codes which have become particularly popular are listed in the table on the following page.

The first three codes in Table 2-7 are weighted or additive codes where each position in the four bit group represents a particular value. The basic BCD or 8421 code represents the decimal digits by its exact binary equivalent with the advantage that no new combinations need to be remembered. The

TABLE 2-7

BINARY CODES OF DECIMAL NUMBERS

	Basic BCD Bit Weight: 8421	Special BCDfor Minimizing 1's Bit Weight: 7421	Complementing BCD Bit Weight: 2421	Excess-3 Code
0	0000	0000	0000	0011
1	0001	0001	0001	0100
2	0010	0010	0010	0101
3	0011	0011	0011	0110
4	0100	0100	0100	0111
5	0101	0101	1011	1000
6	0110	0110	1100	1001
7	0111	1000	1101	1010
8	1000	1001	1110	1011
9	1001	1010	1111	1100
10	0001 0000	0001 0000	0001 0000	0100 0011
11	0001 0001	0001 0001	0001 0001	0100 0100
12	0001 0010	0001 0010	0001 0010	0100 0101

7421 code minimizes the 1's in the binary coded representation which may be considered desirable by some designers, for example, in error detecting and correcting schemes. The 2421 code is self-complementing, that means the 9's complement is simply found by exchanging 0's and 1's. The decimal digit 6 expressed in the 2421 code is 1100 and its 9's complement, the digit 3 is 0011. The complementing of numbers is a very important operation in digital computers, and ease of complementation is considered essential. Designers will make their choice of code on the basis of the features which appear most important within their overall design considerations.

Despite the advantages of weighted codes, also some unweighted codes are quite popular. This is particularly true for the excess-3 code which is obtained by adding binary 3, or 0011, to the basic BCD. In this way, 1's appear also in the representation of the decimal 0 which can help in number recognition. But more important, the excess-3 code is also self-complementing and in addition it provides for a simple automatic initiation of the corrections which are necessary in the addition of codes.

Each digit of the original information is represented in the computer by a group of bits which are treated in the machine as an entity. The size of this group of bits depends not only on the number of different characters to be coded but also on the amount of the desired identification which shall go with the encoded information. It may be remarked briefly here that it is helpful to adhere strictly to the term "digit" for the original information and to the term binary digit or "bit" for the coded information.

Fig. 2-1 shows as an example the encoding of an information digit consisting of two identification bits and four information or, as they are also called, numerical bits which are the minimum required for the encoding of the ten decimal digits.

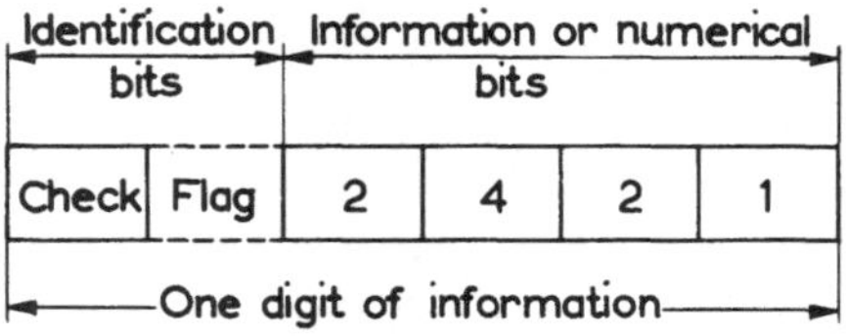

Fig. 2-1. Numerical Code

The number entries in the information bits indicate that the self-complementing 2421 code is considered; when the basic BCD is used, the entries would have to be 8421. When a non-weighted code is applied no numbers at all are shown for the information bits in a portrayal of the code. The check bit is a very common feature, which provides the simplest method for detecting a single bit error by the parity check. Normally the check bit is chosen to make the 1's even for BCD and odd for straight binary.

One additional identification bit, commonly called the flag bit, is often provided to "flag" the sign or the end of a word. It must be recognized that a great amount of information consists of "words," meaning also numbers, with more than one digit. The computer must know which digits belong together to form a word, and a "1" in the flag bit of the most significant digit of the word is used to indicate the end of the word, following the general convention that in a serial processing of digits the most significant digit is processed last. A "1" in the flag bit of the least significant digit stands for minus not only of this digit but also of the entire word to which the digit belongs. If an information word is negative and consists of just one digit the difficulty to recognize the double meaning of the "1" in the flag bit can be overcome by adding another digit with zeros in the information bits; then the "1" in the flag bit of the first digit stands for minus and the "1" in the flag bit of the added digit for the end of the word. The flag bit in Fig. 2-1, is indicated in dotted lines because it is arranged only in the memory of the machine within the information digit while it is processed as a separate character.

Codes which in addition to numbers encode also letters and symbols are called alphanumerical or, in short, alphamerical codes. The 26 letters of the alphabet and the 10 decimal digits make 36 information digits, which require for their binary representation a field of 6 information bits. With 6 bits up to 64 characters can be expressed which provides ample possibilities for additional symbols even if some bit combinations, e.g., binary 10 to 15 are ruled out for usage. The encoding of information digits, as shown in Fig. 2-2, is very often used for alphameric information.

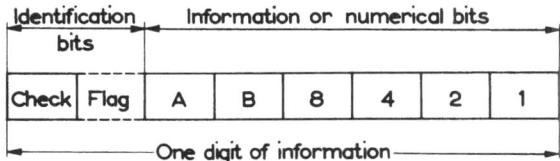

Fig. 2-2.   Alphanumerical Code

The identification bits have the same purpose as described before. Instead of the very illustrative and concise term "flag" other terms such as "word marker" or "indicator" are sometimes used. The information bit field consists of four bits on the right marked with numbers according to the BCD used, and two additional bits on the left marked with letters. When the alphamerical code is applied to numbers the bits A and B are filled with zeros, while for letters and symbols these bits are used to make up the required number of bit combinations.

If a machine must do mostly computation with the handling of numbers and the processing of alphamerical information is only seldom required, the above code would not be very economical because the A and B bits would be carried along without being used most of the time. For such cases another alphamerical code is devised in which the information is represented by two digits of the simple form shown in Fig. 2-1, with provisions for switching between numerical operations mode, using one digit, and alphabetic operations mode, using both digits for the character representation. The term "character" is used generally for one digit of information (number, letter, or symbol), while the term "byte" refers to two decimal digits.

2-5.   REPRESENTATION OF NEGATIVE NUMBERS

Subtraction is the arithmetic operation which involves negative numbers. The common representation of negative numbers, as employed in hand calculation, is the absolute value plus sign notation. This notation is easily manipulated by the human computer who memorizes a subtraction table and uses a borrow table in a fashion similar to the addition table and carry rule for the addition.

It is possible to design computers which will perform subtraction similar to the human using a difference and borrow table which are for binary subtraction as follows:

TABLE 2-8

	Difference Minuend				*Borrow* Minuend	
	0	1			0	1
Subtrahend 0	0	1		Subtrahend 0	0	0
1	1	0		1	1	0

For subtraction it is necessary to determine the relative magnitude of the minuend and the subtrahend. This determination is simple for the human, but it is relatively complicated for a machine. For this reason and in order to avoid in the arithmetic circuitry the inclusion of the logic which implements both, the addition and subtraction tables, machine designers prefer normally to obtain subtraction through the addition of a complement.

The most commonly used complement notations for negative numbers are the ten's and nine's complement in the decimal number system and the corresponding two's and one's complement in the binary number system. The complements Y' of a number Y are defined in the binary system as follows:

$$\text{Two's complement} \qquad Y' = 2^{n+1} - Y \qquad (2\text{-}6)$$

$$\text{One's complement} \qquad Y' = 2^{n+1} - Y - 1$$

where in general n is the number of digits in Y, 2^n is the sign digit, and 2^{n+1} the digit position to the left of the sign digit.

To obtain the two's complement of a binary number with n digits, this number has to be subtracted from 2^{n+1} according to the rules of the binary difference and borrow tables, as shown in the example for binary 6 or 110.

Example 2-5.   Two's Complement of 110

Borrow	1	1		
2^{n+1}	10	0	0	0
subtract	0	1	1	0
2's complement of 110	1	0	1	0

The "1" in the sign digit denotes in this example a negative number represented by the complement.

Without using the binary difference and borrow tables the two's complement can be found by the following rule:

Starting with the least significant digit no digits are changed until after a one is found; the first one is left unchanged; for the remaining digits, ones are replaced by zeros and zeros by ones.

The difference between the two's and one's complement is that according to the given definitions in the expression for the one's complement a one is subtracted in the least significant digit position. For a binary number with n = 3 number digits to the left of the binary point and m = 2 digits to the right of the binary point the term $(2^{n+1} - 1)$ becomes:

2^{n+1}	10	000.00
−	0	000.01
$2^{n+1} - 1$	1	111.11

The general expression for $(2^{n+1} - 1)$ is $(2^{n+1} - 2^{-m})$ which indicates that the one is always being subtracted from the least significant digit. The term $(2^{n+1} - 2^{-m})$ is always a series of ones which corresponds in the decimal system to a series of nines.

In the binary system the one's complement of a number Y is obtained by subtracting Y from this series of one's as shown in the following example.

Example 2-6.   One's Complement of 110

$$
\begin{array}{l|l}
2^{n+1} - 1 \quad 1 & 111 \\
\text{subtract} \quad 0 & 110 \\
\hline
\text{1's complement of 110} \quad 1 & 001
\end{array}
$$

Without going through these steps the one's complement of a binary number can be found by the following rule:

The one's complement for binary numbers is obtained simply by an interchange of ones and zeros.

A few examples of binary subtraction, performed by adding the complement, serve to illustrate the use of the complement notation. Positive differences are obtained when the subtrahend or the number to be complemented is smaller than the minuend, with the result requiring no recomplementing, but the correction of the end around carry for one's complement, in order to restore the one in the least significant bit position.

Example 2-7.   Subtract 11001 − 110 by adding the complement.

For One's Complement			*For Two's Complement*		
binary 25	0	11001	binary 25	0	11001
1's complement of 6 + 1		11001	2's complement of 6 + 1		11010
	0	10010	+ 19	0	10011
end around carry		----- 1			
+ 19	0	10011			

For zero difference 1/8 − 1/8 is used as an example.

Example 2-8.   Subtract .001 − .001 by adding the complement.

For One's Complement			*For Two's Complement*		
binary 1/8	0	001	binary 1/8	0	001
1's complement of 1/8 + 1		110	2's complement of 1/8 + 1		111
negative zero	1	111	positive zero	0	000

The negative zero appears in complemented form as indicated by the "1" in the sign bit position. The true number is obtained by recomplementing the number bits.

Negative differences require no corrections, but only the recomplementation of the result, because the larger number had entered the computation in complemented form.

Example 2-9.   Subtract 1010 − 1100 by Adding the Complement.

For One's Complement			For Two's Complement		
binary 10	0	1010	binary 10	0	1010
1's complement of 12 + 1	0	0011	2's complement of 12 + 1	0	0100
Complemented result	1	1101	Complemented result	1	1110
true result	1	0010	true result	1	0010

2-6.   FIXED POINT NUMBER RANGES

The most common arrangements for the range of fixed point numbers are the placing of the radix point either at the beginning or at the end of the number so that the number appears in the machine either as a fraction or as an integer. For integers, any overflow is always at the left whereby the lost digits are the most significant digits. For fractions, overflows which may develop during multiplication take place at the right for the least significant digits. This advantage has led to the fractional number representation in many machines. The sign bit is usually located to the left of the number bits in the most significant bit position. In the case of the fractional representation, and with the sign bit in the left most position, the binary point follows immediately to the right of the sign bit. After the binary point the number bits follow from left to right in the positions 2^{-1} to 2^{-m} as shown in Fig. 2-3.

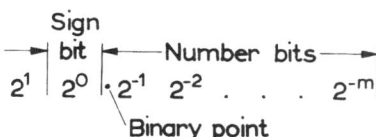

Fig. 2-3.   Positional Arrangement for Fractions

When the arithmetic unit treats the sign bit as an ordinary binary digit the machine will represent numbers in the range from 0 to 2. A carry from the 2^0 position would be lost since the 2^1 position is not provided. This implys such an arithmetic unit carries out addition modulo 2 of positive numbers. Since the 2^0 or zero position is included in the used range and is here also the highest ranking digit order, $2^1 = 2$ indicates the modulus of the finite number system which is handled by the machine. For continuous addition of positive numbers the result may have to be corrected for 2 or for some added multiple of 2.

When the sign digit shall retain its meaning as sign indicator, that is 0 for plus and 1 for minus, then the range for positive numbers x is $0 \leq X < 1$ in the machine. A number $X \geq 1$ would have a one as the sign digit in the machine, indicating a negative number. Therefore, the range for negative numbers $\overline{X}$ in the machine is $1 \leq \overline{X} < 2$ with "1" in the sign digit. In other words, by the use of the sign digit, the precise number range is $-1 \leq X < 1$. It follows that for the defined ranges positive numbers are represented in the machine in correspondence to the real numbers, while for negative numbers a difference of two exists between the real numbers in the range $-1 \leq X < 0$, and their representation in the machine in the range $1 \leq \overline{X} < 2$, or $\overline{X} = X + 2$. The largest positive number in a fractional representation is generally expressed by the term $1 - 2^{-m}$ with all digit positions filled with 1's.

When numbers are represented in the machine as integers, the binary point is placed to the extreme right at the end of the number. Again with the convention of the sign bit in the extreme left position, the number bits for a n-bit computer word are arranged from right to left, from the least significant bit position 2^0 to the most significant number bit position 2^{n-2}, as shown in Fig. 2-4.

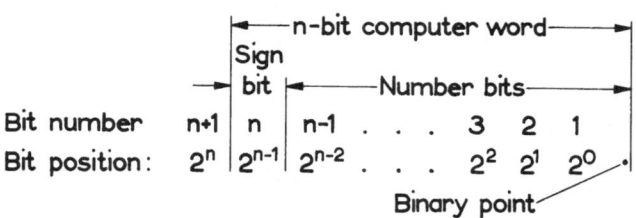

Fig. 2-4. Positional Arrangements for Integers

In the above figure the notations for bit positions and bit numbers are shown side by side in order to indicate clearly the difference between the two of them. The notation of the bit position also expresses the value of the number in the register of the machine when the respective bit position contains a "1" while all other positions are "0". For example, 2^5 represents the 6 bit binary number $(100\ 000)_2 = (32)_{10}$. The sign bit is normally a part of the computer word and therefore, the largest number which can be represented by the number bits is $(2^{n-1}-1)$, with 1's in all number bits. With this the range of positive numbers X which can be represented without overflow into the sign bit is $0 \le X < 2^{n-1}$.

The bit position 2^n and its corresponding bit number $n + 1$ which are indicated to the left of the given computer word are quite important for the consideration of number complementation, though this stage is actually not built in the computer.

2-7. SCALE FACTORING

For fixed point numbers it is necessary to keep continuous track of the magnitude of the numbers, in order to check whether they fall within the given range of the machine; and in order to make the most efficient use of the available bits by minimizing leading zeros and thus increasing precision. Furthermore, the alignment of the radical point for addition and subtraction has to be observed. There is no question that in a fixed point operation the inclusion of the required scale factors results in programming complications. However, there exist sound arguments for fixed point arithmetic and, despite the trend toward the so-called floating point arithmetic, the operation with fixed point numbers will persist to some degree, and a few words about scale factoring are in order.

For machines with fractional number representations any integer x in the range $b^{i-1} \le x < b^i$ must be multiplied by b^{-i} in order to obtain the machine representation of the number. Since the machine then handles the number xb^{-i} instead of x the scale factor b^{-i} must be considered for all operations involving x. If the machine representation of the true value x is denoted by $\overline{x}$, we have the following relations

$$xb^{-i} = \overline{x} \quad \text{or} \quad x = b^i\overline{x} \qquad (2\text{-}7)$$

and in the binary system

$$x2^{-i} = \overline{x} \quad \text{or} \quad x = 2^i\overline{x} \qquad (2\text{-}8)$$

In the practical scaling process first the bounds on the absolute values of the numbers have to be ascertained; then the scale factors for the individual numbers are determined according to relation (2-8); and finally, the true values are replaced by the scaled values in the relations to be solved. If in this process the scale factors do not cancel out, the remaining factor indicates the number of shifts for the correct or most accurate result. While the numerical values of our problems are given in decimal notation, the scale factors have to be determined as powers of 2 because of the binary number representation in the machine.

Example 2-10. Accumulation Scaling

Given three elements with the bounds $|x_1| < 300$, $|x_2| < 600$, $|x_3| < 800$, and the bounds |partial sums $p_i| < 1,000$, and |final sum $S| < 1,000$. Here, with all bounds known, the common scale factor is easily determined according to the largest bound as 2^{10}, since $2^{10} = 1024$. The original equation $S = x_1 + x_2 + x_3$ is scaled to

$$2^{10}\overline{S} = 2^{10}\overline{x}_1 + 2^{10}\overline{x}_2 + 2^{10}\overline{x}_3 \qquad (2\text{-}9)$$

The sum $\overline{S}$ obtained in the machine is converted back to the desired sum by the relation $S = 2^{10}\overline{S}$.

If only the bounds of the elements were known the scale factor would have to be selected according to the sum of the bounds $300 + 600 + 800 = 1700$ as 2^{11}, since $2^{11} = 2048$. With only the bound of the largest element known, we have with the three elements $3 \times 800 = 2400$ for the selection of the scale factor which becomes 2^{12}. This means that with less information on bounds, the original numbers would have to be entered into the machine increasingly shifted to the right, leaving fewer positions for significant bits.

Example 2-11. Multiplication and Division Scaling.

In the case of multiplication the exponents of the scale factors must be added and in division they must be subtracted in order to obtain the scale factor for the product or the quotient respectively.

Given the factors to be multiplied with the bounds $|x| < 1000$ and $|y| < 50$, we obtain their scaled values $x = 2^{10}\overline{x}$ and $y = 2^6\overline{y}$ and the product

$$Z = xy = 2^{10}\overline{x}2^6\overline{y} = 2^{16}\overline{Z} \qquad (2\text{-}10)$$

If, however, it would be known that the product has the bound $|Z| < 4000$, it could be scaled $Z = 2^{12}\overline{Z}$ and the above relation becomes

$$2^{10}\overline{x}2^6\overline{y} = 2^{12}\overline{Z} \quad \text{or} \quad 2^4\overline{x}\overline{y} = \overline{Z} \qquad (2\text{-}11)$$

which means that with the four left shifts we obtain a result with four more significant digits.

In division processes the lower bounds of divisors are also required for accurate scaling.

Automatic scale factoring of fixed point numbers involves the normalizing of numbers with repeated shifts to the left until the first "1" in the number appears in the bit position to the right of the sign bit. The shifts are controlled by a comparison of the sign bit and the adjacent most significant number bit. The number of shifts is stored as the scale factor of the number. After the determination of the scale factor the number may be denormalized again, shifting it back to the original position. The normalizing of numbers is also an important feature of the floating point number representation.

2-8. FLOATING POINT NUMBERS

Floating point numbers are represented in the computer in two parts; the mantissa which contains the number digits and the exponent which expresses the range or scale of the number, similar to the scale factors described above. The scaling by the exponent is normally done so that the mantissa appears as a fraction in the machine with the most significant non-zero digit of the numbers immediately behind the radix point. As an example, disregarding for the moment the sign digits, the 10 digit decimal number 0000000235 may be represented by a 7 digit mantissa and a 3 digit exponent as follows .2350000,003.

For floating point numbers the full range of the mantissa is available to retain as many significant digits as possible, while in the fixed point arrangement many digit positions may be filled with zeros and not be used for significant figures of the number. The counter-argument is that for floating point numbers the available number digits are a priori reduced by the number of digits which have to be set aside for the exponent, and furthermore, that the arithmetic and control circuits for handling two-part words are more complicated.

Floating point numbers provide an extremely wide range for the number representation in the machine. For a fixed point 36-bit computer word with the sign bit in the 2^{35} position, the ranges of numbers x are for integers:

$$-(2^{35} - 1) \leq x \leq 2^{35} - 1 \tag{2-12}$$

and for fractional number representation:

$$-(1 - 2^{-35}) \leq x \leq 1 - 2^{-35} \tag{2-13}$$

If the 36-bit word is expressed as floating point number and it is divided into 28 bits for the mantissa and 8 bits for the exponent, each of which has one bit assigned as sign bit, the following number ranges can be defined. With the mantissa, as is commonly the case, represented as a fraction the positive number range is:

$$2^{-27} \cdot 2^{-127} \leq x \leq (1 - 2^{-27}) \cdot 2^{+127} \tag{2-14}$$

and the negative range is:

$$-(1 - 2^{-27}) \cdot 2^{+127} \leq x \leq -2^{-27} \cdot 2^{-127} \tag{2-15}$$

For the above inequalities it should be remembered that positive and negative number ranges are expressed according to Fig. 2-5:

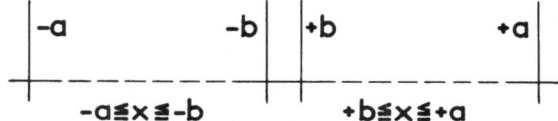

Fig. 2-5.   Positive and Negative Number Ranges

Positive and negative number ranges are normally stated in a combined form for the absolute value of x:

$$2^{-27} \cdot 2^{-127} \leq |x| \leq (1 - 2^{-27}) \cdot 2^{+127} \tag{2-16}$$

If for the smallest number of the range all significant digits shall be preserved this number cannot be expressed by 2^{-27} with one significant digit in the last position with nothing following, since the preceding zeros cannot be considered as significant digits. Then the smallest number must be represented by 2^{-1} with a one in the most significant position followed by zeros preserving the full amount of significant digits for the number. With this consideration the following range is obtained:

$$2^{-1} \cdot 2^{-127} \leq |x| \leq (1 - 2^{-27}) \cdot 2^{+127} \tag{2-17}$$

The above inequalities illustrate the great increase in range obtainable with the floating point number representation, with the number of significant digits, of course, limited to the length of the mantissa. Since in floating point operation the most significant non-zero digit is always shifted to the leftmost position of the number digits, all numbers in the machine are represented with the same number of significant digits.

In the given example one sign and seven number bits are provided for the exponent or power of two, allowing the exponent to change in the range from -127 through 0 to $+127$, because $2^7 = 128$. In some machines the sign bit is used as an additional number bit which would give in our example exponent values from 0 to 255, whereby the exponents appear in the machine biased by a certain amount, say $+128$. This means a negative exponent -30 would appear as $-30 + 128 = 98$, or the largest possible exponent $+127$ appears as $127 + 128 = 255$. The exponent which determines or characterizes the number range is also called the characteristic of the number.

Floating point operations normally take more time than fixed point operations. In addition and subtraction, shifting is required to match the exponents before the operations can be performed. For products and quotients, shifts are necessary to move the most significant digits to the leftmost position. Also, overflows may be more frequent due to the filling of the significant digits, again requiring an increased number of shifts. But, despite this speed disadvantage, the floating point system has become very popular.

2-9. INITIAL COMPUTER INPUT

The previously described binary numbers and codes are used in that portion of the communication with the computer which is done automatically in the input and output circuits of the computer. The user of the computer will then ask the question what communication means and formats are available to him who ultimately has to define the input before the automatic portion of the computer takes over. For the initial transcription into machine-sensible media, mainly punched cards, punched tape, and recently, writing with magnetic ink are used. The punching of holes in cards and tapes is done through key punches in which each key produces a corresponding combination of holes. The direct writing of inputs into the computer from keyboards is only done rarely and for a limited amount of information.

Predominantly, IBM cards are used as the initial input medium. IBM cards have 80 columns and 12 rows. The rows are designated from top to bottom as plus row or sometimes called 12 or high punch, then the minus row, sometimes called 11 or x punch, and from there down rows 0 through 9. With 80 columns and 12 positions in each column the card has 960 hole positions. Fig. 2-6 shows two typical cards for decimal and binary entries.

In the decimal card of Fig. 2-6, the holes or combination of holes are indicated which represent numbers, letters and symbols. This designation of holes for alphanumeric characters goes back to Hollerith, who introduced the use of punched cards. For numbers and the plus or minus sign one hole is punched; for letters, two holes; and for symbols, two or three holes are punched. For the decimal notation, 80 characters can be entered on the card, one for each column, using only a small portion of the $2^{12} = 4096$ possible twelve-bit codes which are available in each column. When numbers are entered in the octal notation the hole designation is the same as for decimal with the exemption that in rows 8 and 9 no single punches are made, because there are not such number digits in the octal system. Instructions are also given in numerical form, e.g., 64 for add, where this number can be either a decimal or an octal number. It is common procedure that the computer is informed by the loading routine about the notation of the subsequent numbers. To distinguish between instructions and data the former are normally loaded first, and then after a card with a special marker, e.g., a single punch in lower left corner, the cards with the data follow.

Binary words are entered in rows, two 36 bit words in a row leaving the columns 73 to 80 unused for words. A card with binary entries is shown in the lower part of Fig. 2-6. There zeros are printed in all 12 rows for columns 1 to 72. The first word is entered at left in row 9, the second at right in row 9, etc., so that we have the word sequence 9 left, 9 right, 8 left, 8 right . . . 12 left, 12 right. On each card, a maximum of 24 full words can be punched. The punching of binary cards is normally not done manually but automatically by the machine, representing a program or the computer output in binary form. Reading of a binary card by the human requires some experience. For the word in the 6 left position in Fig.

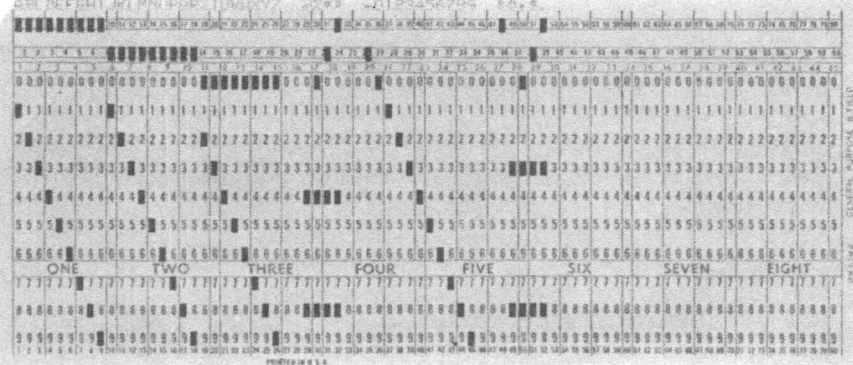

a. Decimal Entries

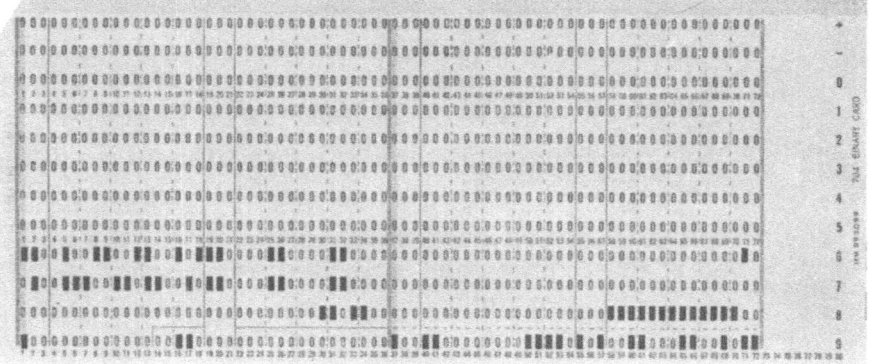

b. Binary Entries

Fig. 2-6. Typical IBM Cards

2-6, the octal equivalent is read as $(623145606060)_8$ which gives an order of magnitude appraisal of the binary word.

The punched card is almost universally used as the initial input medium to computers, and partially as a record of programs and computer outputs. The card reading rate of equipment has been increased from 200 to approximately 800 to 1000 cards per minute, while the punching speeds are still around 250 cards per minute. These speeds are not compatible with the data processing speed of the computer itself, particularly considering the card punch as an output device. Therefore, the use of cards is mostly restricted to serve as initial input, when a program is assembled and debugged for the first time.

PROBLEMS

2-1. Compute in octal calculus:

7432	6421	3256	4567
−4674	−5637	+4365	+5431

2-2. Convert 647_{10}, 792_{10} to octal; 118_{10}, 503_{10} to binary; 24_8, 476_8, 101010_2 to decimal; $.468_{10}$ to octal 6 places; $.5625_{10}$ to binary 4 places; $.07785_{10}$ to binary 8 places; $.622_8$, $.111_2$, $.110011_2$ to decimal 6 places; 961.85_{10} to octal with 6 fractional places; 34.74_8 to decimal 4 places.

2-3. Explain the common features and the differences of the 8421, 7421, and 2421 code.

2-4. Show and explain how for the excess-3 code the initiation of the required add-correction works, using $(4 + 3)$ and $(7 + 8)$ as examples.

2-5. Perform binary subtraction by adding the complements of the negative numbers for $22 - 7$; $6 - 25$; $20 - 8$; $6 - 18$; $7/8 - 1/16$; $9/16 - 15/16$; $5/8 - 1/4$; $1/2 - 1/2$.
a. Using one's complement,
b. Using two's complement.

2-6. Sketch the number ranges for computer words with 24, 36, 49 bits including sign bit for fractional and integer representation.

2-7.   Scale for fractional machine representation $A = \dfrac{a\,b\,c}{d\,e}$ for the given bounds $|a| < 100$; $|b| < 150$; $|c| < 300$; $200 < |d| < 400$; $500 < |e| < 1000$, and the implied maximum bound $|A| < 45$.

2-8.   Rescale problem 2-7 for given $|de| < 200{,}000$ and $|ab| < 10{,}000$, and the implied maximum bound $|A| < 30$.

2-9.   Scale for fractional machine representation after factoring the polynomial $P(x) = a + bx + cx^2$ for the given bounds $|a| < 4$; $|b| < 2$; $|c| < 2$; $|x| < 4$.

2-10.   Rescale problem 2-9 for the additional given bound $|P(x)| < 30$.

2-11.   Give the octal values of the binary words in the punched card shown in the upper part of Fig. 2-6.

2-12.   Determine the maximum character rates for magnetic tapes with densities of 200 and 600 characters per inch and speeds of 75 and 100 inches per second.

2-13.   Determine the effective character rates for the tapes of problem 2-12 with 600, 1200, 1800, and 2400 characters per record.

CHAPTER 3

The Principles
of Logic in Computers

3-1. RELATIONSHIP OF LOGICAL CONCEPTS TO COMPUTER CIRCUITS

Digital computers are essentially comprised of bi-stable electronic and electromechanical elements. The complexity of computers arises from the large number and the interconnection of these elementary components. But in its entirety the computer is still merely an aggregate of rather simple devices that assume either one of two states at any given time. Since the momentary conditions of the elements are represented by only two possible states the concepts of logic apply to the determination of the input-output relation of the elements.

The language and principles of formal logic are concerned with the truth or falsity of statements and their combinations. The logic of classes considers whether elements are members of particular classes or not, whereas the logic of propositions considers whether propositions are true or false. The latter one is mainly applied in computer logic. The validation of propositions compounded from simple statements depends on the so-called logical connectives of the statements. Three important connectives, also extensively used in computer circuits, are the conjunction that makes a proposition true if and only if all compounded statements are true, the disjunction that makes a proposition true if either one or more of the compounded statements are true, and the negation that makes a proposition true if the opposite or inverted statement is false.

The principle of duality and the precise definition of logical connectives are concepts of logic which make them ideally suited for the analysis and synthesis of digital computer circuits consisting of two-state elements. However, the application of these logical concepts to computer design would not have become such a generally accepted practice if logical thoughts had not been symbolized and formalized in an algebraic fashion. The logicians of old used in the systematization of their ideas complex linguistic statements, while in symbolic logic statements, classes, and propositions are expressed by symbols, letters, graphs, tables and equations as they are used in mathematical systems.

3-2. BOOLEAN ALGEBRA AS SYMBOLIC LOGIC

The transition from the linguistic logic with its pitfalls of semantics in language to the symbolic or mathematical logic has been effected particularly by the monumental work by George Boole[3] titled, "An Investigation of the Laws of Thought on which are Founded the Mathematical Theories of Logic and Probabilities". This work, published in 1854, was regarded for many years as no more than an interesting theoretical novelty. Much later, in 1928, a classic text on the same subject by Hilbert and Ackerman[4] was published. The year 1938 is generally considered as the date when this new knowledge of the exact analytical treatment of logical problems began its widespread application in practical engineering fields. In that year Claude E. Shannon[5] of the Bell Telephone Laboratories published a paper titled, "A Symbolic Analysis of Relay and Switching Circuits". In this paper Shannon shows how electrical switching networks can be described concisely and analyzed exactly by means of symbolic logic or Boolean algebra as this system of mathematical logic is called in commemoration of its prime originator.

In the past twenty years digital equipment has gained ever increasing importance in the fields of information processing, computers, and automatic control. Symbolic logic has become a vital tool for the designers of these complex digital systems, providing the means for a rigorous treatment of such design problems as correct, unambiguous data flow and the minimization of the amount of equipment required to perform a given function.

The salient feature of the mathematical-logical system of Boolean algebra is the principle of duality. While in ordinary algebra the letter symbols representing variables can have numerical values ranging from plus to minus infinity, the variables of Boolean algebra can assume only either one of two states. This corresponds directly to the concept of logic where every statement can be either true or false. In the Boolean algebra the symbols for the two states of the binary variables are 0 and 1, and in the practical computer circuits these states are represented either by two different voltage levels, or by different leads or terminals, or by the presence and absence of a pulse.

As in every mathematical system, the Boolean algebra is based on certain assumptions or postulates which specify characteristics of the system. The basic principle of duality can be stated by a postulate in the following form:

$$x = 0 \text{ if } x \neq 1 \qquad (3\text{-}1)$$

$$\text{or} \quad x = 1 \text{ if } x \neq 0$$

This postulate can also be considered as the definition of a binary variable.

Other postulates specify relationships associated with operations or connectives. The logical connectives "AND" for conjunction and "OR" for disjunction are expressed algebraically by the symbols $\cdot$, Λ, $\cap$ and $+$, V, U respectively. Due to their familiarity the symbol $\cdot$ for logical AND and the symbol $+$ for logical OR are used throughout this text. For the basic operations of AND and OR the following relations are postulated:

$$0 \cdot 0 = 0 \qquad (3\text{-}2)$$

for   AND $\qquad 1 \cdot 0 = 0 \cdot 1 = 0$

$$1 \cdot 1 = 1$$

$$0 + 0 = 0 \qquad (3\text{-}3)$$

for   OR $\qquad 1 + 0 = 0 + 1 = 1$

$$1 + 1 = 1$$

It must be clearly understood that the above relations have been defined for logical and not for numerical algebra. The fact that only the last equation under (3-3) differs from conventional algebra should not be misleading (numerically binary 1 plus binary 1 gives binary 2 expressed by 10). In all relations (3-2) and (3-3) 0 and 1 express states, not numbers, and the symbols $\cdot$ and $+$ stand for logical connections and not for algebraic operations in the conventional sense. The relation $1 + 1 = 1$ expresses that the righthand member will be true if either one of the lefthand members is true.

The third important connective, also widely used in computer circuits, is the negation which may be written formally:

$$0' = 1 \quad \text{or} \quad 1' = 0 \tag{3-4}$$

This postulate introduces the concept of inversion or complementation which is indicated by the prime attached to the state. Expression (3-4) states that 0 and 1 are opposite states and that they become equal if either one of them is inverted.

It is interesting to note that the principle of duality is developed in Boolean algebra to the point that any postulate can be converted to another by interchanging 0's and 1's, and the connectives $\cdot$ and $+$.

Further Boolean connectives are equivalence, implication, and tautology. If for two Boolean variables B_1 and B_2 the proposition $B_1 B_2 + B_1' B_2'$ is true then B_1 and B_2 are equivalent, or $B_1 \equiv B_2$, because both variables have to be either true or false to make the proposition true. For the proposition $B_1' + B_2$ it is said that B_1 implies B_2, or $B_1 \supset B_2$, because if B_1 is true (B_1' is false) B_2 must be true to make the proposition true. Tautology is the proposition $B + B'$ which is always true independent of the state of its components.

As a logical consequence of the postulates, theorems may be derived from which some of the most important and useful are presented in the following section.

3-3. SOME USEFUL THEOREMS OF BOOLEAN ALGEBRA

One set of theorems is a direct extension of the postulates with the binary variable x introduced in the above equations. In this way we obtain corresponding to (3-2):

$$x \cdot 0 = 0 \tag{3-5}$$

$$x \cdot 1 = x$$

$$x \cdot x = x$$

and corresponding to (3-3):

$$x + 0 = x \tag{3-6}$$

$$x + 1 = 1$$

$$x + x = x$$

or using (3-4):

$$x + x' = 1 \qquad (3\text{-}7)$$

$$x \cdot x' = 0$$

All these theorems can be proven by perfect induction, substituting for x the two possible values 0 and 1. In (3-7) the primed value x' is, of course, opposite to that of x. The equations for $x \cdot x$ and $x + x$ can be extended to:

$$x \cdot x \cdot x \cdot \ldots = x \qquad (3\text{-}8)$$

$$x + x + x + \ldots = x$$

For relations with more variables the commutative, associative, and distributive law hold true. For two and three variables also some other interesting relations result.

$$x + xy = x, \text{ because } x(1 + y) = x \qquad (3\text{-}9)$$

$$x + x'y = x + y, \text{ because}$$
$$x(y + y') + x'y + xy = x(y + y') + y(x + x') \qquad (3\text{-}10)$$

$$xy + yz + zx' = xy + zx', \text{ because}$$
$$xy + yz(x + x') + zx' = xy(1 + z) + zx'(1 + y) \qquad (3\text{-}11)$$

The last relation is so powerful in eliminating redundant terms that it is worthwhile to remember also the product of sum form of this relation:

$$(x + y)(y + z)(z + x') = (x + y)(z + x') \qquad (3\text{-}12)$$

The preceding relations show that any binary function may be expressed as a disjunctive combination of conjunctions (3-11) or as a conjunctive combination of disjunctions (3-12). Either of these two general forms can be derived for given functions. These forms are also called sum of products and product of sums when algebraic terms are used.

The basic concept of negation is generalized by De Morgan's theorem:

$$(x + y)' = x' \cdot y' \text{ or } (x \cdot y)' = x' + y' \qquad (3\text{-}13)$$

This theorem states that the inversion or complementation of a function is accomplished by the inversion of the variables as well as of the logical connectives.

3-4. BASIC ELEMENTS OF THE COMPUTER

It has been stated that computers are built up from a few simple devices and that the complexity of computers is only a consequence of the large number and the intricate connection of these devices. It is important first to understand clearly what these devices or building blocks of the computer are before discussing the more complicated circuits which are synthesized from the basic elements.

In the operation of the computer the information is channeled through a maze of many different paths and in this process it is also necessary to provide means which will open or close these paths according to the presently desired data flow. This then indicates that we need two basic types of elements, one which interconnects the paths and another which enables or disables the paths. The former, the connecting elements, decide where and in what combination the information shall flow; they are called decision elements. The latter, the enabling elements, are activated by control information and they have to remember this information at least long enough to perform their enabling function; therefore they are called memory elements. These memory elements are not to be confused with the main memory or storage of the computer where information is only stored and where no modification or operation on the information takes place.

At the points where several inputs come together it must be established if an output shall be passed on to the next circuit only when all the inputs are high or when any one of the inputs is high. This corresponds directly to the logical connectives of AND and OR and the elements which realize the connectives are called AND gates and OR gates. The latter, which is always open and does not have the typical open-closed characteristics of a gate, is also called a mixer. The negation concept is realized by NOT gates for the inversing of one variable and by INHIBIT gates, a modified version of the AND gate where a high inhibiting input closes the gate. All gates are one-directional devices. The preferred physical elements for their construction are at present solid state diode rectifiers although they may also be built from tubes or transistors. Figure 3-1 shows commonly used symbols for the four gates which are the essential decision elements of the computers.

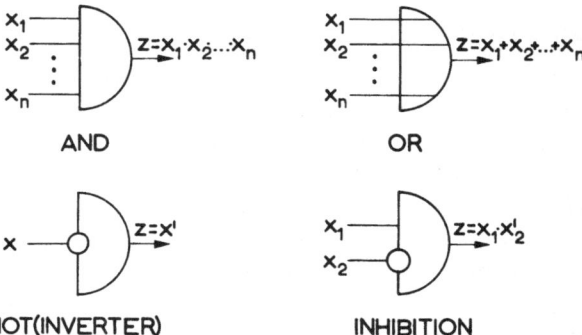

Fig. 3-1. Symbols for Gates

The temporary memory elements accomplish their gate controlling activity based on the information which is temporarily stored in them, or in other words according to the momentary conditions, 0 or 1, to which they have been set just prior to performing their function. The natural elements for such operation are toggle switches, or popularly called flip-flops. The most commonly used flip-flops are the simple set-reset type with "1" obtained by set and "0" by reset, and the trigger type flip-flop which in addition to the set-reset feature has a third, the trigger input by which the flip-flop can be flipped from its present to the opposite state. All flip-flops have two outputs, one for the 1-state and one for the 0-state, however both may not always be connected to other circuits. The output which is high indicates the state of the flip-flop. Symbolic pictures of the flip-flops are shown in Figure 3-2.

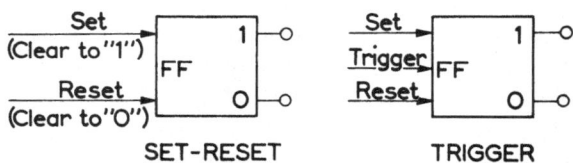

Fig. 3-2. Symbols for Flip-Flops

The described decision and memory elements are called the basic logical elements of the computer. Their combined operation in the computer which is typical for the build up of many computer circuits is illustrated in Figure 3-3.

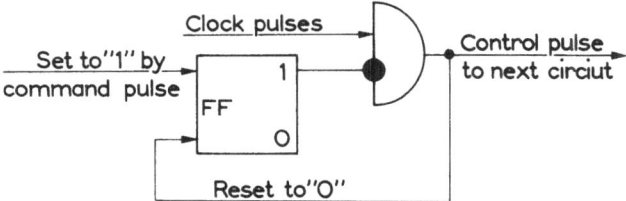

Arrows indicate pulses, and solid circle at gate input "enable" or voltage level.

Fig. 3-3. Combination of Decision and Memory Element

The AND gate is probed by clock pulses at regular intervals determined by the pulse repetition rate of the computer. If this rate is, for example, 500 kc then the interval between two successive pulses is two microseconds. The pulses can pass through only when the gate has been opened or enabled by the flip-flop set to "1". The pulse which passes through as a control pulse to the next circuit resets the flip-flop to "0" through connection with the reset line, thus closing the gate automatically and making another pass through the gate depend on commands which have to appear on the set line of the flip-flop. Typical timing figures for presently used circuits, coordinating pulses and voltage levels, are pulse width .25 microseconds, response time for flip-flop approximately 1.5 microseconds, and pulse intervals 2 microseconds. This provides flip-flop response slow enough for a complete pulse to pass and fast enough to block the next pulse. Higher pulse rates require, of course, correspondingly faster responding flip-flops.

3-5. LOGICAL DESCRIPTION OF BASIC ELEMENTS

The logical description of the elements which represent the logical connectives is simple because here only the momentary relationships of the inputs and the output has to be considered. The relation can be described by a truth table or table of combinations in which the output condition is listed for all possible combinations of the input variables. Two binary variables have $2^2 = 4$ possible combinations, and 3 variables $2^3 = 8$ possible combinations, etc. The truth table has as many rows as there are possible combinations. If some combinations are not permitted they are omitted from the truth table reducing the number of rows accordingly.

TABLE 3-1

TRUTH-TABLES for AND, OR, and NOT gate

AND gate			OR gate			NOT gate	
Inputs		Output	Inputs		Output	Inputs	Output
x_1	x_2	$z = x_1 \cdot x_2$	x_1	x_2	$z = x_1 + x_2$	x_1	$z = x_1'$
0	0	0	0	0	0	0	1
0	1	0	0	1	1	1	0
1	0	0	1	0	1		
1	1	1	1	1	1		

These tables may appear trivial because the listed algebraic equations for the outputs z give a briefer, more concise symbolic description of the gates. The value of the table of combinations becomes fully evident in situations where the output function is not given a priori as in the simple case of individual gates. When the action of circuits consisting of several elements is described by a verbal statement the listing of the given input-output relations in a table of combinations is very helpful in the derivation of the algebraic equation for the circuit.

This may be illustrated for the simple case of deriving the symbolic or algebraic expression for the previously described action of flip-flops. Here the situation is more complicated than for gates because the output or present condition of flip-flops depends not only on the inputs but also on the previous condition of this memory device. Though the algebraic expression describing the flip-flops could be derived by sheer reasoning, the table of combination leads more systematically to the desired result.

Due to the delay in flip-flop action the output appears approximately one clockpulse (actually a little bit less than one clockpulse) later. Therefore the subscripts are introduced to differentiate between the previous condition of the flip-flop Y_i and the present or output condition Y_{i+1}. The set, reset, and trigger inputs S_i, R_i, T_i are in time correlated with the flip-flop condition which exists when these input pulses are applied. On the left side of the tables all possible combinations of the inputs and the time correlated flip-flop conditions are listed, while under output the states are entered which the flip-flop assumes according to the previously described actions. That is, set pulses set to "1" and reset pulses to "0" disregarding

TABLE 3-2
TRUTH TABLES FOR FLIP-FLOPS

SET-RESET			TRIGGER		
Previous Condition	Inputs	Output	Previous Condition	Inputs	Output
Y_i	S_i R_i	Y_{i+1}	Y_i	S_i R_i T_i	Y_{i+1}
0	0 0	0	0	0 0 0	0
0	0 1	0	0	0 0 1	1
0	1 0	1	0	0 1 0	0
1	0 0	1	0	1 0 0	1
1	0 1	0	1	0 0 0	1
1	1 0	1	1	0 0 1	0
			1	0 1 0	0
			1	1 0 0	1

the existing state of the flip-flop, and trigger pulses change the existing state. Input pulses shall never occur at two or three inputs simultaneously. Therefore these combinations are not listed in the above tables. The condition that S_i and R_i can never be "1" at the same time is expressed algebraically for the set-reset flip-flop by:

$$S_i R_i = 0 \qquad (3\text{-}14)$$

and for the trigger flip-flop by the relations:

$$S_i R_i = S_i T_i = R_i T_i = 0 \qquad (3\text{-}15)$$

From the truth tables the equations are derived which specify the logical characteristics of the flip-flops. For the set-reset flip-flop the input combinations of rows 3, 4, and 6 give as a result the output "1". Writing the unprimed variables for their 1-state and the primed variables for their 0-state we obtain:

$$Y_{i+1} = Y_i' S_i R_i' + Y_i S_i' R_i' + Y_i S_i R_i' \qquad (3\text{-}16)$$

Rearranging terms and reducing according to given theorems:

$$Y_{i+1} = S_i R_i' (Y_i' + Y_i) + Y_i S_i' R_i'$$

$$= S_i R_i' + Y_i S_i' R_i'$$

$$= R_i'(S_i + S_i' Y_i) = R_i' S_i + R_i' Y_i$$

Then introducing $S_iR_i = 0$, rearranging and reducing again:

$$Y_{i+1} = R_i'S_i + R_i'Y_i + S_iR_i$$

$$= S_i(R_i' + R_i) + R_i'Y_i$$

we obtain finally the characteristic equation for the set-reset flip-flop:

$$Y_{i+1} = S_i + R_i'Y_i \tag{3-17}$$

Equation (3-17) states algebraically that an output state Y_{i+1} of "1" will be obtained either by a set pulse S_i or when the previous state Y_i of "1" has been left unchanged by the non-occurence of a reset pulse which is expressed by the conjunction $R_i'Y_i$.

For the trigger flip-flop the output state of "1" is obtained according to the input combinations of rows 2, 4, 5, and 8. Therefore:

$$Y_{i+1} = Y_i'S_i'R_i'T_i + Y_i'S_iR_i'T_i' + Y_iS_i'R_i'T_i' + Y_iS_iR_i'T_i' \tag{3-18}$$

Rearranging, introducing $S_iR_i = S_iT_i = R_iT_i = 0$, and reducing:

$$Y_{i+1} = S_iR_i'T_i'(Y_i' + Y_i) + S_i'R_i'T_i'Y_i + T_iS_i'R_i'Y_i'$$

$$= S_iR_i'T_i' + S_iR_i + S_iT_i + S_i'R_i'T_i'Y_i + T_iS_i'R_i'Y_i' + T_iS_i + T_iR_i$$

$$= S_i(R_i + R_i'T_i') + S_i(T_i + T_i'R_i') + S_i'R_i'T_i'Y_i$$

$$+ T_i(S_i + S_i'R_i'Y_i') + T_i(R_i + R_i'S_i'Y_i')$$

we finally obtain the characteristic equation for the trigger flip-flop:

$$Y_{i+1} = S_i + R_i'T_i'Y_i + T_iY_i' \tag{3-19}$$

This equation expresses the fact that the 1-state is obtained for the output either by a set pulse or by a previous 1-state left unchanged by reset and trigger pulses or by a trigger pulse when the previous condition was in the 0-state. After having obtained the characteristic equation, one may wonder about the necessity of the rather lengthy process starting with the table of combinations. However, it must be stated that this process is the most systematic approach, safeguarding against the omission of terms or the introduction of incorrect or superfluous terms.

It is evident that the derivation of algebraic equations from the table of combinations leads first to rather lengthy expressions because all terms which determine the output are listed separately with the corresponding input combinations. Those terms have then to be combined as much as possible in order to obtain a simplified expression which will describe not only a single element but also circuits with several elements most concisely providing the basis for the realization of circuits with the least amount of equipment. Therefore, the techniques which have been developed for the simplification of logical functions are very important and they are briefly mentioned in the following section.

3-6. MINIMIZATION OF LOGICAL FUNCTIONS

The two basic minimization methods are algebraic and graphic. The algebraic method, used in the preceeding section, manipulates a given function with the help of the theorems of Boolean algebra until all the possible combining, simplifying, and eliminating of terms has been done. Some people have gained great proficiency in the use of this method, recognizing which additional terms may have to be introduced to facilitate simplifications, which theorems may be most helpful in this process, and when no further simplification of a given expression is possible. Experience will also help when the algebraic expression is derived from the table of combinations. Considering Table 3-2, the truth table for the trigger flip-flop, it can be seen that in rows 4 and 8 the same input combination $S_i R_i' T_i'$ produces an output "1" for both the Y_i state of "0" and "1", therefore the state of Y_i has no effect on these outputs. The two 4-literal terms representing row 4 and 8, introduced in equation (3-18) as the second and fourth term, were eventually reduced to one 3-literal term. The experienced circuit designer would have made this simplification immediately when writing the algebraic equation from the truth table. He would have used the entries in the table for a quick, preliminary survey of possible redundancies.

The graphical methods develop fully this concept of the adjacent states. Two states or two combinations of binary variables are adjacent when they differ only in the state of one variable. The algebraic combination of two adjacent states results immediately in the elimination of one variable according to part 1 of theorem (3-7). In one way or another all graphical methods provide means to facilitate the recognition of adjacent states. Two slightly different mapping methods were developed by Veitch[6] and by Karnaugh[7] which are very useful for the simplification of functions with up to four variables. For functions with five or more variables charting methods are used as originally developed by Quine[8] or somewhat modified by McCluskey. The book by Samuel H. Caldwell, "Switching Circuits and Logical Design" (*see* Bibliography) gives a thorough treatment of the algebraic and graphic simplification methods which are only briefly mentioned here.

3-7. LOGICAL SYNTHESIS OF COMBINATIONAL CIRCUITS

Combinational circuits are formed for the combination of logical connectives; therefore, they are merely built up from gates which represent the connectives. The present output of those circuits is a function only of the present inputs.

If combinational circuits are realized by relays the contacts have to be arranged in the following way for the representation of the logical AND and OR. For the transmission concept of a network the logical AND is realized by serial contacts because all contacts have to be closed for transmission, and logical OR by parallel contacts because then the closing of any one of the contacts gives transmission. With regard to the hindrance concept the contact arrangement is opposite, with serial contacts for OR and parallel contacts for AND.

Electronic gates which are now used almost exclusively for the connectives in computer circuits permit a wide variety of input combinations at each gate and with this a great flexibility in the arrangement of the gates to form combinational circuits. When germanium diodes or other solid state rectifiers are used for the construction of gates, the not quite ideal electronic characteristics of the diodes make it desirable to minimize the number of cascaded gates. Therefore, wide use is made of the fact that the derivation of any given binary function from its truth table leads either to the sum of products form or to the product of sums form according to the development of the function for the "1" or "0" entries in the table. Equations (3-16) and (3-18) in section 3-5 were derived as sum of products according to the "1" entries. Either of these two general forms results basically in only two levels of gating structure, with the sum of products form representing the function by a group of AND gates whose outputs are brought together into an OR gate or with the product of sums form which represents the function by a group of OR gates whose outputs are combined in an AND gate.

This shall be illustrated by the logical description of a circuit into which the BCD representation of the ten decimal digits is fed and which shall have an output of "1" only when the number of 1's at the inputs is even. Decimal 0 is represented by the code 1010, which is quite customary since in BCD this combination is ruled out for decimal 10. The following table of combinations contains only the entries for the input variables A, B, C, D which are permissible.

TABLE 3-3

TRUTH TABLE FOR CIRCUIT WITH OUTPUT 1 FOR EVEN NUMBER OF 1'S AT INPUT

Inputs				Output
A	B	C	D	Z
1	0	1	0	1
0	0	0	1	0
0	0	1	0	0
0	0	1	1	1
0	1	0	0	0
0	1	0	1	1
0	1	1	0	1
0	1	1	1	0
1	0	0	0	0
1	0	0	1	1

The output function for the 1-states of Z is written as a sum of products:

$$Z = AB'CD' + A'B'CD + A'BC'D + A'BCD' + AB'C'D \quad (3\text{-}20)$$

and for the 0-states of Z as a product of sums;

$$Z = (A + B + C + D')(A + B + C' + D)(A + B' + C + D)$$
$$(A + B' + C' + D')(A' + B + C + D) \quad (3\text{-}21)$$

By using the 0 values of the output transmission we have to introduce the primed value for the variables which appear as 1's in the input combinations and the terms are multiplied to make the output transmission zero if any one of the terms is zero. Both derivations lead to the same transmission function which may be checked by multiplying out equation (3-21).

The above equations have no adjacent terms which differ only in the state of one variable, therefore no simple reduction is possible. The number of literals could be reduced in the equations by factoring, but this would result in additional levels of the gating structure and the designer may decide that the saving in diodes is not worth the difficulties which arise in the design of multi-level circuits due to the voltage drops at each stage. Gate circuits with two levels according to equations (3-20) and (3-21) are shown in Figure 3-4.

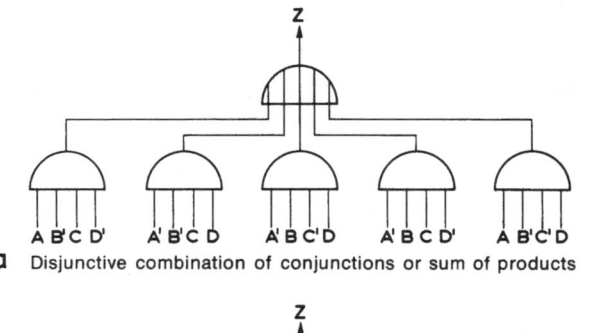

a Disjunctive combination of conjunctions or sum of products

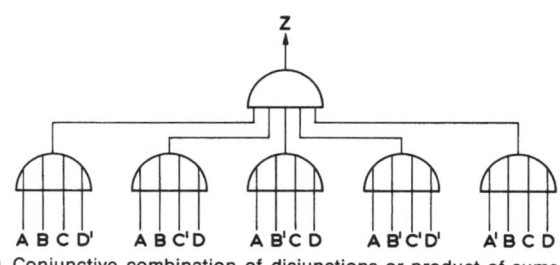

b Conjunctive combination of disjunctions or product of sums

Fig. 3-4. The Two General Forms for Combinational Networks

The above example is somewhat simplified and hypothetical. It was chosen to illustrate the derivation of the two general algebraic expressions for combinational networks from the table of combinations. A more complete example would be the design of a network where all possible input combinations are considered and where an additional check bit is introduced such as to produce one output state for the permissible combinations and the opposite output state for the. non-permissible terms or an occuring error. Such a network could be considered as a realistic error detecting circuit.

3-8. LOGICAL ANALYSIS OF COMBINATIONAL CIRCUITS

If a circuit is given, the logical tools of Boolean algebra can be used to analyze the circuit with regard to possible rearrangements or simplification. The algebraic expression for a circuit affords a more systematic manipulation than can be accomplished by sheer inspection of the circuit. This will be illustrated with the help of the circuit shown in Figure 3-5 in its original and in its simplified form.

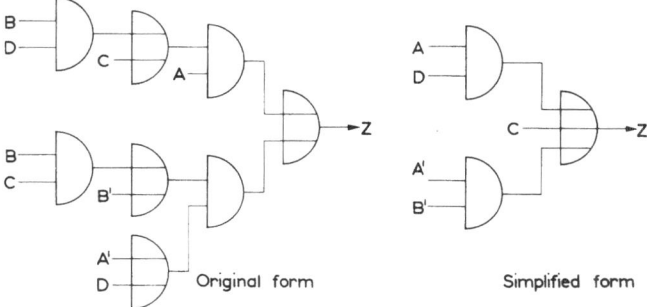

Fig. 3-5. Network Simplification

The algebraic expression for the original circuit is:

$$Z = (BD + C)A + (BC + B')(A' + D) \qquad (3\text{-}22)$$

Rearranging and using theorem (3-10) for simplification we obtain:

$$Z = ABD + AC + A'BC + BCD + A'B' + B'D$$

$$= ABD + C(A + A') + CD + A'B' + B'D$$

$$= C + D(B' + BA) + A'B'$$

and finally with the cancellation of the term DB′ according to (3-11):

$$Z = C + AD + A'B' \qquad (3\text{-}23)$$

Through algebraic manipulation the original network could be reduced from 8 to 3 gates and from 16 to 7 input elements.

3-9. THE LOGIC OF COMBINATIONAL CIRCUITS WITH SEVERAL OUTPUTS

Combinational circuits with several outputs have a wide range of application in computers. They are the natural arrangement for situations where all possible combinations of the inputs need to be available at the outputs, or where special inputs shall produce specified output combinations as in the case of coding and decoding circuits.

The most general form of this type of network are multiplicative switch nets with groups of variables connected to produce any or all possible combinations of signals. Typical arrangements of these nets are the matrix and the tree form. When a tree is called a 2 by 4 tree it has 4 sets of inputs with 2 variables each. Two sets are combined at the first level to form 4 two variable products, then these products multiplied with the 2 variables of the third set give 8 three variable terms and finally these terms combined with the fourth set produce 16 four variable terms.

Of particular interest are the multi-output combinational circuits which are used for the encoding of decimal to BCD and the decoding from BCD to decimal. The encoding circuit is shown in Figure 3-6.

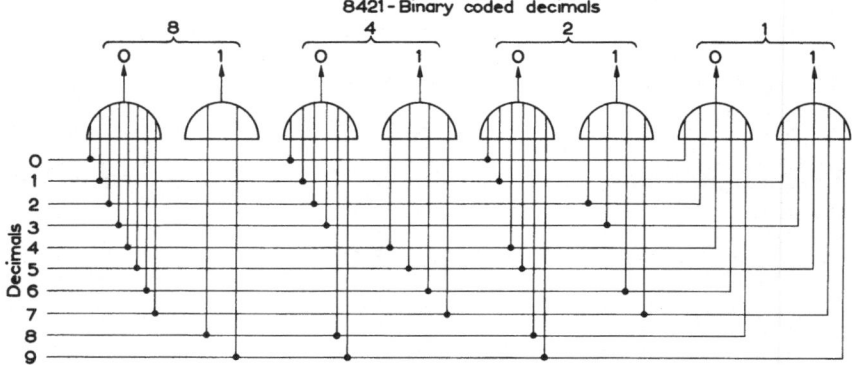

Fig. 3-6. Encoding Circuit for Decimal to BCD

Decimal input signals which come from punched cards as one individual signal per decimal digit have to be dissolved into a group of four bits according to the selected code. Since each of the four bits can have two states 8 outputs are required to form the desired codes. Each decimal signal is fed to the four outputs which represent the code for the decimal digit. The inputs are connected to the outputs by OR gates since any one of the inputs shall produce an output.

The decoding circuit shown in Figure 3-7 represents the reversed process. If and only if a particular group of bits appears as input signals at a gate the corresponding decimal

Decimal

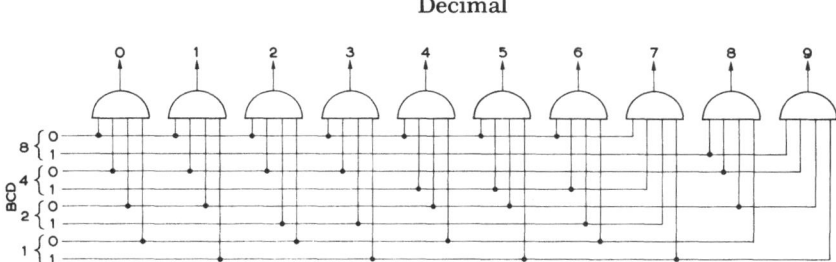

Fig. 3-7. Decoding Circuit from BCD to Decimal

digit is produced. This calls for a realization of the decoding circuit with AND gates.

Similar encoding and decoding circuits are devised for excess-3 and other codes. Also, instruction decoders use the scheme of Fig. 3-7. If, for example, the operation part of an instruction consists of 5 bits which permit 32 different combinations of 1's and 0's we would have 5 input lines and 32 AND gates which form 32 output signals according to the possible combinations of the inputs.

The above described encoding and decoding circuits represent straightforward relations between decimal digits and their corresponding codes and these circuits can be drawn immediately. In these cases we have the simple relation between one single input or output signal and an associated group of outgoing or incoming signals. The situation is quite different when one code is to be converted to another code where a group of input signals corresponds to a different group of output signals. In such cases the means of logic are applied for a systematic design of the conversion or translation circuit.

As an example the conversion from the Gray code to binary is chosen. With the increase of real time applications for digital computers the Gray code, the preferred encoding scheme for analog information, will more and more frequently become the input format to computers, requiring the conversion to the binary system in which the computer works. In order to simplify the example, only the conversion of the first 8 numbers is considered, confining the problem to three bit numbers and the circuit to be designed to 3 inputs and 3 outputs. From the table of combinations the transmission equations of the circuit are derived.

TABLE 3-4

TRUTH TABLE FOR CONVERSION FROM GRAY CODE TO BINARY

Gray code inputs			Binary outputs		
A	B	C	X	Y	Z
0	0	0	0	0	0
0	0	1	0	0	1
0	1	1	0	1	0
0	1	0	0	1	1
1	1	0	1	0	0
1	1	1	1	0	1
1	0	1	1	1	0
1	0	0	1	1	1

The output functions for the 1-states of the outputs X, Y, Z
are after combining adjacent terms:

$$X = A \tag{3-24}$$
$$Y = A'B + AB'$$

$$Z = A'B'C + A'BC' + ABC + AB'C'$$

At this point the designer has to decide if he wants a circuit
with the minimum number of gate levels or with the minimum number of input elements. Assuming he decides for the
latter we factor the expression for Z and design the circuit
according to Figure 3-8.

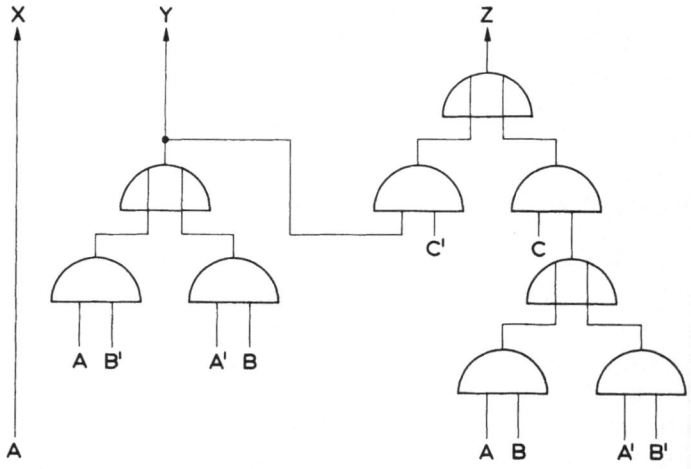

Fig. 3-8.   Circuit for Conversion from Gray Code to Binary

The circuit shows that we have realized the output network for Z with 12 input elements while the expression according to (3-24) would have required 16 input elements. However, this saving was achieved at the cost of two additional gate levels.

3-10. LOGICAL SYNTHESIS OF SEQUENTIAL CIRCUITS

While in combinational circuits the output is only a function of the present inputs, the output of sequential circuits depends not only upon the present inputs but also upon the present internal state of the circuit. Since the internal state had been set by previous inputs the output becomes a function of a certain sequence of inputs. The internal states are set up and held by temporary memory devices; therefore sequential circuits consist of gates as combinational elements and of temporary memory elements. A generalized diagram for sequential circuits is shown in Figure 3-9.

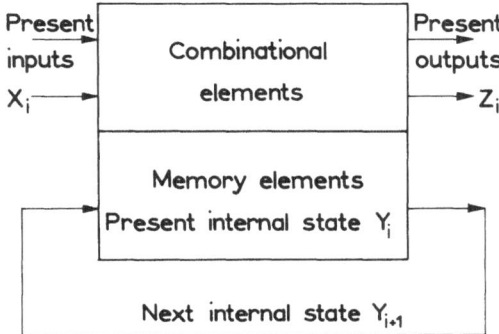

Fig. 3-9. Generalized Diagram of Sequential Circuit

At any time t_i when as a function of the inputs X_i and the internal states Y_i the outputs Z_i are produced, the change from Y_i to the next internal state Y_{i+1} is also initiated. This change should not take place until the outputs Z_i have been established according to the X_i's and the Y_i state, but the change to the Y_{i+1} state should be completed by the time the next set of inputs X_{i+1} arrives.

The computer in its entirety is a sequential network of great complexity not only in the above sense, with the outputs of individual circuits depending on present and previous inputs, but also with the outputs of one circuit becoming the inputs to other circuits. These output-input connections between circuits are normally straightforward and the logical treatment of sequential circuits is concerned with the situation of individual circuits which is depicted in a general form in Fig. 3-9. Important circuits of the computer to which this scheme applies are adding and shifting circuits which are treated in the next chapter, and counting circuits. The logical synthesis of a counting circuit is given here to illustrate the concept.

Counters have a series of advance pulses as input and any prescribed sequence of numbers as outputs. The generation of any subsequent number has to recognize the present number in the counter. Therefore, counters consist mainly of a set of memory elements logically connected to provide the desired sequence. The number of required memory elements depends on the magnitude of the largest number to which count shall be made. A counter with 3 stages can count up to the largest 3 bit number $(111)_2 = 7_{10}$, or a counter with 12 stages counts up to $(4095)_{10}$ which is represented in binary by a 12 bit number with 1's filled in every bit position. If the counting sequence is monotone and the counted number increases by one at every advance pulse, the design is relatively simple. As an example the logical diagram of an instruction counter is shown in Fig. 3-10.

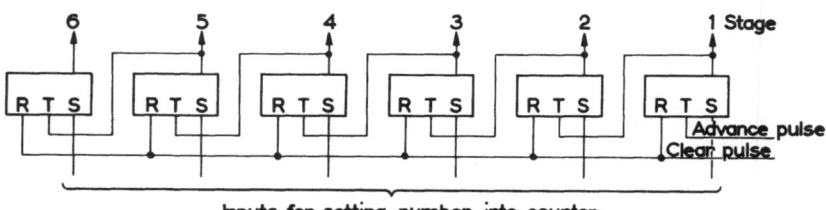

Inputs for setting number into counter

Fig. 3-10. Logical Diagram of Instruction Counter

The counter is first cleared to zero by a reset pulse; all output lines are in zero condition which might be negative or close to ground or whatever potential the designer assigns to this condition. The first advance pulse flips the lowest order stage to "1", the next pulse flips it back to "0" and the surge at the output line going from one to zero flips the next stage to "1". The third pulse triggers the last stage again to "1" with the change from zero to one at the output having no effect on the next stage due to diodes provided in the circuit. A fourth pulse flips the last two stages back to "0" and the surge at the output of the second flip-flop going to zero triggers the third flip-flop to "1", etc. Through the set input lines the counter can be set after clearing to any number which may be the instruction address of a jump instruction outside of the regular sequence. From this new address number, subsequent instruction addresses may be obtained by regular advance of the counter or by going back to an address number from which the next instruction locations are counted in a regular sequential way.

For irregular counting sequences the advance pulse has to be connected to the flip-flop inputs in a special way so that the specified sequence of numbers may be obtained. It is in these situations that logical design techniques are helpful to determine the required gating network which is not only a function of the desired number sequence but also of the memory element which is being used. For these elements the next state depends on the present state and the inputs are shown for the set-reset and the trigger flip-flop by equations (3-17) and (3-19). For the desired number sequence the next state of the memory elements is specified as a function of the present state. The design problem is then the derivation of the input equations for the flip-flop inputs which combine the requirements for the number sequence and the operating characteristic of the applied memory element. Since both of these requirements have one thing in common, namely the dependency on the present state of the memory element, the combination of the requirements makes use of this common feature.

3-11. DESIGN OF AN ODD-SEQUENCE COUNTER

As an example a counter will be designed which counts the number sequence $0-1-3-5-7-0$. This simple example which requires only a 3-stage counter is sufficient to show the logical design procedure, but it must be emphasized that these procedures are particularly useful when applied to more complicated design problems. Table 3-5 lists for the three flip-flops A, B, C of the counter the subsequent states according to the desired counting sequence. In the first row the present state is 000 and the next state 001; this state becomes the present state in the second row for which the next state is 011, etc.

TABLE 3-5

LISTING OF STATES FOR 0 → 1 → 3 → 5 → 7 → 0 COUNTER

Present state i			Next state $(i+1)$		
A	B	C	A	B	C
0	0	0	0	0	1
0	0	1	0	1	1
0	1	1	1	0	1
1	0	1	1	1	1
1	1	1	0	0	0

From this table the relations are derived which express the next states specifically as a function of the present states of the respective flip-flops:

$$A_{i+1} = A_i(B_i'C_i) + A_i'\ (B_iC_i) \qquad (3\text{-}25)$$

$$B_{i+1} = B_i(0) + B_i'(C_i)$$

$$C_{i+1} = C_i(A_i' + A_iB_i') + C_i'(A_i'B_i')$$

Since in the relation for B_{i+1} no term for the present state B_i appears it is introduced with the factor 0.

This counter can be realized with trigger flip-flops which are the most versatile memory elements. The next states which are expressed individually for the three flip-flops with regard to the counting sequence by equations (3-25) and with regard to the flip-flop operation by the general equation (3-19) shall be, of course, the same. Therefore, we obtain the following relations for the three flip-flops in which the subscript i for the present state is omitted because in these relations everything refers to this state.

$$A(B'C) + A'(BC) = S_A + R_A'T_A'A + T_AA' \qquad (3\text{-}26)$$

$$B(0) + B'(C) = S_B + R_B'T_B'B + T_BB'$$

$$C(A' + B') + C'(A'B') = S_C + R_C'T_C'C + T_CC'$$

The solution for the inputs R, S, T of the flip-flops A, B, C can be obtained from a table which shows all possible combinations of the variables of which R, S, T are functions. These variables are entered in general terms with Y_i for the present, Y_{i+1} for the next flip-flop state, and f_1, f_2 for the factors with the unprimed and primed state values on the left side of equations (3-26).

TABLE 3-6

GENERALIZED TRUTH TABLE FOR TRIGGER CIRCUITS

Row	f_1	f_2	Y_i	Y_{i+1}	R	S	T
1	0	0	0	0	$\phi\,(1)$	0	0
2	0	0	1	0	①(1)	0	①(0)
3	0	1	0	1	0	①(0)	①(1)
4	0	1	1	0	①(0)	0	①(1)
5	1	0	0	0	$\phi\,(0)$	0	0
6	1	0	1	1	0	$\phi\,(0)$	0
7	1	1	0	1	0	①(1)	①(0)
8	1	1	1	1	0	$\phi\,(1)$	0

In this table, first the possible combinations of the variables f_1, f_2, and Y_i are entered. Then the entries for Y_{i+1} are determined according to the relation:

$$Y_{i+1} = Y_i f_1 + Y_i' f_2 \tag{3-27}$$

After the values for Y_{i+1} are obtained the entries for R, S, T can be derived from a comparison of the values for Y_i and Y_{i+1} and by using the relation (3-19):

$$Y_{i+1} = S_i + R_i' T_i' Y_i + T_i Y_i'$$

In rows 1 and 5 where the present and next state are zero, S and T must be zero and R is optional, indicated by the symbol ϕ. In rows 6 and 8 the present and next state are one, R and T must be zero while S is optional. When the state changes from zero to one, as in rows 3 and 7, R must be zero and either S or T must be one. This alternate condition is indicated by a circle around the "1". When the one state has been selected for one of the inputs, the other must be automatically zero because two simultaneous 1-inputs are not permitted. A similar condition exists in rows 2 and 4 where the state changes from one to zero; here S must be zero and either R or T must be one but not both.

The optional and alternate states provide the designer with several possibilities for the layout of the circuit. Checking over the R, S, T-entries in table 3-6 it can be seen that by choosing the alternate one entries for T, the R and S inputs can be completely eliminated provided the optional states are made zero. Collecting the terms for the 1-entries in the T column we obtain the following general input equation for trigger circuits in which use is made only of the T and not of the R and S inputs.

$$T = f_1'f_2'Y_i + f_1'f_2Y_i' + f_1'f_2Y_i + f_1f_2Y_i' \qquad (3\text{-}28)$$

$$= f_1'Y_i + f_2Y_i'$$

It may already be recognized intuitively that the above input equation may not be the most efficient solution, because it appears that the proper and specific use of all the different inputs which are available for the memory element should provide optimum design conditions. Therefore a different assignment of the optional and alternate states will be tried, leading to the use of all three inputs. The selected values are shown in table 3-6 in brackets beside the original optional and alternate states. With these entries the following general input equations are obtained:

$$R = f_1'f_2', \quad S = f_1f_2, \quad T = f_1'f_2 \qquad (3\text{-}29)$$

In the above equations the inputs are independent of the state of the memory element. Other assignments for the optional and alternate states are possible and for any particular application these must be checked to see which will give the simplest network.

The final solution for the given example of the $0-1-3-5-7-0$ counter is obtained by introducing into the general equations (3-28) and (3-29) the value for the state and the factors of the individual flip-flops according to the left sides of equations (3-26) which were derived for the specified counter.

Final input equations for circuit with trigger input only:

$$T_A = A(B + C') + A'BC = AC' + BC \qquad (3\text{-}30)$$

$$T_B = B + B'C = B + C$$

$$T_C = CAB + C'A'B'$$

Equations for circuit with all three inputs:

$$R_A = (B + C')(B' + C') = C', \quad T_A = (B + C')BC = BC, \quad S_A = 0 \qquad (3\text{-}31)$$

$$R_B = C', \quad T_B = C, \quad S_B = 0$$

$$R_C = AB(A + B) = AB, \quad T_C = 0, \quad S_c = A'B'$$

The resulting circuits are sketched in Figure 3-11. An inspection of this figure shows that both circuits will count in the specified sequence. Some terms appear redundant even in the much simpler circuit using all possible inputs. Here the C'-input at the reset line of the A and B flip-flops assures that the first pulse sets the counter to 001 independent of its previous setting; if this is assumed to be 000, these reset inputs would not be required. In the described synthesis procedure the advance pulse X was not carried along because it would have appeared as a factor with all input terms. For counters counting UP and DOWN an input X_1 may be introduced for the count up and an input X_2 for the count down.

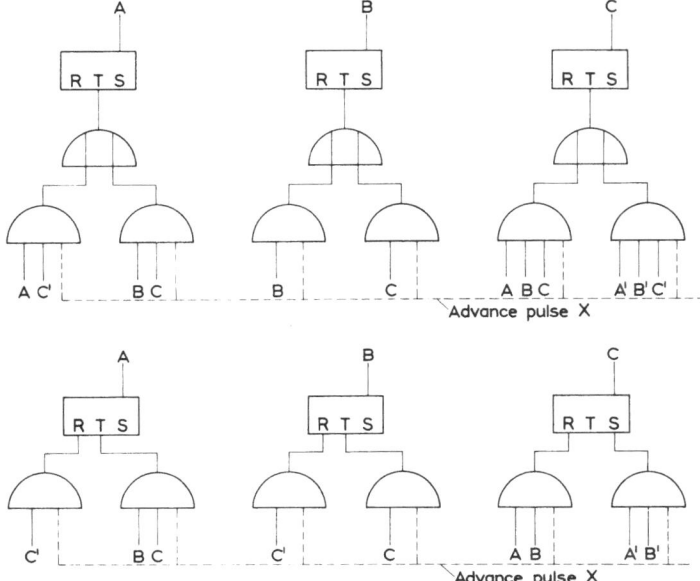

Fig. 3-11. 2 Logical Diagrams of $0-1-3-5-7-0$ Counter

The preceding discussion dealt with sequential circuits for which the required number of memory elements and the basic circuit configuration were known a priori and the design could start with the writing of the truth table. When the number p of the inputs, the number q of the internal states and the number r of the desired outputs is known the size of the truth table is determined with 2^{p+q} rows for all possible combinations of the inputs and present internal states and with $q + r$ columns to the right of the table to be filled in for the next internal states and outputs according to the specified circuit action.

When nothing is known about the number and the behavior of the internal states, the design problem is much more difficult. In particular, the first step in the circuit design requires quite some ingenuity on the part of the designer. The problem in this more general case states only the desired output or outputs as function of a certain sequence and combination of inputs, and the designer has to determine the required number and behavior of the internal states. Several methods have been developed to aid not only in the establishment but also in the reduction of the necessary internal states. References 9 through 12 present some of the basic and original work on synthesis methods for sequential circuits. The logical design of digital computer circuits is also thoroughly treated in the book by Montgomery Pfister "Logical Design of Digital Computers" (*see Bibliography*).

3-12. THE LOGIC OF THE ENTIRE COMPUTER

Since the individual parts of the computer are built up and connected according to logical principles it has become quite customary to refer to the functional characteristics of entire computers as to the logic of the computer. Functional diagrams of the computer which show the basic information flow throughout the computer are also referred to as logical diagrams. As an example a typical functional diagram for a stored program computer is shown in Figure 3-12.

Practically all modern computers are stored program computers with the processed information consisting of instructions and data which should be clearly distinguished in functional flow diagrams. In Figure 3-12 paths which carry only instruction flow are shown in dotted lines. The paths which carry both data and instructions are drawn in solid. Circuit details and elements such as storage bus, buffer registers and similar common processing media are usually omitted from diagrams which delineate the specific processing characteristics of the computer making up the logic of a particular machine. Such specific characteristics are the processing mode and execution of instructions, indexing, input-output connections, the arrangement of arithmetic registers, and the principal interconnections between the major computer units. These elements are normally shown in a simplified way in the so-called logical diagram of the entire computer.

In the arrangement of the diagram in Figure 3-12 instruction and data words are brought from main storage into the same intermediate storage register from where the operation part of an instruction is processed to the operation or instruction register and the address part through the adder network where the address may or may not be modified. If the address

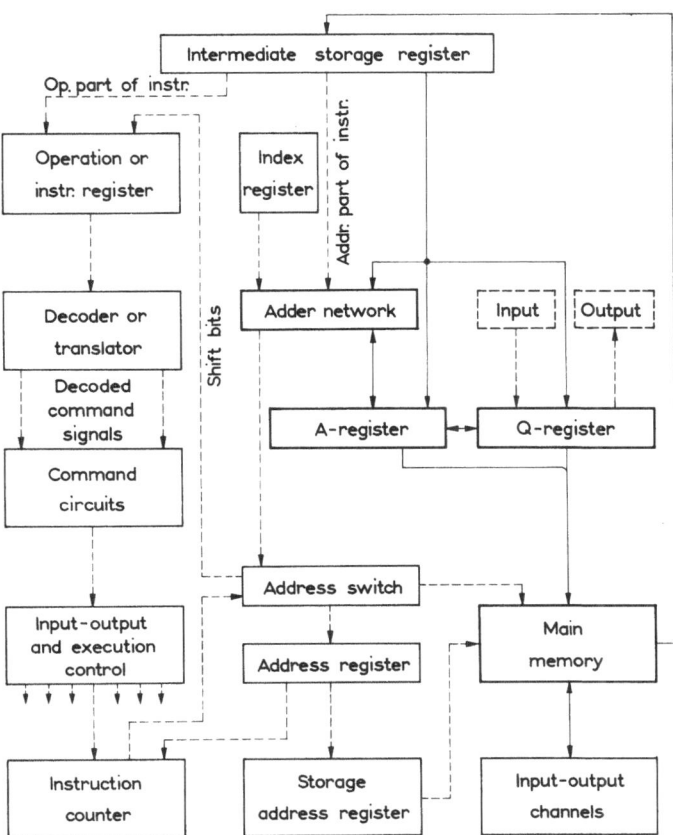

Fig. 3-12. Typical Logical Diagram of Entire Computer

part of the instruction contains the address of the data on which operation is to be performed this address is moved to the address register and further on to the storage address register to control the selection of the location from which data is to be transferred through the intermediate storage register to one of the arithmetic registers. If the address part of the instruction word contains shift bits they may be directed to the operation or to the address register, depending on where provisions are made for the counting of the shifts.

Modified addresses may also be stored in the main storage as indicated by the connection between the address switch and the main memory. An alternative mode for the processing of instructions would be the arrangment of different paths for instructions and data with instructions processed to a program register and only data processed through the intermediate storage register. In this case separate adders would be required for the modification of the address part of the instructions.

In the left part of Figure 3-12 the rather common processing steps for the operation part of instructions are shown. Typical alternate names for the various steps are introduced. It is also indicated how the two major machine cycles perform: The so-called instruction cycle during which the instruction is secured and the execution cycle during which the instruction is executed. The inputs to the address switch are normally alternating, coming either from the address part of the instruction when data for the execution is selected or from the instruction counter when the next instruction is to be secured. This counter is stepped up at the end of the execution cycle and it provides in this way the addresses of consecutive instruction locations. If the program should jump to a location out of this sequence the new address is provided by the address part of the jump instruction. This address is also set into the instruction counter where it may then be stepped up again in a consecutive fashion.

In Figure 3-12, note that input and output are connected directly to the main memory over special input-output channels, which is a common feature of modern computers. The input and output (in dotted lines) connected to the Q-register, represents the arrangement of older machines where input-output is connected to the main storage through an arithmetic register with shift property. The arrangement and functioning of the arithmetic registers is described in the following chapter.

PROBLEMS

3-1. Explain difference between logic of classes and logic of propositions.

3-2. Describe logical connectives.

3-3. Describe characteristics of decision and memory elements.

3-4. Derive the characteristic equation for a flip-flop which has a single input line which changes the state of the memory element with input one and leaves the state unchanged with input zero.

3-5. Analyze the given combinational circuits by means of writing and simplifying the algebraic expressions of the circuits; circuit (a) should be reduced to 3 gates and 8 diodes and circuit (b) to 2 gates and 4 diodes.

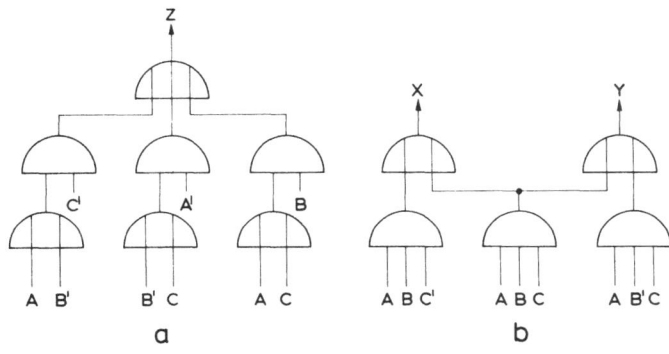

3-6. Design a complementing circuit with 4 bit inputs and 4 bit outputs which are the complements of the inputs, such that for the inputs 0000, 0001, 0010, etc. the outputs are 1001, 1000, 0111, etc.

3-7. Synthesize a circuit which receives at its three inputs the binary numbers 000 through 111 and which produces as outputs numbers which are three times the input.

3-8. Design a circuit with inputs $A_1 A_0$ and $B_1 B_0$ to produce at the output the product of the two 2-digit numbers appearing at the input.

3-9. Design a counter for the sequence 0, 1, 3, 2, 0, 1, 3, 2, etc, when pulsed at intervals so that outputs fed back over delays arrive at inputs simultaneously with the next pulse; without pulses whatever number in the counter shall circulate.

Arithmetic Operations
of the Machine

4-1. THE LOGIC OF BINARY ADDITION AND SUBTRACTION

The various arithmetic functions which the computer must accomplish have to be resolved into simple operations that the physical computer elements can perform. It will be seen that it is possible to reduce the arithmetic which the computer does to a few basic operations. The most important and the most widely used of these operations is the combination of two sets of information bits to form either the sum or the difference of the numbers. Using the logical characteristics which were introduced in the preceding chapter, the use of basic elements to perform the combining function will be analyzed.

The rules for binary addition are given by the following tables.

TABLE 4-1

BINARY ADDITION

Sum Table

	Augend	
Addend	0	1
0	0	1
1	1	0

Carry Table

	Augend	
Addend	0	1
0	0	0
1	0	1

Letting the augend be x and the addend y, we obtain the algebraic expression for the sum S and the carry C for the lowest order digit where no carries have to be added in:

$$S = xy' + x'y = x + y \qquad (4\text{-}1)$$

$$C = xy$$

The complete adding and carry functions are derived from the truth table in which all possible combinations of the augend and addend digits and the carry-in from lower orders are entered.

TABLE 4-2

TRUTH TABLE FOR FULL ADDER

Inputs			Outputs	
x	y	C_i	S	C_0
0	0	0	0	0
0	0	1	1	0
0	1	0	1	0
0	1	1	0	1
1	0	0	1	0
1	0	1	0	1
1	1	0	0	1
1	1	1	1	1

In the above table the carry input from the next lower order is denoted by C_i and the carry output to the next higher order by C_o. The entries for S and C_o are obtained according to the previously stated binary addition rules. Writing the output functions in the sum of product form, the following complete expressions for the sum S and the carry C_o are derived.

$$S = x'y'C_i + x'yC_i' + xy'C_i' + xyC_i \tag{4-2}$$

$$C_o = x'yC_i + xy'C_i + xyC_i' + xyC_i$$

$$= xy(C_i + C_i') + xC_i(y + y') + yC_i(x + x')$$

$$= xy + xC_i + yC_i \tag{4-3}$$

A basic circuit, called a full adder, for the implementation of relations (4-2) and (4-3) is shown in Figure 4-1. For the lowest order digit one half adder is sufficient to realize relations (4-1).

Binary subtraction can be expressed by a logic very similar to binary addition. A truth table for a full subtractor is established according to the binary difference and borrow rules, and from this table the algebraic expressions for the difference D and the borrow out B_o are derived.

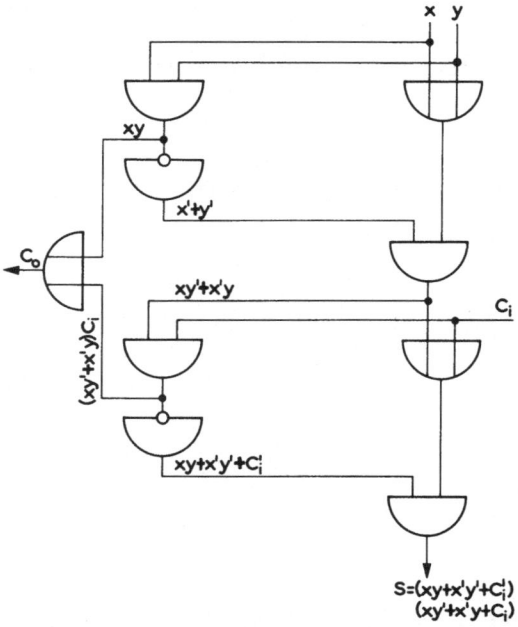

Fig. 4-1. Logical Diagram of Full Adder Composed of 2 Half Adders

TABLE 4-3

TRUTH TABLE FOR FULL SUBTRACTOR

Inputs			Outputs	
x	y	B_i	D	B_o
0	0	0	0	0
0	0	1	1	1
0	1	0	1	1
0	1	1	0	1
1	0	0	1	0
1	0	1	0	0
1	1	0	0	0
1	1	1	1	1

Considering only the x and y inputs we obtain for a half subtractor:

$$D = xy' + x'y \text{ and } B_o = x'y \qquad (4\text{-}4)$$

and with all the inputs the expressions for the full subtractor:

$$D = x'y'B_i + x'yB_i' + xy'B_i' + xyB_i \tag{4-5}$$

$$B_o = x'y'B_i + x'yB_i' + x'yB_i + xyB_i$$

$$= x'y(B_i' + B_i) + x'B_i(y' + y) + yB_i(x' + x)$$

$$= x'y + x'B_i + y B_i \tag{4-6}$$

The expressions for sum and difference are the same, while they are different for carry and borrow. The equations for the borrow bear out the fact that the minuend x is not interchangeable with the subtrahend y and the borrow-in B_i. Subtracting circuits are built according to equations (4-5) and (4-6).

4-2. SERIAL AND PARALLEL BINARY ADDITION

Serial binary addition can be performed with the simplest possible adding circuit. Digit pairs of the same order of two numbers are serially added in one adder stage with the sum digit emerging serially from the output line. The carry-out is fed back through a delay to the input to appear as carry-in simultaneously with the next higher order digit pair of augend and addend. A typical serial binary adder for pulse inputs is shown in Fig. 4-2.

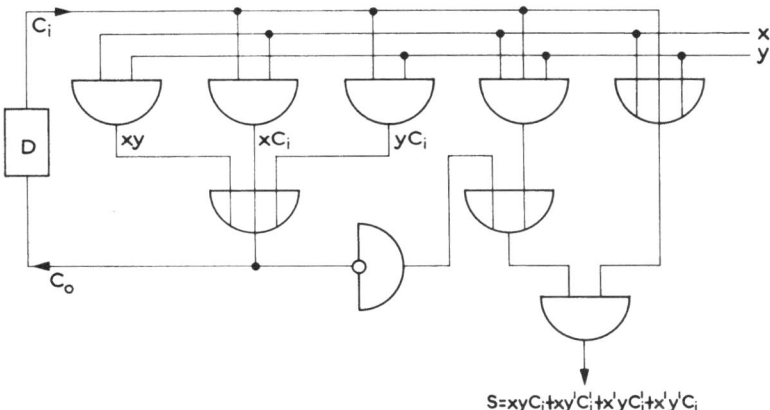

Fig. 4-2. Serial Binary Adder

The adding of the carry to the digits of the next higher order requires processing of the digits in ascending order of significance. Since the sign of the numbers should be recognized before the adding process starts it becomes here necessary to arrange the sign bit at the end instead at the beginning of the number. When two different signs are sensed, the negative number will normally be complemented using the 2's complement in order to avoid the end-around carry which would require, in the serial system, passing the sum through the adder for a second time.

Parallel binary addition, most commonly used in scientific computers, provides the fastest scheme for the addition of two numbers whereby all order pairs are added simultaneously. The two numbers to be added have been brought immediately preceding the addition to two registers in the arithmetic unit which are usually called intermediate storage and A or accumulator register. In their simplest form, these registers consist, per stage, of one delay unit of approximately 1μ sec and an associated gating network. The information in the registers is kept there by recirculating, with the output of the delay unit becoming its input, through an AND gate which is held open until new commands for the resetting of the registers appear on a NOT gate closing the AND gate for recirculation. This arrangement is usually referred to as a dynamic flip-flop. The addition process proper starts with the simultaneous application of two command signals "storage register-adder" and "A register-adder" bringing in the augend x and the addend y to the adding network. At the bottom of Fig. 4-3, a true-complement network is shown. For addition the "true A register-adder" signal would be given. These signals are applied long enough for the execution of the addition; shortly before they are removed a signal pulse "adder-A register" of about one microsecond duration opens AND gates for the transmission of the sum from the adder to the A register. Since this register receives the sum it is also called accumulator register though it does not participate in the adding process more than the storage register, both merely providing the two operands for the adder.

The adding network in Fig. 4-3 is practically the same as shown in Fig. 4-2 for the serial binary adder. This gate arrangement for adding is actually used in many computers. It is an improvement over the arrangement in Fig. 4-1 because with only a few more diodes the number of alternate gate levels has been reduced.

Possibly the item requiring the greatest attention in the design of parallel adders is the problem of carry propagation. The add time of the machine has to allow for the propagation

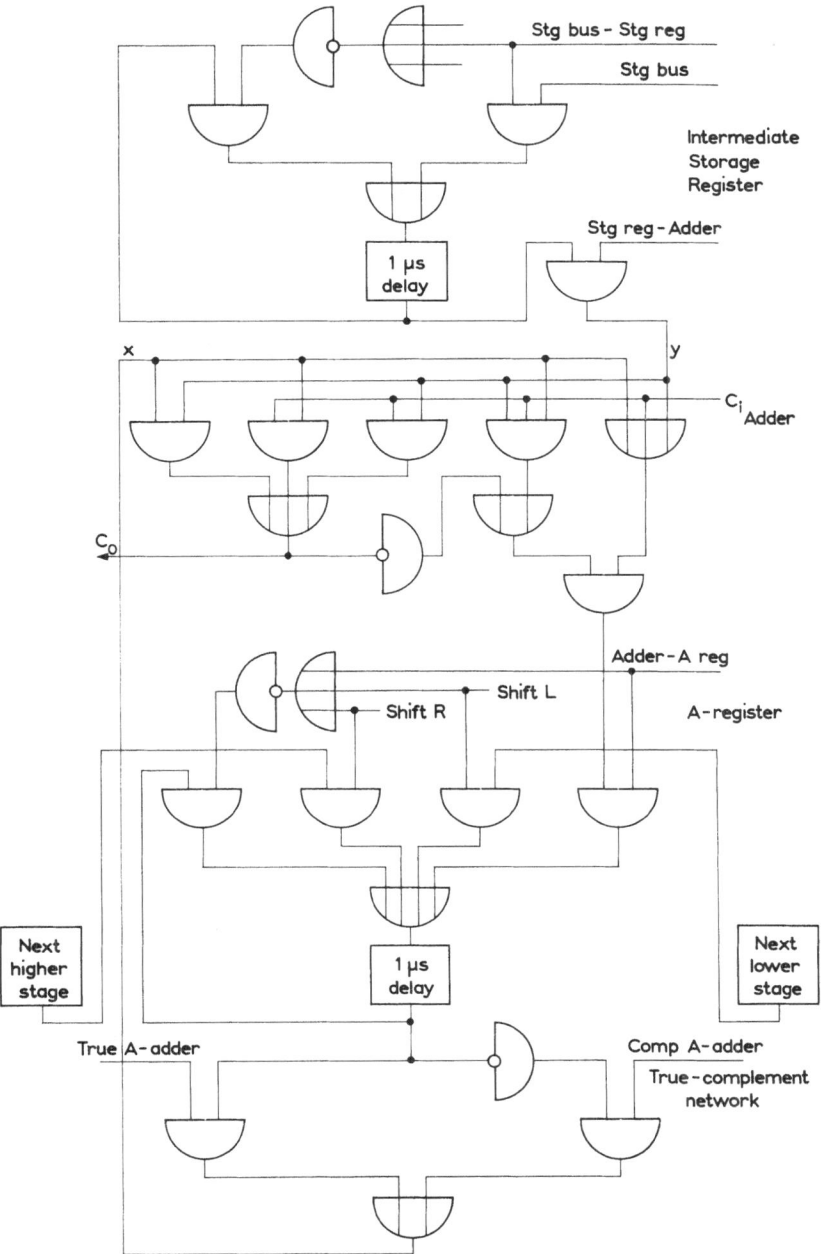

Fig. 4-3. Parallel Binary Adder with Associated Registers

of a carry which might originate in the lowest order and which has to be propagated to the highest order. In the networks shown, the carry has to pass through two gates per stage, or for example with 40 bit words through a maximum of 80 gates. When diodes with extremely low rise and fall time are used for the gates, the overall delay may still be well within other timing considerations of the machine. But since these timing considerations are becoming more and more stringent, a basic concept for the speed up of carry propagation will be briefly mentioned.

Considering an adder stage consisting of two half adders according to Fig. 4-1, it can be seen that at the output of the first half adder the partial sum $xy' + x'y$ is obtained immediately after the application of the inputs x and y without waiting for the carry coming from the next lower order. If this partial sum, the so-called exclusive OR of x and y, is one, any carry coming in is propagated to the next higher order. Speed up circuitry makes use of this fact. Depending on how many adder stages are grouped together for the speed up of the propagation, the outputs of the first half adders of these stages and the carry coming in to the lowest stage of the group are connected to an AND gate whose output is combined with the carry out of the highest stage of the group. In this way a carry will be shot past the stages of the group if all of them are one at the output of their first half adders. Otherwise the carry will be taken care of within the group with the stage having a low output at the first half adder absorbing the carry.

4-3.   ADDITION WITH ACCUMULATORS

Addition can also be performed by adding the addend to the augend which has previously been placed in one arithmetic register, normally the A register, which in this case is usually built up from flip-flops instead of delay units. In this process the previous flip-flop states representing the augend are changed to the states representing the sum. Additional numbers may be added, resulting in the sum of all addends. Due to this accumulating property the arithmetic register in which the summation takes place is called an accumulator.

Special care is required here not only concerning the carry propagation but also the carry initiation. If the carry is initiated by a carry pulse, or automatically within the accumulator, after flip-flops have changed state, it is evident that a longer timing will be required. The timing problem for the carry initiation is overcome by the arrangement shown in Fig. 4-4 where the carry signals are generated prior to addition immediately upon entering the addend into the storage register, here also called the addend register, assuming that the augend has been placed previously in the accumulator.

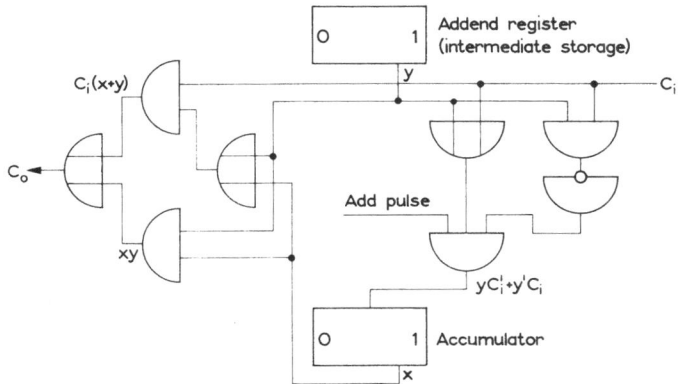

Fig. 4-4. Accumulator with Direct Carry Generation

The carry is initiated and propagated in the network realizing the carry function $C_o = xy + xC_i + yC_i$. The addition takes place in a half adder circuit, which upon an add pulse triggers the accumulator state only when either the addend or the carry from the next lower order are high, but not when both are high, thus eliminating the possibility of a double change of the accumulator flip-flop.

An interesting scheme, particularly applicable to asynchronous operation, provides for a signal upon the completion of the carry process. The completion signal has to be sensed at the highest order to assure that all states are covered, but the carry may propagate only to some lower stage. Therefore the basic idea for the arrival of the completion signal at the highest stage is to propagate a no-carry as well as a carry signal through the accumulator with networks as shown in Fig. 4-5.

At the beginning a no-carry signal is injected at the lowest stage and then as long as neither or only one of the operands is high the no-carry signal will be propagated. At the first

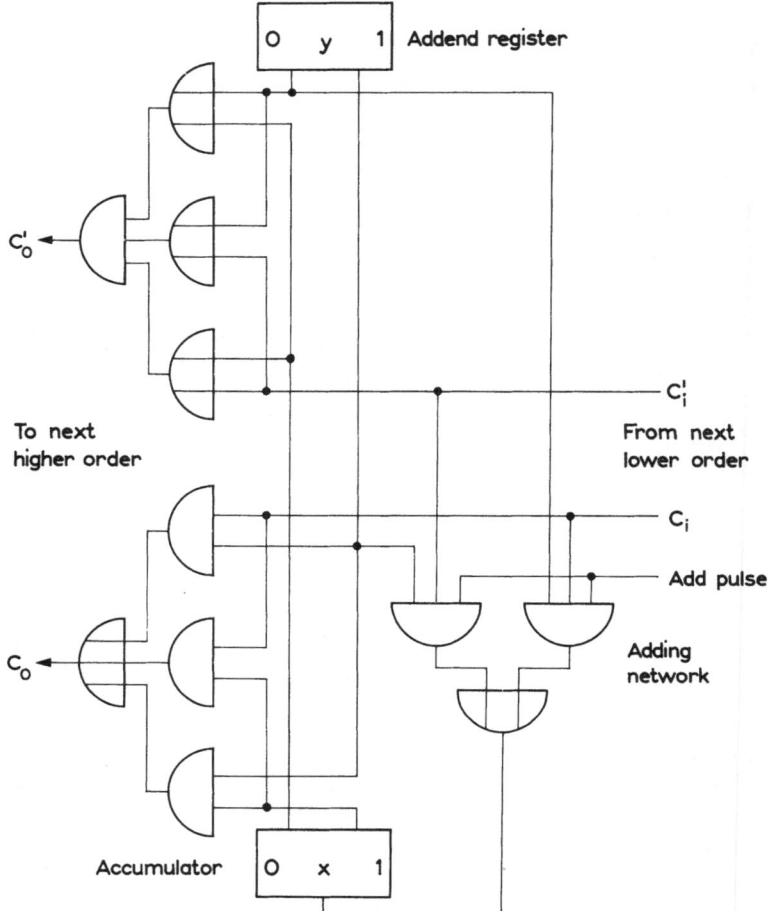

Fig. 4-5.   Accumulator with Signal for Carry Completion

stage with both operands high the no-carry signal will change to a carry signal. When the carry is absorbed by some stage the no-carry signal will come on again, assuming that either one of the two signals will appear at the highest order, whereupon the add pulse is given immediately in the asynchronous mode of operation. The double networks in each stage for carry and no-carry increase the amount of required equipment; but a slight saving can be realized in the adding network because the inverting gate is not needed with the availability of the no-carry signal.

4-4. MACHINE SUBTRACTION

With regard to the binary subtraction in the machine, the major decision has to be made if special circuits for direct or true subtraction will be provided or if subtraction shall be performed by the addition of the complemented number. For most machines the decision has been made in favor of the latter procedure because it is easier to mechanize in the machine. In order to appraise what is actually involved in the mechanization it is quite important to recognize that subtraction is basically the combination of two numbers with different signs.

When the signs of two operands are the same the combining action for the operands is additive with the result having the original sign of the operands. If the signs are different the difference of the two operands is formed no matter if we call it the addition of a positive to a negative number or the subtraction of one number from another which has the same sign. The interrelationship of the sign of the number and the operations of addition and subtraction is used in the machine to an advantage. The machine first senses the signs of the two operands. If they are the same, the machine performs direct addition leaving the sign of the sum in the A register unchanged. If the signs are different the machine forms the difference of the numbers by adding the true number of the storage register and the complemented number of the A register.

In this process the relative magnitude and the resulting sign of the difference are determined by making use of the fact that for the 1's complement an end around carry will always be generated when a smaller number in the A register is added in its complemented form to a larger number in the storage register, while no end around carry will occur when the original number in the A register before complementation is larger. Therefore an end around carry indicates that the sign of the result placed back in the A register has to be changed, no matter what it was before, because the sign of the larger number determines the sign of the difference. Furthermore, when the larger number entered in the addition process is in true form the result is also obtained in true number representation.

Examples 4-1.

	S		Dec.	S		Dec.
Storage Register	0	1010	+10	1	1010	−10
A Register	1	0101	− 5	0	0101	+ 5
		1010			1010	
Adder		1010			1010	
		10100			10100	
End around carry		⟶ 1			⟶ 1	
		0101			0101	

	S			S		
Result in A Register						
with changed signs	0	0101	+ 5	1	0101	− 5

When no end around carry is generated the sign for the result in the A register is left unchanged because in this case the larger number which determines the sign had been placed originally in the A register. But with the larger number entering the addition in complemented form, the result also appears in complement number representation. The result is then through complementing gates recirculated to the A register to obtain the true form.

Examples 4-2.

	S		Dec.	S		Dec.
Storage Register	1	0101	− 5	0	0101	+ 5
A Register	0	1010	+10	1	1010	−10
		0101			0101	
Adder		0101			0101	
		1010			1010	

	S			S		
Result in A Register						
after complementation	0	0101	+ 5	1	0101	− 5

The above discussion about the combination of two numbers with different signs under add instructions basically covers the subtractive operation mode of the machine. Subtract commands are recognized simply by changing the sign of the subtrahend in the storage register. If the signs of both operands had been equal the sign change by the subtract command leads to the desired subtractive action as described for two numbers with different signs. If the original numbers to be subtracted has different signs and the sign change under the subtract instruction makes them equal then we have the case, as in normal arithmetic, where subtracting two numbers with different signs means the addition of the numbers.

In the preceding examples the 1's complement is used as is often preferred because of the easier complementation process and the good use which is made of the end around carry signal in the adjusting of the sign or the recomplementation of the result.

4-5. BCD ADDITION AND COMPLEMENTATION

BCD or decimal addition is mostly performed serially by digits and parallel for the four bits of one BCD digit. A typical serial BCD adder is sketched in Fig. 4-6, with four full adders, one for each of the bits which represent one decimal digit. For the addition of the lowest order decimal digits three full adders and one half adder would be sufficient, but since in the same stage all order pairs are added, the four full adders are required.

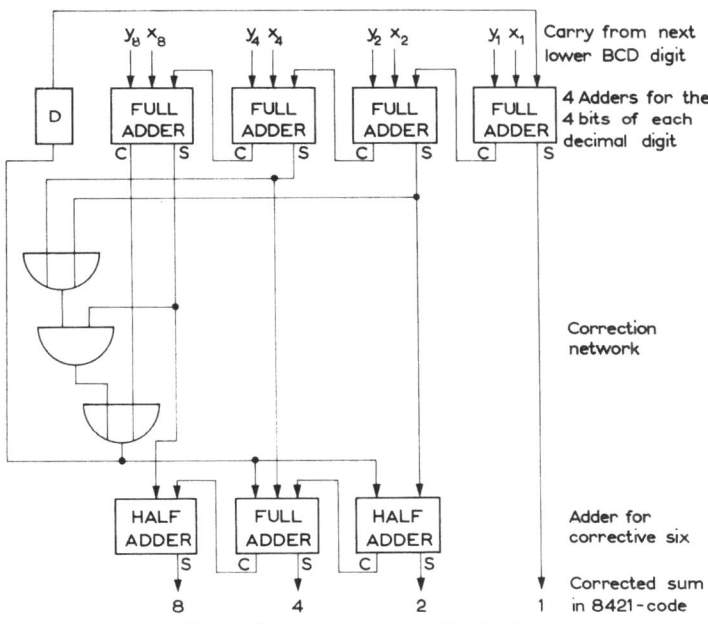

Fig. 4-6. Serial 8421-BCD Adder

The main problem in the operation with binary coded decimal numbers arises from the fact that only the codes for the decimal digits 0 through 9 are valid and that corrective measures have to be introduced when in the course of arithmetic operations invalid bit combinations are produced. Since with 4 bits 16 different combinations are possible, there are 10 valid and 6 invalid combinations. In the case of the basic BCD or 8421 code the combinations 0000 through 1001 are valid while the six other possible combinations 1010 through 1111 are invalid. The addition and correction procedure is explained for this code since it is used most frequently.

TABLE 4-4

**COMPARISON BETWEEN VALID AND INVALID BCD
REPRESENTATION**

Dec	Invalid Combination	Valid BCD Representation	
10	1010	0001	0000
11	1011	0001	0001
12	1100	0001	0010
13	1101	0001	0011
14	1110	0001	0100
15	1111	0001	0101
16	1 0000	0001	0110

From the above table, it can be seen that the addition of 6 or 0110 to any invalid combination gives the correct BCD representation and that the corrective 6 has to be applied when the weight position 8 and either of the positions 4 or 2 or both of them are high and when a carry is generated. The state of the bit position with the weight 1 does not affect the need for correction. In the correction process not only the addition of 6 to the present digit order but also the carry to the next higher digit order are provided. The network for the generation of the correction signal and the adder for the corrective six, as shown in Fig. 4-6, are required to complete the BCD adder. If no correction is necessary there will be no correction signal, and the number passes unchanged through the corrective six adder.

The coding and operation on binary coded decimal numbers is done on a digit by digit basis; this is also the case with the complementation of BCD numbers.

In decimal notation, each digit plus its 9's complement gives 9 and each digit plus its 10's complement gives 10. The same holds true for the BCD notation because it deals with decimal numbers although they are expressed in a binary code. The following table shows a comparison between the 9's complement of BCD numbers and the 1's complement of corresponding binary numbers.

TABLE 4-5

COMPARISON BETWEEN 9'S COMPLEMENT FOR BCD AND 1'S COMPLEMENT FOR BINARY

Dec.	BCD Number	9's Compl. for BCD	1's Compl. for Binary
0	0000	1001	1111
1	0001	1000	1110
2	0010	0111	1101
3	0011	0110	1100
4	0100	0101	1011
5	0101	0100	1010
6	0110	0011	1001
7	0111	0010	1000
8	1000	0001	0111
9	1001	0000	0110

An inspection of Table 4-5 reveals that the difference between the 9's complement for BCD and the 1's complement for binary is always six with the latter always being larger by this amount. Therefore, the 9's complement for BCD can be formed by first sending the coded digit through inverting gates obtaining the 1's complement and then subtracting binary 6 or 0110.

A more systematic and faster way to obtain the 9's complement for BCD is by means of a special complementation network. The input-output relations for the network can be derived from Table 4-5. Letting the bit positions of the original BCD number be denoted in ascending order according to the weight of the position by x_1, x_2, x_4, and x_8 and the bit positions for the 9's complement of the number which shall be the output of the complementing network by z_1, z_2, z_4, and z_8, we can write:

$$z_1 = x_1'$$ (4-7)

$$z_2 = x_2$$

$$z_4 = x_8' x_4' x_2 + x_8' x_4 x_2'$$

$$z_8 = x_8' x_4' x_2'$$

A complementer for the realization of the above relations is shown in Fig. 4-7.

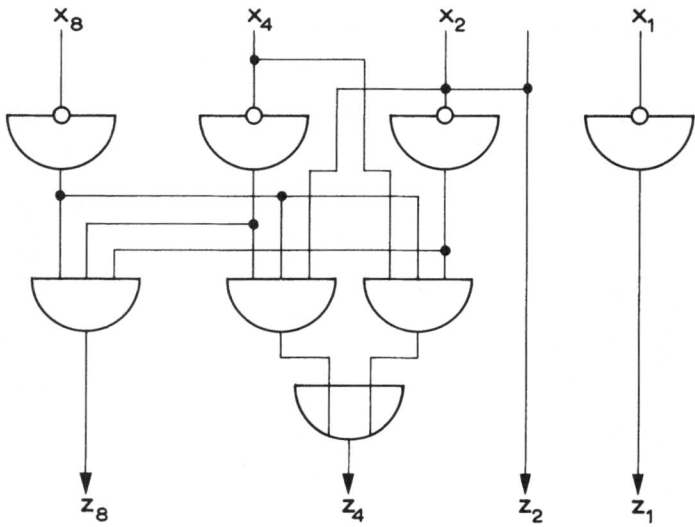

Fig. 4-7. 9's Complementer for BCD

Negative numbers and subtraction are handled in the machine for BCD in a similar way as for binary. The sensing of the signs of the two operands determines if they shall be added in their true form or with one operand complemented. The occurrence or non-occurrence of an end around carry indicates the sign and form, true or complemented, of the result in the manner explained for binary operation.

4-6.   CONSIDERATIONS FOR MACHINE MULTIPLICATION

The general formula for the multiplication of the multiplicand X with the n-digit multiplier Y is:

$$XY = Xy_0 b^o + Xy_1 b^1 + \ldots Xy_i b^i + \ldots Xy_n b^n$$ (4-8)

$$= P_o + P_1 + \ldots P_i + \ldots P_n$$

where y_0 through y_n the digits of the multiplier, b^0 through b^n the positional values of the digits and P_0 through P_n the partial products.

The multiplication process then consists according to (4-8) of the following three steps: forming the product of the multiplicand with one multiplier digit, shifting the partial product in the correct position for the third step, and the addition of the partial products. In the binary system the first step is particularly simple because the multiplier digits y_0 through y_n have only the values of either 0 or 1 making the partial products either zero or equal to the multiplicand. The calculation with paper and pencil follows directly the above steps.

Example 4-3.   Multiply 9×6 in binary.

$$\begin{array}{r} 1001 \\ 0110 \\ \hline 0000 \\ 1001 \\ 1001 \\ 0000 \\ \hline (0110110)_2 = (54)_{10} \end{array}$$

For machine multiplication the simultaneous addition of all partial products is impractical and the partial products are added as they are developed. Calling the accumulated partial products subproducts and denoting them with S, we may write the steps in which the final product XY is obtained in the following way:

$$P_0 \tag{4-9}$$

$$P_0 + P_1 = S_1$$

$$S_1 + P_2 = S_2$$

$$S_{i-1} + P_i = S_i$$

$$S_{n-1} + P_n = S_n = XY$$

In mechanizing the steps for the machine, either the partial products P can be shifted to the left, as it is usually done when calculating with paper and pencil, or the subproducts S can be shifted to the right which is the same with regard to the alignment for the addition. The first method is formalized by:

$$P_o = Xy_o \tag{4-10}$$
$$S_i = S_{i-1} + Xy_i b^i$$

and the second method by:

$$P_o = Xy_o b^n \tag{4-11}$$
$$S_i = S_{i-1} b^{-1} + Xy_i b^n$$

where b^{-1} means one right shift and b^i and b^n mean respectively i and n left shifts.

The second method is preferred for machine mechanization because the shifting of the subproduct is normally easier to accomplish. But since the first method might also be used, the following examples explain how both methods lead to the same result. In working the examples it must be recognized that the product of a m-digit multiplicand and a n-digit multiplier will require in general m + n digit positions in the machine from which for small digit values of multiplicand and multiplier only m + n − 1 positions might be filled with significant digits.

Examples 4-4.
   a. Multiplication with left shift of partial products (multiplicand).

Multiplier Y		$y_2 y_1 y_0$	
		1 1 0	
Multiplicand X		1 1 1	Remarks
$P_0 = Xy_0$		0 0 0	Bring in 1st part. prod. to low order
$Xy_1 b$	1	1 1 0	Shift L 2nd part. prod.
$S_1 = P_0 + Xy_1 b$	1	1 1 0	Add 1st and 2nd part. prod.
$Xy_2 b^2$	1 1	1 0 0	Shift L 3rd part. prod.
$S_2 = S_1 + Xy_2 b^2$	1 0 1	0 1 0	Add 3rd part. prod. to 1st subproduct

b. Multiplication with right shift of subproducts.

			$y_2y_1y_0$		
Multiplier Y			1 1 0		
Multiplicand X			1 1 1		
$P_0 = Xy_0b^3$		0 0 0			Bring in 1st part. prod. to high order
P_0b^{-1}		0 0	0		Shift R
$S_1 = P_0b^{-1} + Xy_1b^3$		1 1 1	0		Add 1st and 2nd part. prod.
S_1b^{-1}		1 1	1 0		Shift R subprod. S_1
$S_2 = S_1b^{-1} + Xy_2b^3$	1	0 1 0	1 0		Add 3rd part. prod. to 1st subprod.
S_2b^{-1}		1 0 1	0 1 0		Shift R subprod. S_2

Result $(101010)_2 = (42)_{10}$

Comparing the two multiplication methods it will be recognized that in method a the partial product has to be added every time at different orders and that the shifting has to be done before the partial product is entered into the adding register. Furthermore this method requires a double length register for the product since the register is entered from the low to the high order. These disadvantages are practically all avoided with method b where the partial product is always entered at the same high order positions. Since only the high order positions are needed for the entry of the multiplicand the adding register in which the product is formed requires only the length of the normal word size if provisions are made to shift the lower order digits over to another register which would at the end of the multiplication contain the low order part of the product while the adding register retains the high order part.

According to method b, we obtain then a general arrangement for machine multiplication, shown in Fig. 4-8, which in some form or another is adopted in the majority of binary machines.

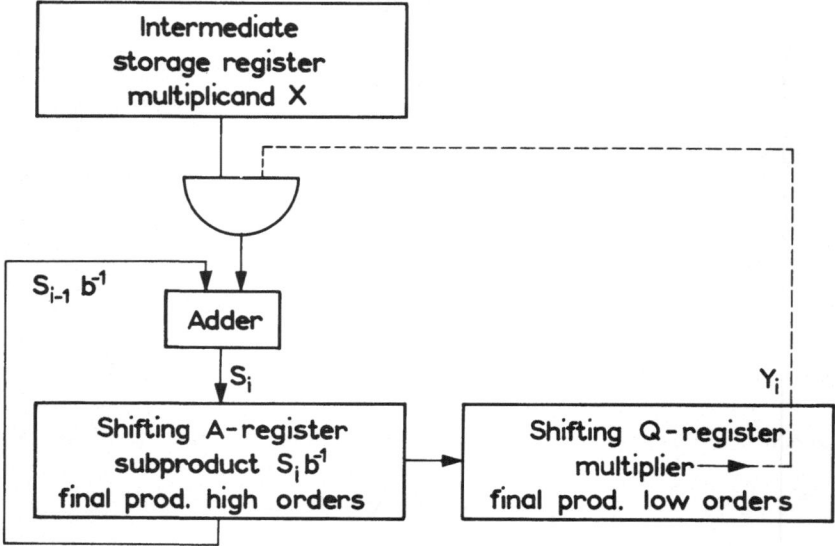

Fig. 4-8. General Arrangement for Machine Multiplication

Three registers are required for the multiplication process if the securing of the multiplicand at every step from the main storage is ruled out. Two of the registers require shifting property; sometimes they are combined to one double length register which, however, is inefficient because only one of the registers needs both the shifting and the adding capability. Though shifting and adding may be done in one unit, the accumulator, in Fig. 4-8 the adder is depicted separately to emphasize the three steps in the multiplication process:

1. Forming partial product of multiplicand and one multiplier digit by closing or opening an AND gate depending on whether the multiplier digit Y_i is zero or one;

2. Adding the partial product to the accumulated subproduct which has been shifted previously one position to the right $S_{i-1}b^{-1}$);

3. Shifting the new subproduct S_i and the multiplier to the right one position at a time, bringing consecutive multiplier digits in the least significant position for sensing and controlling the partial multiplication, and moving the lower order digits of the product into positions vacated by the multiplier.

Example 4-5. Machine Multiplication 12×5 in Binary, Showing Contents of A and Q Registers at Each Step

Operation	Contents of A-Register	Contents of Q-Register
Clear Acc. Register	0000	101
Add Multiplicand	<u>1100</u>	101
	1100	101
Shift R	0110	010
Add zero or immediately Shift R	0011	001
Add multiplicand	<u>1100</u>	001
	1111	001
Shift R	0111	100

Result $(111100)_2 = (60)_{10}$

If the multiplier is expressed as 0101, four right shifts are executed, leading to the same result.

A simple arrangement for fast shifting as shown in Fig. 4-3, consists of AND gates and delay units. This arrangement requires delicate timing because the previous state should not be permitted to change until it has been safely transmitted to the next state. Shifting registers with an auxiliary memory rank for the temporary storage of the shifted number are less sensitive to timing, but they are slower.

4-7. SERIAL BINARY MULTIPLICATION

Serial binary multiplication is an interesting example of the special timing problem when two different motions of the data in the machine have to be coordinated. The problem arises in the relative shifting of two circulating numbers. Suppose the circulating registers consist of delay units and two n-bit numbers X and Y are introduced in the registers such that the bits of the same order emerge from the registers at the same time. If in the register circulating the number X one delay unit is added the digit x_i will emerge simultaneously with the digit y_{i+1} which means that the number X is shifted one position to the left with respect to number Y. For a right shift, one delay unit has to be left out of the circulating path. As long as this is being done the number will be shifted one position to the right for every complete circulation compared with the number for which no delay unit is left out. Leaving one delay unit out requires that an extra one is provided originally in addition to the n digits of the number and usually takes the form of a space bit between wo rd s.

The serial binary multiplier, shown in Fig. 4-9, uses the previously described multiplication method a with the left shift of the multiplicand.

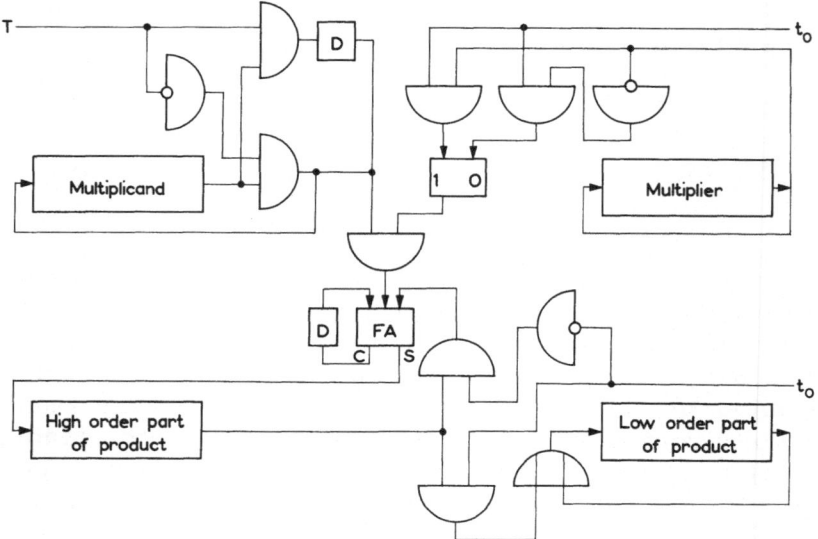

Fig. 4-9. Serial Binary Multiplier

The multiplier consists of 4 circulating registers with n delay units each for the multiplicand X, the multiplier Y and the high and low order part of the product. For the timing, it is convenient to differentiate between word time T and bit time t, required for the circulation of an entire word or one bit respectively. The word time T contains $n + 1$ bit times due to the additional delay for the multiplicand. At bit time t_0 of the first word time T_1 the least significant bit of the multiplier sets a flip-flop according to the value of the bit either to one or zero. One bit time later the multiplicand bits emerge from the additional delay unit and serially enter, with the flip-flop in the 1-state, the full adder during the bit times t_1 through t_n and proceed from there during the same time into the register for the high order part of the product.

At the bit time t_0 of the second word time T_2 the lowest order bit of the partial product is moved from the high order to the low order product register, and the next to the least significant multiplier digit which emerges at this time from the register sets the flip-flop. During bit times t_1 through t_n of the second word time T_2, the remaining bits of the partial product are circulated through the adder back to the high order product register with the multiplicand bits added or not added whichever may be the case according to the flip-flop state.

The signal $T = T_1$ through T_n is applied continuously during the multiplication process. It affects the emergence of the multiplicand digits during the bit times t_1 through t_n while at bit time t_0 of each word time a blank appears in the series of multiplicand digits. This time is used to set the flip-flop which controls the addition of the multiplicand by the circulating multiplier digits, and to move the low order digit of the partial product, which is not needed for further addition, into the low order product register. The digits circulating in this register have reentered the register one bit time before the new bit from the high order register arrives.

The serial multiplier can also be built with two circulating registers for multiplicand and high order part of the product and one shifting register in which the originally entered multiplier is gradually replaced by the low order digits of the product. During the multiplication process the shifting register is shifted one position to the right at the bit time t_n of every word time T_i so that at the bit time t_0 of the word time T_{i+1} the next multiplier digit has been moved in the controlling least significant position and the most significant bit position in the shifting register has been vacated for the bit coming in from the register for the high order digits of the product.

The time required for the serial multiplication according to Fig. 4-9 is determined by the number of additions depending on the number of significant multiplier digits and by the time per addition or word time allowed for the serial processing of the multiplicand digits.

This time can be substantially reduced, in fact to two word times, when a flip-flop register is provided into which the multiplier digits emerging from the delay units of a circulating register are transferred simultaneously at one bit time and are held in static condition during the multiplication process. The arrangement shown in Fig. 4-10 for 3-bit words can be extended for any word length.

In addition to the static register for the multiplier $(n-1)$ full adders are required for n-bit words. The delays are one bit time. The multiplicand digits enter and the product digits emerge serially. For n-bit words the product will have 2n bits, therefore for the development and processing of the product two word times have to be allowed.

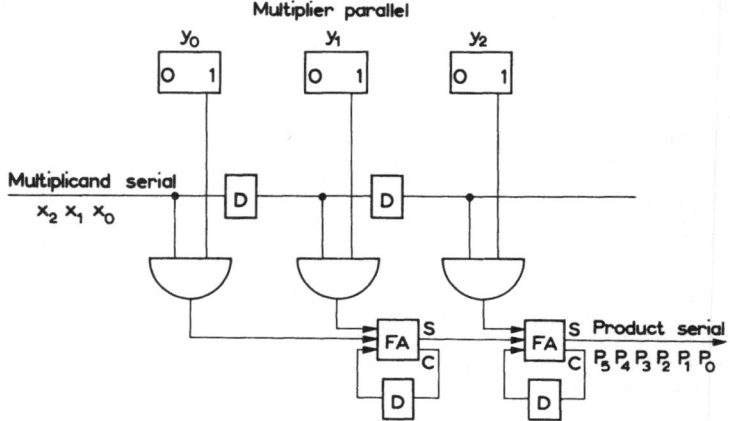

Fig. 4-10. Fast Serial Multiplier

Denoting in ascending order multiplicand digits with x_0, x_1, x_2, multiplier digits with y_0, y_1, y_2, and product digits with p_0, p_1 through p_5 the following multiplication sequence can be traced through Fig. 4-10.

After 1st bit time $p_0 = x_0 y_0$ (4-12)

After 2nd bit time $p_1 = x_0 y_1 + x_1 Y_0$

After 3rd bit time $p_2 = x_0 y_2 + x_1 y_1 + x_2 y_0$

After 4th bit time $p_3 = x_1 y_2 + x_2 y_1$

After 5th bit time $p_4 = x_2 y_2$

After 6th bit time $p_5 =$ eventl. carry from p_4

The value for the product digits in (4-12) check exactly with the normal paper and pencil multiplication shown below.

			x_2	x_1	x_0	(4-13)
			y_2	y_1	y_0	
			$x_2 y_0$	$x_1 y_0$	$x_0 y_0$	
		$x_2 y_1$	$x_1 y_1$	$x_0 y_1$		
carry	$x_2 y_2$	$x_1 y_2$	$x_0 y_2$			
p_5	p_4	p_3	p_2	p_1	p_0	

4-8. PARALLEL BINARY MULTIPLICATION

The parallel generation and processing of partial or final products can be considered as the typical characteristicum of parallel binary multiplication. Otherwise parallel and serial operations are quite intermingled in the multiplication process. The previously described fast serial multiplication circuit uses a multiplier presented in parallel while in the arrangement according to Fig. 4-8 which is basically used in parallel machines the multiplier digits enter the multiplication process in a serial fashion.

The time required for parallel multiplication is determined primarily by the number of additions and shifts which have to be performed. The efforts to reduce the time are directed toward speeding up the individual operations or cutting down the number of operations. So far the first approach has been more successful. In the execution of a multiply instruction the first machine cycles are used to set up the instruction and to bring the operands from main storage to registers in the arithmetic units. The add and shift operations can then be performed so fast that the operations called for by two or more multiplier digits can be handled in one machine cycle which consists of a multiple, e.g., 10 or 12, clock pulses.

The other approach to cut down the number of operations or, to be more specific, the number of successive operations is based on the simultaneous sensing of two or more multiplier digits and the initiation of control circuits to handle the operations according to the combined multiplier digits.

The logic for the simultaneous sensing of several multiplier digits has not yet become very popular. The main reason is the great advance in speeding up the conventional multiplication process with individual sensing of the multiplier digits. In modern computers full advantage is taken of the fact that shifts can be performed much faster than additions and they are both performed at their maximum possible speed. If the sensing is done in the so-called look ahead manner and not serially with the shifting, it is possible to perform a series of shifts at the clock pulse rate of the computer. Assuming a machine cycle consisting of 10 clock pulses, 10 successive shifts could be performed in one machine cycle. With the cycle time of fast machines down to 2 microseconds, shifts are done in .2 microseconds or 200 nanoseconds. If the machine cycle comprises more pulses, the time per operation becomes even shorter. With these speed advances it is understandable that any gain in speed which is claimed for multiple digit sensing is looked upon very critically, not so much with regard to the the additional equipment but even more with regard to the actual increase in speed which might be obtainable in practice after the more complicated circuits and controlling schemes all have been realized.

4-9. BCD MULTIPLICATION

The BCD addition is generally performed parallel for the four bits making up one binary coded decimal digit, while the coded decimal digits are processed serially. The circuit for addition, shown in Fig. 4-6, handles all possible bit combinations $x_1x_2x_4x_8$ and $y_1y_2y_4y_8$ of the two operands.

A multiplication circuit which could multiply the multiplicand bits $x_1x_2x_4x_8$ in parallel with all possible combinations of the multiplier bits $y_1y_2y_4y_8$ would be rather complicated. The difficulty arises from the fact that the bits of the operands are not combined pair-wise as in the addition process but that the entire bit combinations of multiplicand and multiplier, standing for decimal 0 through 9, have to be considered simultaneously.

For simplification of the problem use is made of the fact that the products can be considered as multiples of some basic products. If, for example, fixed circuits are provided which multiply the multiplicand M by 2, 5, and 8 having as their outputs 2M, 5M, and 8M, then the products P_1 through P_9, according to the values 1 through 9 for the multiplier, can be obtained by adding the partial products in the following way:

$$P_1 = M, P_2 = 2M, P_3 = M + 2M, \tag{4-14}$$

$$P_4 = 2M + 2M, P_5 = 5M, P_6 = M + 5M,$$

$$P_7 = 2M + 5M, P_8 = 8M, P_9 = M + 8M.$$

When the four bits of one multiplicand digit are presented to the circuit, the partial products, M, 2M, 5M, and 8M are formed and their addition takes place through a gating network under the direction of the decoded multiplier bits. Other selections for the basic partial products are possible. They all lead to a considerable simplification of BCD multiplication circuits. The reason is the relative simplicity of the circuits which are required for the multiplication by a constant, as illustrated by the doubling and quintupling circuits which are derived for the 8421 code. The algebraic expressions for the circuits are obtained from the table of combinations.

TABLE 4-6

TRUTH TABLE FOR DOUBLING

Original BCD				Doubled BCD				
x_8	x_4	x_2	x_1	C_0	D_8	D_4	D_2	D_1
0	0	0	1	0	0	0	1	0
0	0	1	0	0	0	1	0	0
0	0	1	1	0	0	1	1	0
0	1	0	0	0	1	0	0	0
0	1	0	1	1	0	0	0	0
0	1	1	0	1	0	0	1	0
0	1	1	1	1	0	1	0	0
1	0	0	0	1	0	1	1	0
1	0	0	1	1	1	0	0	0

$C_0 = x_8'x_4x_1 + x_8'x_4x_2 + x_8x_4'x_2'$; since in BCD no combinations are permitted with one in the x_8 position and one's in either the x_4 or x_2 position the relations $x_8x_4 = 0$ and $x_8x_2 = 0$ can be used for simplication:

$$C_0 = x_8 + x_4x_2 + x_4x_1 \qquad (4\text{-}15)$$

The carryout C_0 is fed back over a delay unit to be available at the lowest bit position of the doubling circuit as carry-in C_i when the next higher order multiplicand digit arrives for doubling. In this way the carry to the next higher order digit is automatically taken care of. The doubled output in the lowest bit position D_1 is zero and becomes one only when a carry-in occurs.

$$D_1 = C_i \qquad (4\text{-}16)$$

Since the carry-in C_i has no effect on the other bit positions the values for the doubled outputs D_2, D_4, and D_8 can be directly derived from Table 4-6.

$$D_2 = x_8'x_4'x_1 + x_8'x_4x_2x_1' + x_8x_4'x_2'x_1'$$

adding in $x_8'x_2'x_1'x_1 = 0$ and using $C_0' = x_8'x_4' + x_8'x_2'x_1'$ as well as $x_8x_4 = 0$ and $x_8x_2 = 0$, we obtain the simplified expression:

$$D_2 = x_1 C_o' + x_1' C_o \tag{4-17}$$

$$D_4 = x_8' x_4' x_2 + x_8' x_4 x_2 x_1 + x_8 x_4' x_2' x_1'$$

Using again $x_8 x_4 = 0$, $x_8 x_2 = 0$ and bringing in $x_8' x_2' x_1' x_2 = 0$ the expression simplifies to:

$$D_4 = x_2 C_o' + x_2 x_1 + x_8 x_1' \tag{4-18}$$

$$D_8 = x_8' x_4 x_2' x_1' + x_8 x_4' x_2' x_1$$

Adding $x_8' x_4' x_4 = 0$ and using $x_8 x_4 = x_8 x_2 = 0$ reduces this expression to:

$$D_8 = x_4 C_o' + x_8 x_1 \tag{4-19}$$

It will be noted that the rearrangements leading to the introduction of the terms C_o and C_o', which are available anyhow, contributed greatly to the achieved simplifications. The network realizing the above equations is shown in Fig. 4-11.

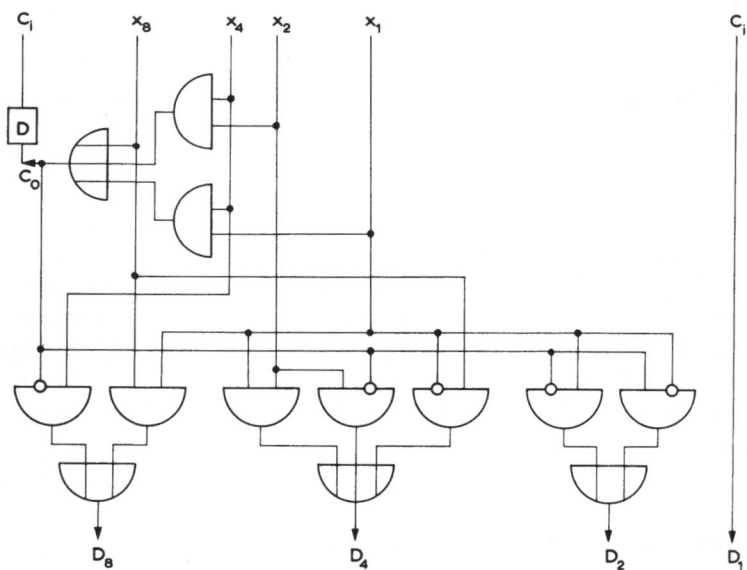

Fig. 4-11. Doubling Circuit

The quintupling circuit is obtained from Table 4-7 in which in the middle part the carries and outputs are entered which are generated at the multiplication of the lowest order digit of the multiplicand, and at the right the outputs for all higher order digits with the carries from the preceding digit added. The equations are derived for the latter outputs because they present the general case. The inspection of Table 4-7 reveals that only the input x_1 contributes to the outputs while the inputs x_8, x_4, x_2 generate the carries C_4, C_2, C_1. The carry C_8 never occurs, therefore the right hand outputs are functions only of x_1, C_4, C_2, and C_1. For simplification use is made of the fact that carry never occurs simultaneously for C_4 and either C_2 or C_1, which means $C_4C_2 = 0$ and $C_4C_1 = 0$.

TABLE 4-7

TRUTH TABLE FOR QUINTUPLING

BCD input				Carries				Quintupled output without carry				Quintupled output with carry			
x_8	x_4	x_2	x_1	C_8	C_4	C_2	C_1	Q_8	Q_4	Q_2	Q_1	Q_8	Q_4	Q_2	Q_1
0	0	0	1	0	0	0	0	0	1	0	1	0	1	0	1
0	0	1	0	0	0	0	1	0	0	0	0	0	0	0	1
0	0	1	1	0	0	0	1	0	1	0	1	0	1	1	0
0	1	0	0	0	0	1	0	0	0	0	0	0	0	1	0
0	1	0	1	0	0	1	0	0	1	0	1	0	1	1	1
0	1	1	0	0	0	1	1	0	0	0	0	0	0	1	1
0	1	1	1	0	0	1	1	0	1	0	1	1	0	0	0
1	0	0	0	0	1	0	0	0	0	0	0	0	1	0	0
1	0	0	1	0	1	0	0	0	1	0	1	1	0	0	1

$$Q_8 = x_1 C_4' C_2 C_1 + x_1 C_4 C_2' C_1' \qquad (4\text{-}20)$$

$$= x_1 C_2 C_1 + x_1 C_4$$

The following relations for Q_4 and Q_2 can be written in a more condensed form by using

$$Q_8' = x_1' + C_1' C_4' + C_2' C_4' \qquad (4\text{-}21)$$

$$Q_4 = x_1 C_4' C_2' + x_1 C_4' C_1' + x_1' C_4 C_2' C_1'$$

$$= x_1 C_4' C_2' + x_1 C_4' C_1' + x_1' C_4 \qquad (4\text{-}22)$$

$$= (x_1 + C_4) Q_8'$$

$$Q_2 = x_1 C_4' C_2' C_1 + C_4' C_2 C_1' + x_1' C_4' C_2 C_1$$

$$= x_1 C_4' C_2' C_1 + C_4' C_2 C_1' + x_1' C_2 \qquad (4\text{-}23)$$

$$= (x_1 C_1 + C_2) Q_8'$$

$$Q_1 = x_1 C_4' C_1' + x_1' C_4' C_1 + x_1 C_4 C_2' C_1'$$
$$= x_1 C_1' C_4' + x_1' C_1 + x_1 C_1' C_4 \qquad (4\text{-}24)$$
$$= x_1 C_1' + x_1' C_1$$

The last relation expresses the exclusive OR for x_1 and C_1 which means Q_1 is only high when either x_1 or C_1 is high but not both. Other approaches for the simplification are possible. The circuit according to the above output equations is shown in Fig. 4-12.

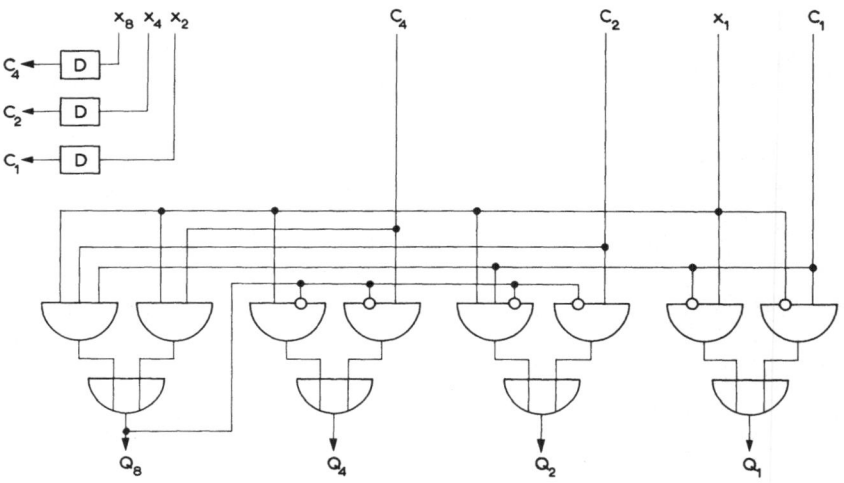

Fig. 4-12. Quintupling Circuit

This circuit is relatively simple because for the carry generation no gates are required. From the truth table 4-7 the straightforward relation between the inputs x_8, x_4, x_2 and the carries C_4, C_2, C_1 can be recognized where x_8 becomes C_4, x_4 becomes C_2, and x_2 becomes C_1 exclusively.

A complete BCD digit multiplier arrangement is depicted in Fig. 4-13. The fixed multiples of the multiplicand digit are gated and added under the control of the decoded multiplier digit according to (4-13) or other combinations of constant multiples. After the partial product of all multiplicand digits with one multiplier digit is formed the circuit comes under the control of the next multiplier digit. The digits of the partial products may be added to the corresponding digits of previous partial products as they emerge serially from the circuit thus forming the subproducts and the final product.

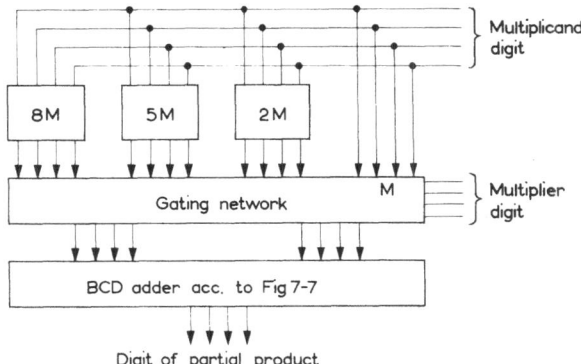

Digit of partial product

Fig. 4-13. BCD Multiplier Arrangement

4-10. CONSIDERATIONS FOR MACHINE DIVISION

Since in the division process the dividend can be considered as the product of divisor and quotient it is evident that a certain similarity exists between multiplication and division and that the approach to the machine mechanization of the two operations will follow similar lines. In division the known factor is the divisor which has to be subtracted successively from the dividend and the remainders in order to obtain the quotient. As in binary multiplication the product is obtained through successive additions of the shifted multiplicand.

However, in division some problems arise which are not present in multiplication, notably the beginning of the division, the handling of negative remainders, and the disposal of the final remainder. With paper and pencil the start of a division problem is done somewhat intuitively by inspecting the relative magnitude of the operands. The machine does not have the same capability, and the first orders of the dividend from which the divisor shall be subtracted have to be determined mechanically. It is quite customary to start machine divisions with subtraction of the divisor from the high orders of the dividend as it is usually done with paper and pencil. To this end the most significant digits of the dividend and divisor are aligned for the first subtraction. The sign of the difference then determines the start of the division. A positive difference gives "1" and a negative difference "0" for the digit of the quotient. Since a leading zero has no significance the development of the quotient starts with the first positive difference.

At this point, the two modes of restoring and non-restoring division have to be considered with regard to their handling in the machine. In the restoring method every time a negative difference occurs the divisor is added back in again to restore the original dividend or remainder which is then shifted to the left before the divisor is subtracted again. In the non-restoring method the division process is continued without the restoring of the dividend or remainder; the negative sign of the remainder directs the machine to add the divisor after the remainder had been shifted to the left while a positive remainder calls for subtraction of the divisor. The following example of dividing $66_{10} = 1000010_2$ by $13_{10} = 1101_2$ explains step by step the process for both methods.

Example 4-6.   Divide 1000010 by 1101

	Restoring Method				Non-Restoring Method		
	S	1000010			S	1000010	
Subtract		1101		Subtract		1101	
	1	1011010			1	1011010	
Add		1101		Shift L	1	011010	Quotient
	0	1000010		Add		1101	1
Shift L	1	000010	Quotient		0	001110 - - - - - - - ↑	
Subtract		1101	1	Shift L	0	01110	
	0	001110 - - - - - - - ↑		Subtract		1101	10
Shift L	0	01110			1	10100 - - - - - - - - ↑	
Subtract		1101	10	Shift L	1	0100	
	1	10100 - - - - - - - - ↑		Add		1101	101
Add		1101			0	0001 - - - - - - - - - ↑	
	0	01110					
Shift L	0	1110					
Subtract		1101	101				
	0	0001· - - - - - - - - - ↑		Remainder 0001			

In the restoring method, the divisor D is first added back in again with its full value D and then subtracted from the left-shifted remainder which results in an operation $+D - 1/2\ D$. The non-restoring method simply adds the divisor to the left-shifted remainder corresponding to $+ 1/2\ D$ in this way saving one operational step every time a negative remainder occurs. Due to the resulting shorter execution time for non-restoring division it has become the preferred method for machine division.

In the shifting process, the bit which is shifted beyond the sign position is lost. The value which appears in the sign position directly as a consequence of the add or subtract operation determines in the described manner not only the quotient bit but also the next operation; a "1" as sign bit is followed by add and a "0" by subtract. If the sign bit changes during a shift operation, the subsequent operation, determined by the sign bit prior to shift, remains unchanged. The repeated shifts of the remainder will eventually result in a greater length of the dividend, and the quotient digits which are then obtained fall behind the binary point. The next example shall illustrate these points.

Example 4-7.   Divide 10100 (dec. 20) by 110 (dec. 6)

```
              S | 10100
   Subtract      | 110
              ―――――――――
              1 | 11100
   Shift L    1 | 1100
   Add          | 110              Quotient
              ―――――――――
              0 | 10000 ---- → 1
   Shift L   *1 | 000                      *The "1" shifted in the sign posi-
   Subtract     | 110                       tion enters further computation
              ―――――――――                      but does not effect the subtract
              0 | 010 ------- → 1           operation which has been deter-
   Shift L    0 | 10                        mined by the "0" previously in the
   Subtract     | 110                       position.
              ―――――――――
              1 | 110 -------- → .0
   Shift L    1 | 10
   Add          | 110
              ―――――――――
              0 | 010 -------- → 1
   Shift L    0 | 10
   Subtract     | 110
              ―――――――――
              1 | 110 --------- → 0
   Shift L    1 | 10
   Add          | 110
              ―――――――――
              0 | 010 ---------- → 1        Result 11.0101
                etc.
```

In preceding examples correct results were obtained because the divisor was larger than the high order bits of the dividend from which the first subrraction was made. When the divisor is much smaller than the high order bits of the dividend, it can happen that the dividend is shifted to the left, before all respective quotient bits have been collected. This always happens when positive remainders would be obtained for more than one subtraction of the divisor from the unshifted high order bits of the dividend. Therefore, the divide-check test determines before division takes place, if the absolute value of the divisor is greater than the absolute value of the part of the dividend in the accumulator.

Example 4-8 illustrates the incorrect division with the smaller divisor and the correct division with alignment to satisfy the divide-check.

Example 4-8.   Divide 1000010 (dec. 66) by 11 (dec. 3)

a. Incorrect Division				*b. Correct Division*			
		1000010				001000010	
Subtract		0011	1	Subtract		0011	
	0	0101010 - - - - - - ↑			1	111100010	
Shift L	0	101010		Shift L	1	11100010	
Subtract		0011	11	Add		0011	1
	0	011110 - - - - - - - ↑			0	00010010 - - - - - - - ↑	
Shift L	0	11110		Shift L	0	0010010	
Subtract		0011	111	Subtract		0011	10
	0	11000 - - - - - - - - ↑			1	1111010 - - - - - - - ↑	
Shift L	1	1000		Shift L	1	111010	
Subtract		0011	1110	Add		0011	101
	1	0101 - - - - - - - - ↑			0	000110 - - - - - - - - ↑	
Shift L	0	1010		Shift L	0	00110	
Add		0011	1110.1	Subtract		0011	1011
	0	1101 - - - - - - - - ↑			0	00000 - - - - - - - - - ↑	
Shift L	1	1010		Shift L	0	0000	
Subtract		0011	1110.10	Subtract		0011	10110
	1	0111 - - - - - - - - ↑			1	1101 - - - - - - - - - - ↑	
etc.				Shift L	1	1010	
				Add		0011	10110.0
				etc.	1	1101 - - - - - - - - - - ↑	

Correct result $(10110)_2 = (22)_{10}$

After the quotient has been developed to the specified number of bits it has to be decided what shall be done with the final remainder. If the latter is used in further computations it is stored as a separate word; otherwise it may be discarded. In the rare cases where the final remainder may be needed, it can be reconstructed by subtracting the product of quotient and divisor from the dividend.

The basic idea underlying the implementation of machine division is the common usage of the arithmetic registers which are already provided for multiplication according to Fig. 4-8. Following the analogy of the two operations, the dvidend corresponding to the product in multiplication, is placed in the shifting A-register and the divisor, corresponding to the multiplicand, in the storage register as indicated in Fig. 4-14.

After alignment of the two operands the division always starts with the subtraction of the divisor from the dividend.

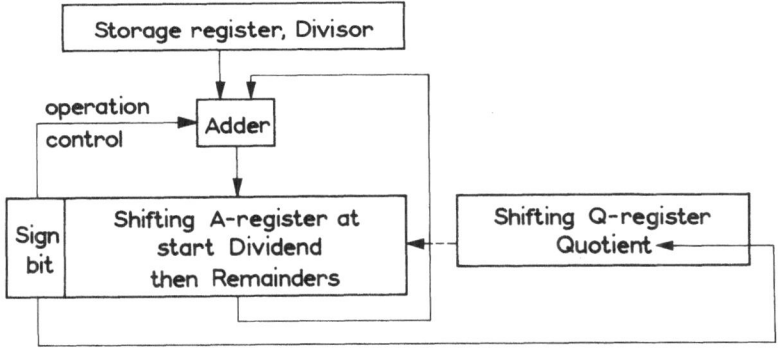

Fig. 4-14. General Arrangement for Machine Division

From there on the sign of the remainder controls the operations and the quotient bits which are entered and shifted from the right to the left in the other shifting register, called the Q-register, of the arithmetic unit. At the beginning of the division process the register is empty and may be filled with the lower orders of a double-length dividend which are gradually shifted to the left into the A-register as the quotient bits are moved in.

Subtraction may be performed by adding the complement, with the necessary considerations for the sign, and recomplementation as explained under binary subtraction. In the foregoing examples straight addition and subtraction were used in order to keep the examples simple and to concentrate on the essentials of the division process.

BCD division is performed by successive subtraction of the divisor from the highest orders of the dividend until it goes negative. Then the positive value is restored by adding back in the divisor and the subtraction of the divisor is started again from the next lower digit of the dividend. A remainder in the higher digit position has to be adjusted to the next lower position by the subtraction of a corrective 6. Note that every digit consists of 4 bits.

Each time a positive remainder is obtained a one is added to the respective order of the quotient corresponding to the order of dividend from which the subtractions are made. The following example with the division of 52 by 4 shall explain the procedure.

Example 4-9.   BCD Division (0101 0010) ÷ (0100)

		Dividend		*Quotient*	
		0101	0010		
Sub Divisor		0100			
		0001		0001	
Sub Divisor		0100			
Borrow	(1)	1101			
Add Divisor		0100			
		0001	0010		
Sub Corrective 6			0110		
			1100		
Sub Divisor			0100		
			1000		0001
Sub Divisor			0100		
			0100		0010
Sub Divisor			0100		
			0000	0001	0011 = $(13)_{10}$

Many variations of binary and decimal arithmetic circuits, past and present, are presented in the book by Richards, "Arithmetic Operations in Digital Computers" (*see bibliography*).

4-1. Draw a diagram for parallel binary adder with speed up circuits with the grouping of 6 stages of a 24 bit computer word.

4-2. Explain the difference of adding with adder networks and with accumulators.

4-3. Perform according to Fig. 4-3 binary addition similar to examples 4-1 and 4-2 for $(+7)+(-5)$; $(-8)+(+6)$; $(-9)+(-3)$.

4-4. Perform according to Fig. 4-3 binary subtraction similar to examples 4-1 and 4-2 for $(+10)-(+7)$; $(-13)-(-5)$; $(-12)-(+3)$.

4-5. Add the following BCD numbers (0010 0101) plus (0100 0011); (0101 0100) plus (0001 1001); (0011 0110) plus (0110 0111).

4-6. Subtract the following BCD numbers using the 9's complement for BCD (1001 0001)− (0101 1000); (0011 0101)− (0001 1001); (0100 0110)− (0010 0011).

4-7. Perform binary machine multiplication showing the contents of the A and Q register as in Example 4-5, for $13/16 \times 3/8$, or $(0.1101)_2 \times (0.0110)_2$.

4-8. Perform binary machine multiplication as in problem 4-7 for 12 times 11 and 21 times 12.

4-9. Draw the gating network of Fig. 4-13 in detail according to equations (4-14).

4-10. Rewrite equations (4-14) for the case that the doubled multiplicand 2M is doubled again to obtain 4M, but no constant product 8M is formed.

4-11. Draw diagram for obtaining the 9 multiples of the multiplicand according to the relations derived in problem 4-10.

4-12. Perform binary machine division with the restoring and non-restoring method as in Example 4-6, for $140 \div 14$ or in binary $(10001100)_2 \div (1110)_2$.

4-13. Perform binary machine division using the non-restoring method for $8 \div 3$; $13 \div 4$; $24 \div 8$.

4-14. Develop quotient to three positions behind the binary point for $(1010)_2 \div (11)_2$ using the same method as in problem 4-13.

CHAPTER 5

The Instruction
Code of the Computer

5-1. BASIC COMPUTER OPERATIONS

Considering the vast variety and complexity of the problems which are solved by the computer, it is surprising how few basic operations are required to accomplish these great computational feats. Actually everything which the machine does depends upon the elementary functions of moving, replacing, and combining information bits.

The *movement* of information bits takes place between or within computer parts; generally the information is not changed in the moving process with the exemption of the shift motion which alters the meaning of the information.

The *replacement* of information bits is done either for a part or for the entire computer word; the exchange if 1's and 0's in the complementation process and the modification of instructions and data belong in this category.

The *combination* of two sets of information bits is done for matching or for computing purposes; matching is a logical process with the bit pairs combined individually, while computing is an algebraic process where the carries have to be considered which are generated in the combination of two sets of bits.

The manifold instructions or commands which the computers have available for the execution of programs are built up from these few elementary operations.

These instructions comprise more or less complex combinations of the basic operations. They are made up to suit the needs of the programmer and what he wants to accomplish, and are not restricted to the basic functional operations of the computer.

For example, a simple add instruction includes not only the adding process but also the moving of at least one operand to the register where the adding is performed, or a multiply instruction includes besides the moving of the operands all the additions and shifts which are required to form the desired product.

Therefore, it can be seen that no simple direct relation exists between the elementary functions of the computer and its command structure. The latter is rather determined by considerations with regard to the handling and solving of problems on the computer, and it is quite natural that the instruction code of machines varies according to the concepts of different designers as to what might be the most useful set of instructions. The professional user of the computer considers the available instructions as a very important aspect which should weigh highly in the evaluation of a machine.

So far the words "instruction" and "command" have been used in the same sense, meaning the ordering of actions by the computer. For larger computer setups which consist not only of the main processor but also of separate input-output channels and controllers between the channels and the main unit a distinction may be made, such that instructions refer to the main processor, commands to the action of channels, and orders to the controllers. Since we are concerned with the main processing unit the word "instruction" will be used in the sequel. The totality of instructions available in a computer is referred to as instruction code or instruction repertoire.

5-2. INSTRUCTION FORMAT

Instruction words and data words in the computer have outwardly the same appearance as strings of 0's and 1's; only the interpretation of the words distinguishes them.

Instruction words basically have an operation part and an address part referring to the addresses whose contents are to be operated on. One major distinction between different instruction formats is made according to the number of addresses in their address part, as shown in Fig. 5-1.

Since computer words have a fixed length, it is obvious that an instruction word with four addresses is very much limited in the number of individually addressable storage locations. Assuming a word length with 34 bits and setting aside 6 bits for the operation part, leaves a 7 bit address field for each of four addresses, just large enough to hold as the largest number 127 with 1's filled in all 7 positions. For older computers

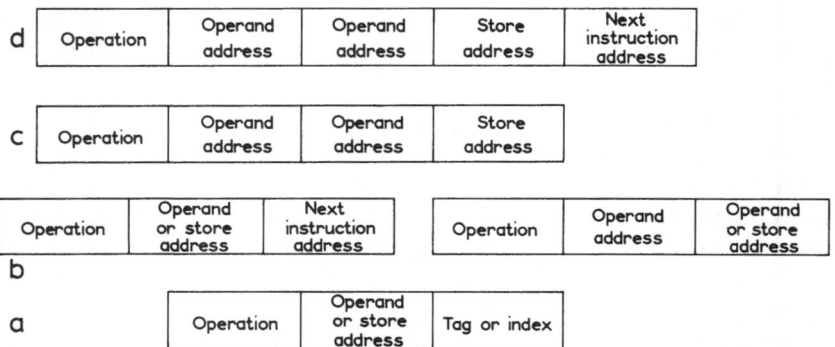

Fig. 5-1. Some Formats of a.) One-Address, b.) Two-Address, c.) Three-Address, and d.) Four-Address Instructions

with small memories this was not so critical, and advantage was taken, for ease in programming, of the possibility of packing one instruction word with information sufficient to fetch 2 operands, to operate on them, to store the result, and to fetch the next instruction.

When the memory size of computers increased, the two-address instructions became very popular with substantially larger address fields and still some packing of information in one instruction word. The format shown at left in Fig. 5-1, b is used by the IBM 650, a decimal machine, with 2 decimal digits for the operation part and 4 digits for each address part. The format at right in Fig. 5-1, b is used by the Univac 1103, a binary machine, with 6 bits for operation and 15 bits each for the address parts. A field of 15 bits can hold as largest number 32,767 for the highest core address, certainly a great advance compared with three-, or four-address instructions.

In modern computers there is a definite trend toward one-address instructions, not only to accomodate the addressing of larger memories, but also to facilitate address modification and, in general, to provide a greater flexibility in the manipulation of data. For the scanning of records and the search of tables, the computer must be able to work efficiently with variable sized fields. The translation into machine instructions is made easier for a simple order structure. One-address instructions provide both simplicity and flexibility. There is no question that for the mind of the programmer a more sophisticated and larger set of instructions is appealing and helpful.

The situation is different however for automatic machine operation.

The basic format for one-address instructions, as shown in Fig. 5-1.a, has an operation, address and index part. There exists a great variety of formats, partly with variable operation and address fields according to the type of operation to be performed, and practically always with some tag or index field for the specification of index operations or modifications.

For machines with a larger word length two complete instructions are placed in one machine word, as in the Philco S2000 and the CDC 1604 which have a 48 bit word length. In the CDC 1604 each instruction has 6 bits for operation, 3 bits for index, and 15 bits for the address part. In the IBM 7030 STRETCH computer which has a word length of 64 bits two instructions with 32 bits each may be placed in one word. The instruction format for this machine is arranged from left to right with address, operation, and index part.

These few examples may suffice to indicate that details in the arrangement of the instruction format vary from machine to machine, but that in general, the one-address format is now preferred providing a sufficient number of bits for instruction modification purposes.

5-3.   CODING OF INSTRUCTIONS

The machine can respond only to information expressed in the code which is recognized and obeyed by its circuitry. The proper encoding is required for both, data and instructions. The writing of programs is mainly concerned with the set of instructions of which they are composed. Therefore, the different coding levels which have been established as programming codes are mainly reflected in the coding of instructions, and a discussion of them leads automatically to discussion of the different programming systems.

The basic idea, underlying the development of the different coding levels, is the continuous endeavor to relieve the programmer from the drudgery of details of programming and eventually to make it independent of any particular machine. In this section the codes are discussed in which the instructions can be written for a specific digital computer.

The *machine or absolute code* expresses instructions in numeric form directly acceptable to the computer, with the operation part in some numeric code and the address part containing the actual number of the respective storage location. After loading into the machine the instructions can be entered directly in this form into the control and address registers for execution. This code is also called the machine language in which ultimately every computation is carried out in the machine.

The *interpretive code* was introduced to ease the burden on the programmer by packing more information in one instruction and making it possible to write a program with fewer instructions. Thus, pseudo-instructions are formed which have no one-to-one relation to the actual machine instructions and they must be decomposed into an equivalent sequence of machine instructions at the time of execution before they can be entered into the control unit of the machine. The decomposition is performed by the interpreter, an interpretive program, which must be loaded in the main memory of the machine at execution time. The main disadvantage of the interpretive system is the time loss in the interpretation of an instruction each time it is used, making this system attractive only for one-time problems. The pseudo-instructions of the interpretive code may be written either in numeric or symbolic form.

The *symbolic or assembly code* is now most commonly used for direct programming for a particular machine. It replaces the numbers in the address and operation parts by symbols facilitating the use of the instructions by the programmer. Generally the one-to-one relation between machine and symbolic instructions is preserved and only a simple replacement of the symbols by the actual numeric machine operations and addresses is required before execution of the program. This transformation is done by the so-called assembly program usually only once when the program is assembled. Subsequent production runs use the assembled program in machine code.

The next level of coding, the machine independent algebraic codes or languages are discussed under automatic programming in Chapter 7.

The symbolic letter or mnemonic code is normally chosen to suggest the operations implied. Single letters or groups of letters, from two to five, small and capital, have been used, or symbols such as+ for clear and add and (+) for adding without clearing. Uniform sets of three capital letters, such as CLA for clear and add and HLT for halt, have possibly become more customary than other symbols and they will be used in this text.

5-4. GENERAL CLASSES OF INSTRUCTIONS

Though practically all computers have different instruction repertoires some very typical classes of instructions can be organized and according to these groups or types of instructions certain more general statements can be made. A good identification of the classes is obtained by a basic picture of the principal activities which take place in a computer program. The essential activities are sketched in a simplified form in Fig. 5-2.

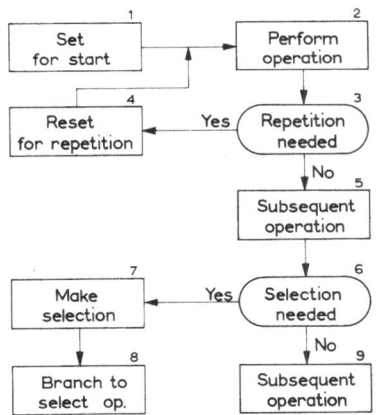

Fig. 5-2. Essential Program Activities

The two most essential characteristics of computer programs, which actually make the use of computers practical and permit the writing of codes for machines, are the capabilities to reply to questions or situations and to make choices. The first property is generally referred to as replication and the second as conditionals. Every computer language and instruction code must include these properties in order to make possible the automatic solution of problems in which decisions have to be made according to intermediate results and changing conditions.

Check 3 and box 4 in Fig. 5-2 are the typical discrimination and response to situations arising in operational loops for repetitive and iterative processes. Check 6 and boxes 7 and 8 are the discrimination and response for situations requiring a choice. It is obvious that these activities represent the directed links or structure of the control functions which connect the operational parts of the program. All instructions referring to them can be classified as *control instructions*.

In reality the instructions are not made up according to the breakdown of checks and boxes in Fig. 5-2 which only illustrate the general situation. In practice, an instruction for selection will include both, the actions of box 7 and 8, to be performed at the point in the program which is normally determined by the programmer, but which also may eventually be determined by the program. The check in 3 and the reset in 4 are also normally performed under the direction of one instruction. The instruction which executes box 1 may be considered as a control instruction as well because it sets or controls the initial condition for the operation in box 2.

The operational boxes, in the example of Fig. 5-2 the boxes 2, 5, and 9, are called the nodes of the program. They perform the actual processes or operations of the program under the direction of the next class of instructions, the *operational instructions*. One operation box may require a set of several instructions for its execution.

Besides the two previous classes of instructions for strictly internal computer actions a third class, the *editing instructions*, cover the communication of the computer with input and output media.

Modern computers have an instruction repertoire of approximately 50 to 100 instructions. Many of them are provided for specific operation modes, such as fixed or floating point arithmetic, the utilization of special registers, test and sense operations, or an elaborate selection of peripheral equipment and data. These instructions are required for the efficient handling of the overall data processing, but for the actual solution of problems in the computer only a certain set of instructions is necessary. A representative set of these internal instructions will be introduced as much as possible with instruction types which are quite common. It must be recognized that in general no standards exist as yet and many instructions are tailormade to fit particular machines.

The three classes of instructions are not mutually exclusive and in some cases it is a matter of choice in which class an instruction is placed.

5-5.   OPERATIONAL INSTRUCTIONS

The operational instructions are the easiest to describe and relatively common for many machines.

The four basic *arithmetic operations*, add, subtract, multiply, and divide are handled by the instructions ADD, SUB, MPY, and DIV. Since one-address instructions are considered with only the address of the second operand in the address part, additional instructions are required for the loading of the first operand into the arithmetic unit and the storing of the result in order to cover the complete operation.

The loading instructions contain in their address part the location L of the information which shall be loaded into some part of the arithmetic unit and different instructions are necessary to direct the information to different destinations. The instructions LDA and LDQ are used respectively to load information in the accumulator and the Q-register. The loading of the accumulator is also done with the instructions CLA, clear and add, and CLS, clear and subtract. The contents of the accumulator is complemented by COM, complement magnitude, leaving the sign unchanged.

The storing of results is done by STA and STQ, depending on whether the result is in the accumulator or in the Q-register. The address part of storing instructions contains the location L into which the result is to be stored.

Replace instructions are a combination of operation and storing of the result in the location of one of the operands. For example, replace add obtains one operand from storage location L, adds it to the initial contents of the accumulator and transmits the sum into L, leaving the sum also in the accumulator.

For initializing, the instruction STZ, store zero, is handy which places zeros in location L.

The contents of storage locations L and the arithmetic registers A, for accumulator, and Q is expressed by C(L), C(A), and C(Q), or even more briefly by (L), (A), and (Q). With this notation the instructions introduced so far are listed more formally in Table 5-1 in alphabetic order.

Shift operations are embedded in the multiply and divide instructions, but shifts are used in a more general way in programs and special shift instructions are provided. Even simple divisions or multiplications by 2 or powers of 2 are

TABLE 5-1.

INSTRUCTIONS FOR ARITHMETIC OPERATIONS

Instruction	*Code*	*Description of Operation*
Add	ADD	(L) + (A) → A; (L) unchanged
Clear A and add	CLA	(L) → A; (L) unchanged
Clear A and subtract	CLS	−(L) → A; (L) unchanged
Complement magnitude	COM	complement (A); sign unchanged
Divide	DIV	(A) or (AQ) ÷ (L) → Q; remainder → A
Load Q-register	LDQ	(L) → Q; (L) unchanged
Multiply	MPY	(L) × (Q) → A or AQ; (L) unchanged
Store A	STA	(A) → L; (A) unchanged
Store Q	STQ	(Q) → L; (Q) unchanged
Store zero	STZ	(L) replaced by zeros; sign of L plus
Subtract	SUB	(A) − (L) → A; (L) unchanged

done more quickly by shift instead of divide and multiply instructions. One right shift divides by 2 and one left shift multiplies by 2 in the binary system just as the shifts divide and multiply by 10 in the decimal system. Right and left shift instructions are provided for the A and Q registers and so-called longshift instructions for the combined shifting of both registers. The shift instructions which are listed in Table 5-2 contain in their address part the number of the required shifts.

Operations which use the properties of logical AND and OR are classified as *logical operations*. The AND operation matches two data words or one data word with prepared masks determining the presence of 1's in both. The OR operation determines the presence of 1's in either one of two data words where one may be considered as a reference word.

The masks for AND operations are filled with 1's for that part of the word which is being matched and with 0's for the rest of the word. The result of AND operations is called logical product, though it is actually obtained in the machine in the simplest way by logical addition without carries and comple-

TABLE 5-2.

SHIFT INSTRUCTIONS

Instruction	Code	Description of Operation
A left shift	ALS	Shift (A); left bits lost; sign unchanged
A right shift	ARS	Shift (A); right bits lost; sign unchanged
Long AQ left shift	LLS	Shift (AQ); $Q_1 \rightarrow A_{35}$; sign Q $\rightarrow$ sign A
Long AQ right shift	LRS	Shift (AQ); $A_{35} \rightarrow Q_1$; sign A $\rightarrow$ sign Q
Q left shift	QLS	Shift (Q); left bits lost; sign unchanged
Q right shift	QRS	Shift (Q); right bits lost; sign unchanged

mentation. The match may be done with the masks loaded from storage location L into A and the data to which the address part of the logical AND instruction refers, leaving the result in A. It is also possible to let the instructions refer to locations into which the masks have been stored temporarily and where they will be replaced by the results.

The OR operation sets the individual bits of the contents of A to "1" where there are corresponding 1's in the reference word. "0" bits in the reference word do not modify the corresponding bits in A. For OR operations, which are also called select operations, one data word is loaded into A and the other is referenced by the address part of the logical OR instruction. The result of the OR operation, called the logical sum, is after the operation usually in A, but the form of the OR instruction may be also such that the data word which the address part of the instruction has reference is replaced by the logical sum.

Special logical load and store instructions are provided when the sign position of the logical word is treated as a numerical bit and the sign of A is ignored. All bits of the logical word are brought into and fetched from continuous accumulator positions by these instructions.

Instructions for the version of logical AND and OR which leave the result in A and for logical load and store are listed in Table 5-3.

TABLE 5-3.
LOGICAL INSTRUCTIONS

Instruction	Code	Description of Operation
AND logical	ADL	(A-numeric) AND (L) → A-numeric; (L) unchanged
OR logical	ORL	(A-numeric) OR (L) → A-numeric; (L) unchanged
Load logical	LDL	(L) → A-numeric; (L) unchanged
Store logical	STL	(A-numeric) → L; (A-numeric) unchanged

5-6.   CONTROL INSTRUCTIONS

The control instructions provide the directed links between the operational parts of the program. Any time when the sequential execution of instructions is to be changed the program is placed under the control of instructions which contain in their address part the address of the instruction to which the program shall be directed. This type of control instructions is referred to as *jump or branch or transfer instructions.*

The requested jump may be unconditional, simply directing the program after the completion of an operation to an instruction out of the normal sequence. But more often the jump is dependent on a prescribed condition. The specification of the condition is in essence the most important aspect of the binary decision processes in digital computers.

A control function is described by defining a rule by which the appropriate successor to a given process is determined. For machines, in particular, the rule making the determination from among several possible successors is replaced by a sequence of binary decision processes. The control functions can then be considered as propositions which may be either true or false according to a simple arithmetic operation which determines the sign or relative magnitude of a variable.

In general, jump or transfer instructions go to the instruction out of the normal sequence when the prescribed condition is true, and they go to the next sequential instruction when the condition is false. Since programmers want the flexibility to make the jump in the program for either condition it is customary to provide instructions for jump on plus and for jump on minus as well as for jump on equal to zero and for jump on non-equal to zero.

For conditional jump instructions information must be given concerning the condition for the jump and the register where the condition is tested. The information about the jump condition may be placed in the three letter mnemonic code for the operation or in the index part of the instruction word. Different forms and types exist for jump instructions according to the logic of particular machines, but basically the concept is always the same.

In this text these instructions are introduced in a form which stresses simplicity and clarity. The word "jump" is used because the letter j in the code is more unique than the letter T for "transfer". The sequence of the letters in the code is arranged according to the following verbal description of the instruction, e.g., JAZ for jump when A is zero, or JQP for jump when Q is plus. The code for unconditional jump is JMP with no reference to register or condition, which is the equivalent to TRA for unconditional transfer, used in some computer manuals. Instructions which are more concerned with the actual running than the basic writing of programs are not introduced, such as jump on overflow.

The *stop or halt instructions* are also considered as control instructions. The instruction halt, HLT, simply stops the computer. Halt and procede, HPR, stops the computer and directs the program to the next sequential instruction when the start key on the operator's console is depressed. Halt and jump, HJP (in some manuals HTR for halt and transfer), stops the computer and directs the program to the instruction in the location indicated in the address part of the HJP instruction when the start key is depressed. The instruction NOP, for no operation, is used when the program shall be directed to the next instruction in sequence without any actions during the NOP cycle time.

The control functions, introduced so far, are summarized in Table 5-4 on the following page.

TABLE 5-4.

CONTROL INSTRUCTIONS

Instruction	Code	Description of Operation
Unconditional jump	JMP	go to instr. in addr. part of JMP
Jump when A is zero	JAZ	if (A) = 0, go to addr. in JAZ, otherwise to next instruction
Jump when A is non-zero	JAN	if (A) ≠ 0, go to addr. in JAN, otherwise to next instruction
Jump when A is plus	JAP	if (A) pos., go to addr. in JAP, otherwise to next instruction
Jump when A is minus	JAM	if (A) neg., go to addr. in JAM, otherwise to next instruction
Jump when Q is plus	JQP	if (Q) pos., go to addr. in JQP, otherwise to next instruction
Jump when Q is minus	JQM	if (Q) neg., go to addr. in JQM, otherwise to next instruction
Halt	HLT	stop computer
Halt and procede	HPR	stop computer and procede to next instr. after pressing start key
Halt and jump	HJP	stop computer and jump to addr. in HJP after pressing start key
No operation	NOP	machine takes next instr. in sequence

5-7.   INSTRUCTION MODIFICATION

The modification of instructions, brought to a high degree of sophistication in modern computers, is a very essential development toward more flexible and efficient control functions.

Actually, the modification of instructions is mainly concerned with the modification of the address in the address part of the instruction. This address modification is done by indexing or by indirect addressing which is a more elaborate concept for the modification.

The concept of *indexing* is relatively simple. The index part of instructions is used for this purpose. The number in the index part refers to an index register (X-register) whose contents is used to modify or index the address part of an instruction by subtracting from or adding to the stated address the contents of the index register. The resulting address is called the effective address and it is used in the execution of the instruction, while the address in the original instruction in memory remains unchanged. The effective address may be formed in different ways. One possibility is the addition of the complement of (X) and the address to be modified, resulting in the difference of both.

The real advantage of indexing is obtained when it is not used just once with a fixed number in X but consecutively with the number in X altered by a given increment or decrement after each indexing process. In this way one instruction can be executed for any number of different operands at the incrementally changed address.

Though the implementation of indexing varies widely for different machines, the following instructions may be considered as a basic requirement for indexing operations.

The quantity which shall be modified must be entered in the X-register (ENX), an address to be modified loaded in X (LDX), and eventually the contents of X be stored (STX).

Particularly useful and in some form available in most machines, is the instruction "jump an index" (JPX) which compares the modified address, or generally speaking the quantity in X with some index and reduces the quantity by a given amount, usually one count, and goes to the address in JPX or to the next instruction, depending on whether or not the jump condition is satisfied. This instruction, which can be also classified as a control instruction, may compare with zero, but more generally with any quantity, the so-called decrement, which is given in the index part of the instruction where also the number of the X-register used is specified.

The writing of some programs is facilitated when both, decrementing and incrementing index instructions are available. For incrementing instructions the decrement is added to the contents of the specified index register, without using the decrement for comparing and checking purposes. The instruction JIX, jump with incremented index, is an example. This instruction has to be preceded by an instruction which checks the condition for the jump.

The operational details of the described index instructions are listed in a more formal way in Table 5-5, with L again referring to the location indicated in the address part of the instruction, with the exemption of ENX whose address part contains the index.

TABLE 5-5.

INDEX INSTRUCTIONS

Instruction	Code	Description of Operation
Enter index	ENX	(addr. part of ENX) or index → X
Load addr. into X	LDX	(addr. part of L) → X; (L) unchanged
Store X	STX	(X) → addr. part of L; (X) unchanged
Jump on index	JPX	if (X) > D, (X) − D → X, go to L; otherwise to next instruction
Jump with incremented index	JIX	(X) + D → X, go to L

The D, used in instruction JPX, stands for index or decrement with which (X) is compared and by which (X) is reduced when (X) is greater than D. The decrement D can be simply included in the index part of JPX, provided that the index field is large enough for both, the number for the referenced X-register and the decrement. In JIX the decrement D is simply added to (X); comparison of D with the increased (X) is not practical.

When for the so-called indexable instructions reference is made in the index field to some index register X the address of the instruction is modified automatically by the contents of X. For example, STA, L, X does not store (A) in L but in L-(X). No further special instructions are required for this indexing operation, but only the reference to an index register in the index part of the instruction.

This may be further illustrated by a simple program using indexing, by which i words shall be copied from an external medium into memory locations beginning at location L. First the index i is entered into the referenced index register X. After each copy operation (CPY) the contents of X is compared with a given decrement, in this case, one, and reduced by the decrement as long as $(X) > 1$. The program goes through the copying loop i-times until, after the ith copy, the instruction JPX finds (X) reduced to one and directs the program to the next instruction. The copy instruction CPY is assumed to be indexable.

Example 5-1. Simple program with indexing

Instruction location	Instruction op. addr. index	Comments on operation
100	ENX, i , X	$i \to X$
101	CPY, L + i, X	$Data \to L = L + i - (X)$
102	JPX, 101 , X, 1	if $(X) > 1$, $(X) - 1 \to X$, go
	↑	to 101; otherwise to next
	for decrement	instruction

Note, that the first loop pass is made with the original setting $i \to X$, and that only (i-1) passes are made with reducing (X), so that *after* a total of i copies $(X) = i - (i - 1) = 1$, when JPX is called up again, and that only the contents of X at call time effects the jump and not the reduced (X) after the execution of JPX!

In the above example it was assumed that the index field in the instruction word is large enough for both the number of the referenced register and the decrement, and it can be stated in general that the length of the index field provided and the amount of information which can be placed in the index field, effects on different versions of the advanced method for address modification, which is called indirect addressing.

The basic idea of *indirect addressing* is that the address in the address part of the current instruction is not considered as the so-called execution address of the present instruction where, e.g., an operand or other quantity may be found for the execution of the current instruction, but this address refers only to a location where the execution address may or may not be found, depending on the contents of the index part of the word stored at the referenced location. When the index part of the located word contains again the code for indirect addressing, the address in this word is again not to be considered as an execution address but as a reference to another location. When the located word contains the number of an index register in its index part, the indexed address of the located word becomes the execution address of the current instruction, or when there is no reference to an index register, the address as found in the located word becomes the execution address.

In this way indirect addressing can direct the program to any desired location where the address of the quantities for operation may be found, and in addition the located addresses can be modified by the above described indexing process.

For indirect addressing no additional instructions are required, because the presence of the code for indirect addressing causes the machine automatically to interpret the address of the current instruction as a reference to a location and not as an execution address.

5-8.   EDITING INSTRUCTIONS

Only a few of these instructions are introduced, just enough to tie the programs in Chapter 10 to some input and output. In modern machines separate input and channels are provided which have so many options with regard to number and type of external equipment to be connected with the computer that the set of commands for these input-output operations are best studied and understood individually for each computer installation.

The concept is then broadened from the computation proper which is done in the main processor to entire installations with their manifold peripheral equipment, such as card and tape equipment and printers, which is linked with the main processor by external control units. Commands for the selection of tape for reading and writing, or for the rewinding and backspacing of tapes are executed by external control units. This is a different class of orders or instructions which effects the efficiency of the movement of data more than the solution of problems.

The broad class of editing instructions refers not only to the various operational aspects of peripheral equipment but also to the format of data as it is processed by these units. These things are all subject to rather specialized and changing requirements and needs. Some instructions such as read card (RCD) or punch (PCH) are seldom used anymore with large computers. Others are being introduced, and the latest trend places the movement of data to and from the main processor, as well as the sequencing of jobs under the control of supervisory or monitor systems, known as operating systems.

Three instructions are introduced which are handy as starting and finishing points for writing programs. These instructions are RDS and WRS for read select and write select with the component, from which information shall be read or on which information shall be written, specified in the address part of the instruction. The other instruction which follows RDS and WRS is the copy instruction, CPY, for the transfer of information between the selected component and the storage locations L given in the address part of CPY. This instruction is indexable, permitting the transfer of a series of data to or from indexed or serially modified locations.

The formal description of the above instructions is as follows:

TABLE 5-6.

INPUT-OUTPUT INSTRUCTIONS

Instruction	Code	Description of Operation
Read select	RDS	select for reading component specified by L
Write select	WRS	select for writing component specified by L
Copy	CPY	copy to or from locations specified by L

5-9. INSTRUCTION EXECUTION

The execution of instructions is a rather complicated process. For each instruction the machine automatically performs many operational steps. Though the programmer does not have to worry about these details which are taken care of by the circuitry of the machine, the detailed operational steps will be explained for one instruction, because they give an interesting insight into the actual workings of the machine.

The example shown refers to the IBM 704. Other machines execute instructions in similar steps, with the details depending on the arrangement of the registers and the logic of the particular machine.

For machines with one-address instructions, such as the 704, sequencing is done by the instruction counter which provides the address of the next instruction to be executed, and a trigger which divides the sequence into the so-called fetch and execute phases. Actually the trigger enables only two alternate gates through which either the instruction location or the address part of the instruction is gated to the address switch (see Fig. 3-12 on page 71). This means that the two phases are distinguished with regard to the interrogation of the memory, one for the instruction address and one for the execution address, properly sequenced through the one channel which connects with the memory.

It has become customary to refer to these two phases as the instruction and execution cycle of the machine or to a sequence of alternating I- and E- times, though the total execution of the instruction may not be completed in the E-time. It is necessary that at least the part of the execution which interrogates the memory is finished during the E-time, so that in the following I-time the next instruction can be brought from memory while the rest of the execution of the previous instruction may be completed.

The operational steps of the I-time fetch the instruction, set up the execution control circuits by the decoding of the instruction, and prepare for the interrogation of the memory with regard to the execution address. These steps are quite common for all instructions. During E-time the quantity at the execution address is obtained from memory and operations are performed according to the decoded instruction, either completely or partly, with the rest done during the next I-time. It is important that the control circuits are set up as late as possible during the I-time, so that a large part of that time is still available for the completion of the previous instruction before the controls are set for the new instruction.

There are also machine cycles or times during which no reference is made to memory, as for example in multiply and divide after the operands have been brought into the arithmetic registers. However, the alternating I- and E-cycles are the basic mode in the execution of instructions.

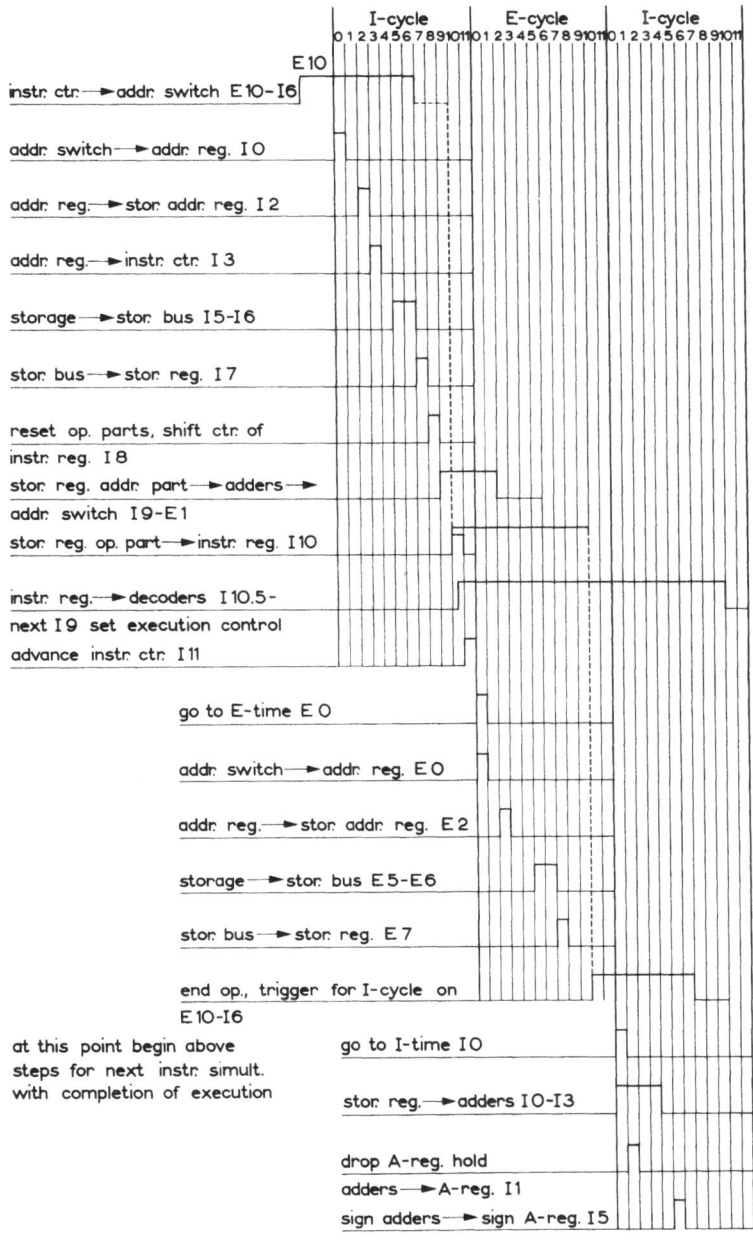

Fig. 5-3. Execution Steps for Clear-Add Instruction

Fig. 5-3 shows the operational steps for the execution of a clear-add (CLA) instruction by the IBM 704, which has a $12\,\mu s$ cycle time with twelve $1\,\mu s$ clock pulses for each machine cycle. The two different trigger settings for the I- and E-cycle are connected by dotted lines. The trigger is set for the I-cycle by an end operation signal at E10. The setting for the cycle following the I-cycle is done by designated bits of the operation part in the instruction register at I10. These bits control a cycle timer and determine if the next cycle shall be an E-cycle with reference or another cycle without reference to memory.

The individual steps in Fig. 5-3 can be traced with the help of the logical computer diagram Fig. 3-12 which shows the various computer parts to which the steps refer.

In Appendix A, a summary is given of the instructions which were introduced in this chapter. The summary lists the instructions in alphabetical order as a convenient reference for the discussion of programs in the next chapter. Problems which use these instructions are formulated at the end of Chapter 6.

CHAPTER 6

Principles and
Examples of Programming

6-1. MATHEMATICAL METHODS FOR DIGITAL COMPUTERS

The astonishing development of powerful general purpose digital computers has brought about a revaluation in the
field of applied mathematics, the investigation of methods for
the solution of mathematical problems on machines. These
efforts are spurred by the recognition that so far the limitations on what computers can do come, in many cases, more
from the weakness of the presentation of problems to the
computer than from the intrinsic limitations of the machines.

It is interesting that almost 10 years before the first practical large scale computers came into being, the basic problem
of computability had already been dealt with in the fundamental work by Turing[13] which defines the class of computable functions from the viewpoint of the characteristics required for problem solutions by machine methods. Turing
specified a class of machines for particular computable functions and an Universal Turing Machine capable of computing
any computable function. The specified basic characteristics
which are also found in modern computers, are storage of
information on a long tape, a part called configuration corresponding to the present state of the machine based on
previous inputs, and a part called present behavior determined entirely by the present input symbol and the present
configuration.

Though these rather abstract considerations did not result
directly in practical computers, the Turing theory is important, because it defines the class of computable functions and
the minimal requirements for a general purpose digital
computer.

Following this very sound and systematic start in the field
of machine computation, further theoretical studies on com-

putability were overshadowed for a few years by the fast pace of advances in the development of practical computers. But the capabilities of these machines increased so rapidly that the concern for their proper utilization lead to a quick revival of efforts toward the development of what may be called the mathematical science of computation.

The objectives of such science can be grouped generally into three major categories. The first objective is concerned with an improvement of present programming techniques for arithmetic and numerical problems by theoretical investigations. The second objective is the nonarithmetical, mainly logical utilization of computers, and the third category covers the far reaching aspects of cybernetics, the new mathematical science which studies and tries to mechanize the most elaborate control and concept forming processes, even to some extent the human nervous system which is supposed to work in a digital fashion.

The fundamental work, leading to established regions of research, by Turing, Wiener[14], Church[15], Markov[16], and Kleene[17], to name just a few, is brought into focus again and research work is now spreading widely on an international scale into many areas which all can be classified as coming under the mathematical science of computation.

Research studies investigate the basic structure of programs and the underlying logical schemes with an attempt to use these schemes for the construction of more efficient programs. Despite the great variations in computational processes there exist equivalences in computations and a theoretical definition of the equivalence would pave the way to construct transformations for the purpose of reducing programming for different comparable variations and to perfect the control structure. Efforts are also being made with regard to formalizing the development and writing of programs by graphical and tabulating means.

All these endeavors refer to the first mentioned objective of improving programming techniques. The present work toward the utilization of computers for nonarithmetical and control processes must be considered as the starting point for accomplishments to be gained in the future. It is very helpful that a great amount of information concerning this work is published in the open literature. An article by Liapunov[18] in the

Communications of the ACM gives a condensed survey of the mathematical investigations which have been done in Russia with regard to the use of computers.

After discussing the objectives for the development of mathematical methods for computation, a brief consideration will be given to the major mathematical disciplines which are involved. McCarthy[19] states in his work on the mathematical theory of computation that there are three established directions of research relevant to a science of computation: numerical analysis, the theory of computability as a branch of recursive function theory, and the theory of finite automata. Though the endeavor to establish a theory of computation tries to provide a mathematical theory with broader usefulness, at present the concept of numerical analysis is still most widely used in the preparation of arithmetic problems for the computer.

In addition to the classical textbooks on numerical analysis by Hildebrand, Householder and Scarborough (*see bibliography*) continuous work is being done on numerical methods for automatic computer solutions of complex systems of equations and mathematical descriptions of physical situations. The computer programs presented in this book use mathematical formulations of the problems reduced to a numerical form suitable for machine solution according to the concepts of numerical analysis.

6-2. DIAGRAMMING THE PROGRAM

A profound description of program construction is given in the treatise by Goldstine[20] and von Neumann about the planning and coding for a computing instrument. The description explains systematically the basic elements of a program for which different names and arrangements were eventually introduced, though the principal concepts and ideas remain the same.

Ten years later Saul Gorn[21] presented a report on standardized programming and coding methods which discuss in connection with the contemplated standardization the basic programming features in a very interesting and systematic way. Particularly the definitions with regard to the syntax of a code, given in this report, are worth noting. The discussion in this and the following section uses some of the concepts presented in reference 20 and 21.

The description of the construction of a program is best started with a remark about the manner in which the machine handles data. It has already been mentioned that the analytical or implicit form of equations for problem descriptions must be replaced by arithmetical and numerical procedures acceptable to the machine. These explicit procedures consist primarily of step-by-step or successive approximation processes which require iterative or loop operations. An iterative process is also called an induction, and the quantity which controls the passes through the iteration loop is called the induction variable.

The linear sequence of operations with no loops or inductive elements represents the simplest form of a program which can be considered, consisting of a straight sequence of imperative sentences with no iterations and decisions made by the program. For such simple problems it is often hardly worthwhile to go to the machine.

Most machine programs of any significance are a sequence of imperative and interrogative sentences, constituting a code of instructions, and have loops as well as loops within loops. In Fig. 6-1 the principal program elements for this typical situation are depicted.

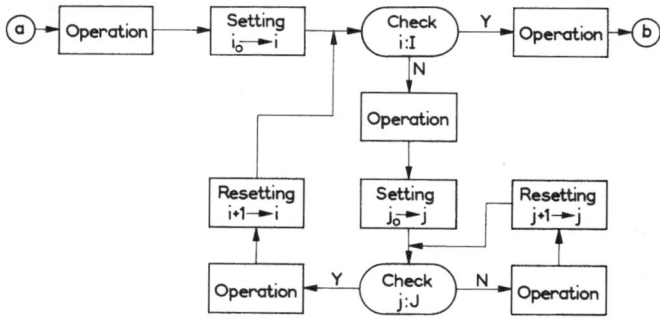

Fig. 6-1. Principal Program Element

For the sake of classification the following elements may be distinguished: operation, setting-resetting, and discrimination, though in practice discrimination and resetting are normally executed by one control instruction. The induction variables i and j are compared in the check or discrimination boxes with the total number of required loop passes I and J. For one pass through the i-loop the program has to go J-times through the j-loop.

At the first entry for each series of consecutive loop passes the induction variables have to be initialized by $i_o \to i$ and $j_o \to j$. For setting or replacement two equivalent notations are used, either $i + 1 \to i$ or $i \leftarrow i + 1$, both meaning the replacement of i, or more precisely of the contents at location i, by $i + 1$.

A distinction is made in programs between bound and free variables. The former are the variables of induction and the dependent variables of the problem which change within a certain domain during the computational process. If one storage location is assigned to such variable the contents of this location is always replaced by the new value of the variable which is obtained after resetting or computation. In the replacement notation $x_1 \to x$, x_1 refers to the new value and x to the location whose content is replaced. This location is called variable storage.

The free variables are the independent variables or parameters of the problem which are determined a priori and whose values do not change during computation. Their storage locations are called fixed storage.

The all important matter in programming is the proper sequencing of the required program actions. Fig. 6-1 shows typical program elements. Each individual program has to be planned by arranging these elements into a flow chart, as a schematic of the course through which the program shall be directed. Depending on the complexity of the program, it may be necessary to draw first a general schematic and then more detailed flow charts in which the actions of all boxes are enumerated.

In drawing flow diagrams it is customary to give check or discrimination boxes, where the program branches or goes into loops, a somewhat different form, diamond-shaped or rounded, as compared with the regular rectangular boxes. When a large program is broken up into several parts, the connections between the parts are marked with encircled letters or numbers, e.g., a and b in Fig. 6-1.

It is natural that a relation exists between the structure of a program and the instructions which direct the program along the skeleton of the structure, resulting in a marked similarity between instruction types and program elements. The flow diagram however is primarily determined by the problem to be solved, and the first design of the chart may not even consider the instruction code of a particular machine.

According to the amount of detail in the diagram one may distinguish between macro flow chart, flow chart, and micro flow chart. The most popular, at least up to the present time, is the flow chart which gives enough detail for the direct writing of the code for a problem. Micro flow charts which go into the details of individual instructions, as shown in section 5-9 on the execution of instructions, are scarcely used, because the details of microcodes are normally left up to the machine.

Macro flow charts comprise in one part or box of the diagram a sequence of several actions without enumerating these actions for direct coding based on the idea that the translation from the macrocode, expressed in the chart, to machine code can be done automatically by the machine.

At a very early stage of program developments it already became apparent that certain sequences of actions, e.g., the steps for extracting a square root, are used in many programs, and that it would be inefficient to write the code for these actions every time they are needed. This lead to the concept of subroutines, a coded sequence for the solution of a problem which can be used as a single entity when the problem occurs as part of a more complicated problem, thus avoiding the need for recoding it each time it occurs in a new context. The required provisions for the incorporation of subroutines into a program, also called routines, are discussed in the next section.

Subroutines may be considered as the first step toward macro programming, even though they were conceived and developed as a help for direct coding and not for automatic coding which is a part of a much broader concept not only of automation but also of machine independency as will be explained in Chapter 7.

Direct coding is still basic for the most versatile and efficient usage of computers and it should be learned and used first, before relying on automatic programming techniques. The flow diagram lays out the plan from which the writing of the code starts.

6-3.   WRITING THE CODE

The code for a problem is basically a sequence of instructions or more precisely, a sequence of symbolized sentences, whose nouns are constants and variables. When writing the code, in addition to the sequence of instructions as the main part of the code, also the numerical data, variables, intermediate results, and final results have to be considered and storage locations have to be assigned to them as well as to the instructions.

All these things must be done in detail when the code is written in absolute or machine language. The work for individual coding steps is greatly reduced or even eliminated when symbolic code or compilers are used, as indicated in the following table which lists the primary things to consider in writing a code.

TABLE 6-1

THINGS TO CONSIDER IN WRITING A CODE

	Absolute	*Symbolic*	*Compiler*
How much data	yes	reduced	reduced
Where to locate data	yes	reduced	—
Assignment of memory	yes	—	—
How many variables	yes	yes	yes
Assign to actual locations	yes	—	—
List intermediate results	yes	reduced	reduced
Assign to actual locations	yes	—	—
Write sequence of instructions	yes	yes	reduced
Include functional subroutines	yes	reduced	—
Assign to actual locations	yes	—	—
List results to be written out	yes	reduced	reduced
Assign to actual locations	yes	—	—
Translation and arrangement of I/O	yes	yes	—
Write out results	yes	reduced	reduced

There are additional secondary things such as scaling considerations, program and machine checking, and debugging which may be included in codes, but they are not required to explain the principles of writing a code.

Furthermore, the coding in absolute is so laborious that it is quite out of use, though professional programmers benefit by learning it, if only as background for simpler coding methods. Compilers are used in automatic programming which is discussed in Chapter 7.

For direct programming with one-to-one relation to machine

instructions the code which is now most commonly used is the symbolic mnemonic code and it will therefore be used in this description. The code has three letters to represent the operation part of instructions and up to five symbols, letters or letter and numbers to represent the location of instructions. The addresses for variables and constants are simply indicated by the contents which shall be placed in the locations.

In absolute and also in symbolic, the code is written on consecutive lines with one instruction per line giving from left to right the following information: location of instruction, operation, address, index part of instruction, and comments which have no effect on the operation of the machine other than that the comments may be printed out. Each line is later punched on an individual card with blanks or commas between the different parts of information which are placed into specified columns where the machine can recognize them and interpret their meaning.

A symbolic instruction should be identified by a symbolic location in the left-most part of the code only if it is necessary to refer to this instruction in the program. Therefore the left or location part in the coding sheet will have only a few entries when the code is written in symbolic. If a symbol appears as symbolic location in the location part, the current location number will be assigned to this symbol.

Starting from one specified memory location, the assignment of subsequent locations to consecutive instructions and the conversion from the symbolic instructions to their numerical equivalents is made by a program, called the *assembly program.*

The replacement of all symbols by integer equivalents requires that each symbol is uniquely defined. The operation code and the address and index part of instructions are interpreted as such by the machine directly, while the symbols for other quantities are defined by pseudo operations which in turn are interpreted for the machine by the assembly program.

Up to this point the description has been completely general with no reference to any particular machine or assembly program, but the explanation of further details is more practical when it uses some specifics for illustration. It is felt that it is justified to introduce for this purpose, without too much loss of generality, some concepts which have been developed by United Aircraft Corporation[22] for the SHARE assembler for the IBM 704. Specifically, some pseudo operations of the SHARE assembler are introduced in order to aid in the practical writing of codes.

The pseudo operation ORG specifies the origin for a code by setting the location counter to the value of the address field. The pseudo operations EQU for equals and SYN for synonym assign the integer value of the address field to the symbolic location, using EQU for problem constants which are invariant with respect to the location, and SYN for a piece of data, an instruction location, or any other quantity whose value depends upon the location of the program in storage. The pseudo operations DEC and OCT convert decimal or octal data to binary and assign the converted data to locations beginning at the location indicated in the location part of DEC and OCT. The pseudo operations BSS and BES reserve a block of storage, and that with BSS for a block started by the symbolic location L and extending to $L + N - 1$, where N is the value of the address field, and with BES for a block ended by the symbolic location $L + N$, corresponding to the location of the first word following the reserved block.

The pseudo operation LIB searches the library tape for the subroutine which is identified by the symbol in the location part and inserts the subroutine in the program being assembled, assigning storage locations to the number of words which are required by the subroutine. REM for remarks causes the information following the operation part REM to be printed in the listing of the assembly without otherwise affecting the assembly program. END is the last pseudo operation read by the assembly program. More details about these and other pseudo operations of the SHARE 704 assembler are found in reference 22.

A location counter specifies the absolute or numerical location of each word in the program. If the initial value of this location L is not specified by ORG or by an absolute decimal value in the location part of the first word the initial value of L will be zero. After the initial setting of L, henceforth L is increased by one for each word used in the program. As mentioned before, if a word has symbols in the location part, the current numerical value is assigned to these symbols. If for a word an absolute decimal location is given, the location counter will be set to that value.

Before going to the writing of codes for particular examples in the following sections, a few remarks concerning the inclusion of subroutines in the code of the main program are in order. If subroutines are used as so-called open subroutines only once in a program the sequence of instructions for the main program and subroutine is straightforward. But the real usefulness of subroutines is obtained when they are written in a general form whereby the same set of instructions and address references are used to solve a problem for different parameter values. In this form subroutines are normally included as closed subroutines in the program. The parameters upon which the subroutine shall work have to be placed into locations referenced by the subroutine and at entry to the subroutine the next instruction of the main routine to which the subroutine shall exit must be provided. Example 6-1 gives a simple form of the required linkage.

Example 6-1. Linkage for Inclusion of Closed Subroutine.

Location	Operation	Address	Remarks
L	STA	L-parameter	(A) → L-parameter
L + 1	CLA	next instr.	next instr. of main routine → A
L + 2	JMP	subroutine	
subroutine	STA	L-exit	(A) → L-exit
.	.	.	
subroutine	JMP	L-exit	
L-exit	next instr. of main routine		program to main routine

The next instruction in the main routine may be either a jump to a desired location or an instruction for the storage of the results of the subroutine which is still in the accumulator.

Some basic subroutines with the number of required instructions given in parenthesis are: Sine and Cosine (86), Arc Sine and Arc Cosine (105), Arc Tangent (24), Square Root (22), Natural Logarithm (29) and Exponential base e (39). In addition up to approximately 20 locations for constants and extra storage are provided for these subroutines.

Approximate time and cost estimates have been made for the different coding methods on the basis of representative jobs. An average of these estimates is given in the following table.

TABLE 6-2

TIME AND COST ESTIMATES FOR DIFFERENT CODING METHODS

	Absolute	Symbolic	Compiler
Relative Coding Time	100	50	10
Debugging Time	100	70	45
% Loss of Machine Efficiency	0	10	10
Lapse Time to Code and Run	100	50	30
Cost per Job, Code and Run	100	65	30

6-4.   SIMPLE ARITHMETIC PROBLEMS

Some more coding and actual operational details will now be explained using practical examples. When coding is done in symbolic, the machine first handles the assembly, or translation to absolute, under the control of the assembly program in storage and after this phase the absolute program is written on tape with the numerical data upon which the program operates added. In placing these data on tape they have to be converted to binary or BCD in which form they are read from the tape. This conversion and placing on the program tape is normally done by off-line equipment and not by the main processing unit.

For production runs, the machine first reads the absolute program or sequence of numeric instructions from the tape and places them in the assigned memory locations. No execution of instructions takes place during this loading into the internal storage. When the loading of the program is finished the machine next reads from the tape information equivalent to that on transfer cards which are used when loading is done from cards. This information directs control to the first instruction of the loaded program. Under the control of this program the reading of data from the tape and the execution of the program takes place.

A problem with the basic arithmetic operations is given as the first coding example, namely, to find the solutions y_i where

$$y_i = \frac{ax_i + b}{cx_i - d}, \text{ for } i = 1, 2, \ldots 50. \qquad (6\text{-}1)$$

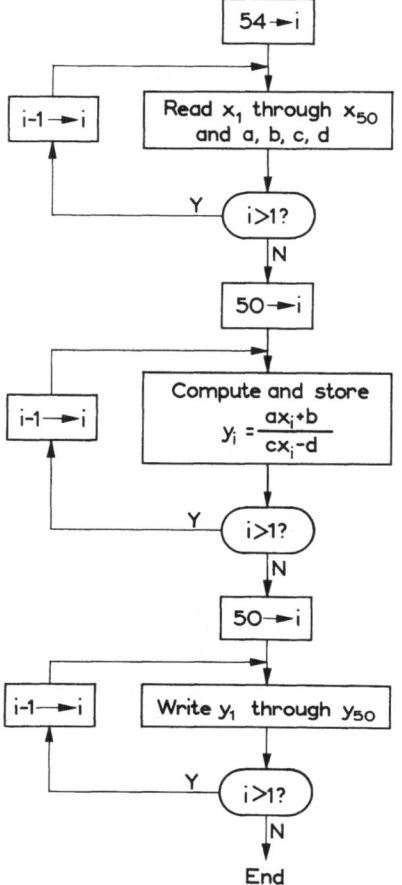

Fig. 6-2.   Flow Chart for Solving $y_1 = \dfrac{ax_1 + b}{cx_1 - d}$

The diagramming of the program is shown in Fig. 6-2.

Though for simple problems such as this first one, the experienced programmer may not need a flow chart, the practice of diagramming the program should be considered as the usual preliminary step providing a clear plan for the coding. In the given problem 50 values of x have to be read, and 50 values of y to be computed and to be written. The diagram indicates the required loops aiding in the corresponding coding.

Example 6-2. Symbolic Code for Solution of $y_i = \dfrac{ax_i + b}{cx_i - d}$

Loc.	Op.	Addr.		Index	Comments
01000	ENX	54	,	1	$54 \rightarrow X1$
	RDS	tape			read select tape given in Addr.
L1	CPY	x + 54	,	1	read into block x thr. x + 53
	JPX	L1	,	1, 1	if (X1), > 1, reduce by 1, go to L1
	ENX	50	,	2	$50 \rightarrow X2$
L2	LDQ	c			$c \rightarrow Q$
	MPY	x + 50	,	2	$cx \rightarrow A$
	SUB	d			$(cx - d) \rightarrow A$
	STA	T			$(cx - d) \rightarrow$ temp. loc. T
	LDQ	a			$a \rightarrow Q$
	MPY	x + 50	,	2	$ax \rightarrow A$
	ADD	b			$(ax + b) \rightarrow A$
	DIV	T			$(ax + b)/(cx - d)$
	STQ	y + 50	,	2	store y
	JPX	L2	,	2, 1	if (X2) > 1, reduce by 1, to to L2
	ENX	50	,	3	$50 \rightarrow X3$
	WRS	tape			write select tape given in Addr.
L3	CPY	y + 50	,	3	write from block y thr, y + 49
	JPX	L3	,	3, 1	if (X3) > 1 reduce by 1, go to L3
	HLT				stops machine
x	BSS	50			
a					
b					
c					
d					
T					
y	BSS	50			
	END				

The above code is general enough for the solution of the problem for any set of values for the parameters a, b, c, d and the independent variables x_1 through x_{50}. Only when the size of the set of variables x changes, slight modifications are required with regard to the size of the reserved storage block and the indices for the X-registers.

In order to simplify the code, one read loop for the variables x and the parameters, a, b, c, d is provided, accounting for the setting of index register X1 to 54.

In the code the instruction ENX is used for the setting of the index registers. If the instruction LDX is used the indices must be stored in memory from where they are loaded into the X-registers.

For the instruction part of the code the comments explain the actions. The instructions are assigned to consecutive locations, so that the symbolic locations L1, L2, L3 to which the program refers will be assigned the numbers 01002, 01005, 01017 after 01000 had been specified as the origin for the code.

The instruction part is followed in the symbolic code by the portion which reserves and assigns the subsequent locations to the problem variables and parameters, as well as to temporary storage locations. This assignment is done by pseudo-operations such as BSS, or simply by placing the symbol to which a location shall be assigned in the location part of the code. In our example the variable x_1 will be assigned to location 01020 and the parameter a to location 01070.

The instructions CPY, MPY, STQ with references to index registers are said to be used in the indexed mode, which means that the addresses to which they refer are modified every time around the loop by the altered contents of the referenced index register.

The general code form in Example 6-2 which is independent of a specific set of data is the usual form. For one-time jobs with only one set of data a combination of assembly, data conversion, and computation may be considered, in particular when the program and data are loaded from cards. The pseudo-operation BSS would be replaced by DEC, which converts decimal to binary and assigns memory locations. Also the numerical values for the parameters would be introduced and converted by DEC. In this case the general copy loop for reading is not required, and the computation can commence immediately after the loading of the program and the one set of converted data.

The code in Example 6-2 performs the computational steps in a sequence which requires the least amount of data

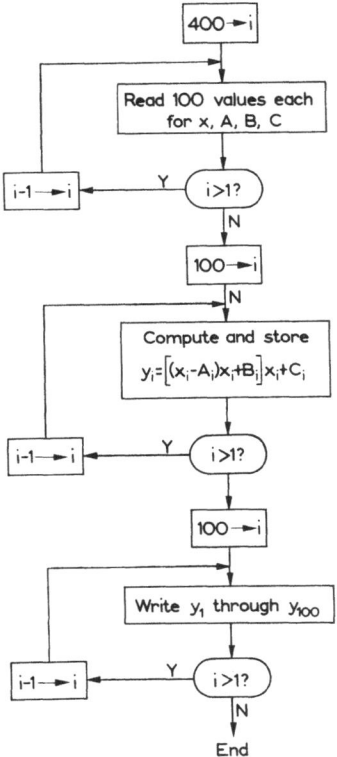

Fig. 6-3. Flow Chart for Solving $y_i = [(x_i - A_i)x_i + B_i]x_i + C_i$

movement and temporary storage. In solving algebraic equations this sequence of steps should always be considered carefully before coding. Also the appropriate factoring of equations can save computing time, as shown by the next example for solving

$$y_i = x_i^3 - A_ix_i^2 + B_ix_i + C_i, \text{ for } i = 1, 2, \ldots 100 \qquad (6\text{-}2)$$

The code is best written for the factored form

$$y_i = [(x_i - A_i)x_i + B_i]x_i + C_i \qquad (6\text{-}3)$$

The flow chart for solving (6-3) is shown in Fig. 6-3 in which the index for the reading loop is set to 400 because it is assumed that 100 values have to be read in for each quantity x, A, B, and C. The computation and write loops for y require 100 passes each.

For programs with simple loops only one index register would actually be necessary which can be set every time before directing the program through one loop. But for loops within loops several index registers are required. All larger machines have at least three or more X-registers and it is quite common to use different registers even for simple loops which permits setting them all at the beginning of the program and avoids resetting during the program. The utilization of several registers is enhanced by instructions by which two or more registers can be entered with an index simultaneously.

The code for solving equation (6-3) is given below, showing only the part required for the actual computation. The read and write loop and the portion for the assignment of storage locations have been omitted. They are similar to Example 6-2.

Example 6-3.   Symbolic Code for Solution of
$$y_i = [(x_i - A_i)x_i + B_i]x_i + C_i$$

Loc.	*Op.*	*Addr.*	*Index*	*Comments*
L	ENX	100 ,	2	$100 \to X2$
L2	CLA	x_i ,	2	$x_i \to A$
	SUB	A_i ,	2	$(x_i - A_i) \to A$
	LRS	35		$(A) \to Q$
	MPY	x_i ,	2	$(x_i - A_i)x_i \to A$
	ADD	B_i ,	2	$[(x_i - A_i)x_i + B_i] \to A$
	LRS	35		$(A) \to Q$
	MPY	x_i ,	2	$[(x_i - A_i)x_i + B_i]x_i \to A$
	ADD	C_i ,	2	$[(x_i - A_i)x_i + B_i]x_i + C_i \to A$
	STA	y_i ,	2	$(A) \to y_i$
	JPX	L2 ,	2, 1	if $(X2) > 1$, reduce by 1, go to L2

In this example all quantities have different values at each computation loop. Therefore all instructions referring to these quantities are indexed. For all these address modifications the same index register, here X2, is used, because the quantities are stored in blocks with corr2sponding consecutive address locations.

The loops in the discussed arithmetic problems are repetitive loops where the values for the computation in each loop are independent of the values for other loops. For the calculation of approximations different types of loops, called iterative loops, are used where the result of the i-th iteration becomes the input to the $(i + 1)$th iteration. An example for coding iterative processes is given in the next section.

6-5. ITERATIVE PROCESSES

The classical example for an iterative process is the extraction of the square root, x, from an argument a using Newton's formula for successive approximations.

$$x_{i+1} = \frac{1}{2}\left(x_i + \frac{a}{x_i}\right) \tag{6-4}$$

where successive x_{i+1} are computed as functions of x_i until for $x_i = a/x_i$ or $x_{i+1} = x_i$ the iteration converges.

Equation (6-4) is derived from the following relations

$$x = \sqrt{a} \text{ or } x^2 - a = 0, \text{ then} \tag{6-5}$$

$$f(x) = x^2 - a \text{ and } f'(x) = 2x$$

$$x_{i+1} = x_i - \frac{f(x_i)}{f'(x_i)} = x_i - \frac{x_i^2 - a}{2x_i} = \frac{1}{2}\left(x_i + \frac{a}{x_i}\right)$$

In hand calculation with unlimited number length the computation approaches asymptotically the desired value x. In machine computation with fixed number length the chop off at the given length causes a nonmonotonic behavior at this point which can be used for the termination of the iteration process instead of specifying an acceptable error term for the approximation. In the approach using the truncation error the result is obtained with the highest possible accuracy of the machine.

The initial guess should be high enough so that the sequence of approximations is first decreasing in a monotonic fashion with $x_{i+1} < x_i$, until due to the truncation error $x_{i+1} > x_i$. A simple, rather unsophisticated initial guess is $x_o = a$ followed by the first approximation derived from (6-4)

$$x_1 = \frac{1}{2} + \frac{a}{2}. \tag{6-6}$$

More sophisticated initial guesses can save a few iteration steps. In the process of iteration the difference between x_i and x_{i+1} decreases and, if a permissible error is considered somewhat larger than the machine truncation error, the error should be specified in terms of this difference.

The flow chart of the iteration process for extraction a square root is shown in Fig. 6-4.

The above flow chart can be modified when the square root shall be obtained for a series of numbers. Every time a result is obtained the program is returned to the start, and an operation is added to place the new number in the location of a, so that the rest of the program can remain unaltered.

In the following code the details for reading and writing are omitted, because they follow the previously shown pattern.

Example 6-4. Symbolic Code for Square Root Extraction
$$x = \sqrt{a}$$

Loc.	Op.	Addr.	Index	Comments
L	CLA	a		$a \rightarrow A$
	JAM	L3		if (A) neg., go to L3
	JAZ	L2		if (A) = 0, go to L2
	ARS	1		$a/2 \rightarrow A$
	ADD	c		$(1/2 + a/2) \rightarrow A$
	STA	X_i		$(A) \rightarrow X_i$
L1	CLA	X_i		$(X_i) \rightarrow A$
	STA	T		$(A) \rightarrow T$
	CLA	a		$a \rightarrow A$
	DIV	X_i		$a/x_i \rightarrow Q$
	LLS	35		$(Q) \rightarrow A$
	ADD	X_i		$(x_i + a/x_i) \rightarrow A$
	ARS	1		$1/2(x_i + a/x_i) = x_{i+1} \rightarrow A$
	STA	X_i		$x_{i+1} \rightarrow X_i$
	SUB	T		$x_{i+1} - (T) = (x_{i+1} - x_i) \rightarrow A$
	JAM	L1		if (A) neg., go to L1
	CLA	T		$(T) \rightarrow A$
L2	STA	X		$(A) \rightarrow X$
L3	HLT			
a				
X_i				
T				
X				
c	DEC	.5		

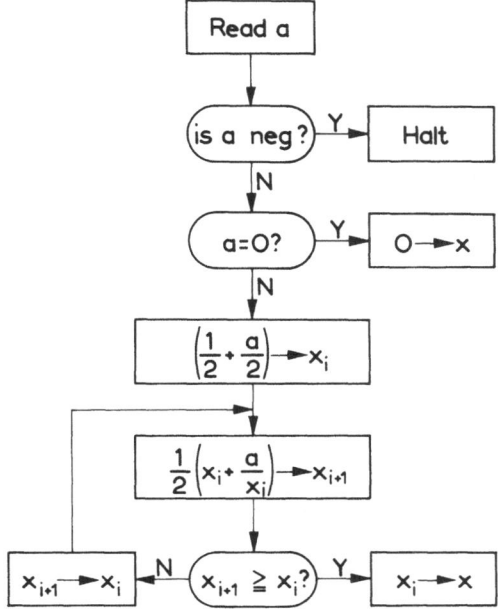

Fig. 6-4. Iterative Process to Compute $x = \sqrt{a}$

There are different ways to write the code for the above problem. The presented code tries to stress simplicity in explaining the following important points, first the writing of instructions for the iteration loop which can be used unchanged for all loop passes, and second the preservation of two successive approximations as required by the program. At the end of each iteration loop the new approximation x_{i+1} replaces the preceding in cell X_i. Therefore the value of x_i has to be preserved at the beginning of the loop in the temporary storage T. Then both values are available for the check after the loop. Contrary to the flow chart, the coding places the replacement of the old by the new approximation ahead of the check, so that the jump can be executed directly to the loop which can use the same instructions after the contents of X_i has been changed.

In the case of the square root extraction for a series of numbers, storage blocks have to be reserved for the required number of arguments a and results x, and the instructions

referring to these quantities have to be indexed in the previously described manner.

6-6. POLYNOMIAL EVALUATION

The solution for many problems and functions is obtained by evaluation as polynomial of the general form

$$y = a_n x^n + a_{n-1} x^{n-1} + \ldots + a_1 x + a_0 \qquad (6\text{-}7)$$

The calculation can be performed with a simple program
when the polynomial is factored into the form

$$y = [(a_n x + a_{n-1}) x + a_{n-2}] x + \ldots + a_0 \qquad (6\text{-}8)$$

The inputs to the program are the degree n of the polynomial, the $(n + 1)$ coefficients a_0 through a_n, and the independent
variable x. The inputs can be read into the machine as one
record, or as separate records for the coefficients a and the
variable x, the latter being particularly the case when the
polynomial is evaluated for several values of x. This more
general case is shown here for m values of x. Furthermore, in
order to minimize the required storage space, it is assumed
that only one value of x is read in at a time and that the
corresponding value for y is printed out every time it has been
obtained.

The index registers X1, X2, and X3 are used to index the
reading of the $(n + 1)$ coefficients, to direct the program
through the n iteration loops required for an nth degree
polynomial and to control the repetitions of the program for
the m values of x. It is quite common to start the program
with the setting of the index registers, however, in this case
the contents of X2 is reduced to one after n iteration loops and
it must be reset before the iteration loops are repeated for the
new value of x. Therefore, the setting of X2 is not placed at
the beginning of the program but before the iteration loops, as
shown in the flow chart Fig. 6-5.

In the flow chart and the following code, capital letters are
used for storage locations and small letters for the corresponding quantities, stored at these locations. For the accumulator
the symbol Acc is used to distinguish it from locations A for
the coefficients a.

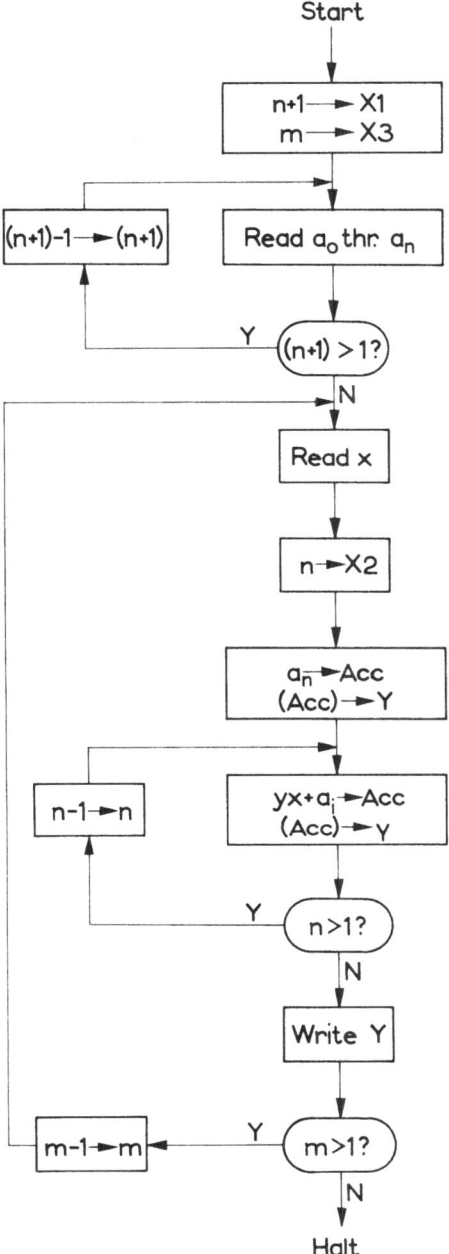

Fig. 6-5. Polynomial Evaluation

Example 6-5.   Symbolic Code for Polynomial Evaluation

Loc.	Op.	Addr.	Index	Comments
	ORG	1000		specifies initial loc. L = 1000
	LDX	I	, 1	$n + 1 \to X1$
	LDX	K	, 3	$m \to X3$
	RDS	tape		read select tape given in Addr.
L1	CPY	$A + n + 1$,	1	$a_n \to A$ thr. $a_o \to A + n$
	JPX	L1	, 1, 1	if $(X1) > 1$, reduce by 1, go to L1
L3	RDS	tape		read select tape given in Addr.
	CPY	X		$x \to X$
	LDX	J	, 2	$n \to X2$
	CLA	A		$a_n \to$ Acc
	STA	Y		(Acc) $\to Y$
L2	LDQ	Y		$(Y) \to Q$
	MPY	X		$yx \to$ Acc
	ADD	$A + n + 1$,	2	$yx + a_i \to$ Acc
	STA	Y		(Acc) $\to Y$
	JPX	L2	, 2, 1	if $(X2) > 1$, reduce by 1, go to L2
	WRS	tape		write select tape given in Addr.
	CPY	Y		$(Y) \to$ tape
	JPX	L3	, 3, 1	if $(X3) > 1$, reduce by 1, go to L3
	HLT			stops computer
I	EQU	$n + 1$		
J	EQU	n		
K	EQU	m		
A	BSS	$n + 1$		
X				
Y				
	END			

The above code is written in a general form. For the assembly into absolute the parameters, n, (n + 1), and m are specified to provide for the required storage allocation for the coefficients a and for the settings of the index registers. With this information the assembled program, stored in the main memory, is ready for production runs.

The storage assignment for the coefficients a is made under the assumption that the coefficients are arranged on the record so that a_n is read into A and a_o into A + n. A check of the iteration loop, beginning at L2, indicates that the first coefficient a_i called in by the indexed ADD instruction is $a_i = a_{n-1}$ and the last $a_i = a_o$, with n reduced to one after the next to the last iteration loop.

In order to simplify the code, it is again assumed that the calculator does not skip instructions after the last word of a unit record has been copied. If skipping takes place, simply the required number of NOP instructions would have to be inserted in the program.

6-7. SOLUTION OF SIMULTANEOUS LINEAR EQUATIONS

Another interesting example for multiple-loop programs is the solution of simultaneous linear algebraic equations of the form

$$a_{11}x_1 + a_{12}x_2 + \ldots + a_{1n}x_n = b_1 \tag{6-9}$$

$$a_{21}x_1 + a_{22}x_2 + \ldots + a_{2n}x_n = b_2 \tag{6-10}$$

$$a_{n1}x_1 + a_{n2}x_2 + \ldots + a_{nn}x_n = b_n \tag{6-11}$$

The solution is explained according to the Gauss method which eliminates successively the unknowns through the use of pivotal equations which express one unknown explicitly in terms of the others. The first pivotal equation for the elimination of x_1 is

$$x_1 = -\frac{a_{12}}{a_{11}}x_2 - \ldots - \frac{a_{1n}}{a_{11}}x_n + \frac{b_1}{a_{11}} \tag{6-12}$$

By substituting this value for x_1 in all the remaining equations, x_1 is eliminated from the set

$$-\frac{a_{21}}{a_{11}}(a_{12}x_2 + \ldots + a_{1n}x_n - b_1) + a_{22}x_2 + \ldots + a_{2n}x_n = b_2 \tag{6-13}$$

$$\vdots$$

$$-\frac{a_{n1}}{a_{11}}(a_{12}x_2 + \ldots + a_{1n}x_n - b_1) + a_{n2}x_2 + \ldots + a_{nn}x_n = b_n \tag{6-14}$$

For automatic machine solutions according to Fig. 6-6, the first things we are looking for, are the repetitive processes which can be handled by loops. In the elimination of each unknown repetitive operations can be distinguished for the division of the coefficients of the first column by the pivot and the determination of new values for the coefficients a and the constants b. The determination of the new coefficients is done first for one equation in one loop which might be called the

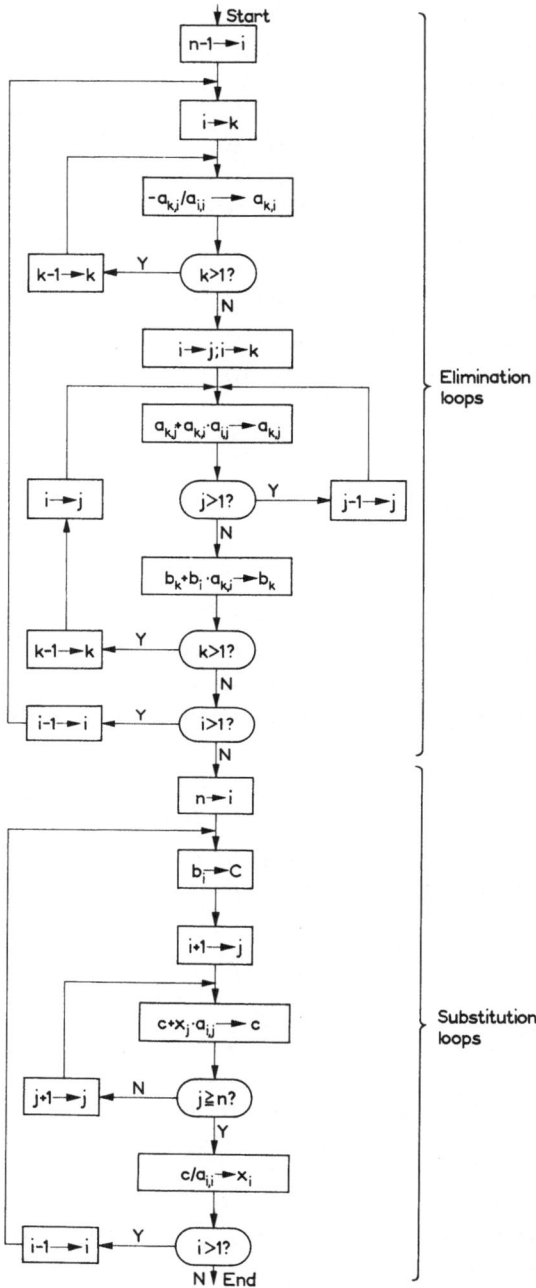

Fig. 6-6. Flow Chart for Gauss Elimination

coefficient loop, at the exit of which the new constant for this equation is determined. Then the program is directed back to the coefficient loop for the determination of the new coefficient values for the next equation.

After the new coefficients and constants for the remaining equations have been determined the program goes back to the starting point for the elimination of the next unknown. The pivot for the elimination of x_1 was a_{11}, however, the pivot for the elimination of x_2 is not a_{22}, but the newly obtained coefficient of x_2.

After all unknowns, except x_n, have been eliminated the program goes to the substitution phase in which first the value for x_n is computed, which is then substituted in the pivotal equation for x_{n-1}. In this way the values for all unknowns are obtained in successive loops.

The following general subscript notations are introduced: k for rows, j for columns, and i for general counting purposes which are not confined to either rows or columns.

With this notation the division process of the respectively first column coefficients by the corresponding pivot and the replacement of the old by the new value can be written in the general form

$$-\frac{a_{k,i}}{a_{i,i}} \to a_{k,i} \qquad (6\text{-}15)$$

indicating the replacement process for k rows and the respective i'th column which is fixed each time for the loop. Using this notation and inspecting equation (6-13), it can be seen that the coefficients a_{22} and a_{2n} for the unknowns x_2 and x_n are replaced by the following expressions

$$a_{22} + a_{k,i} \cdot a_{12} \to a_{22} \qquad (6\text{-}16)$$

$$a_{2n} + a_{k,i} \cdot a_{1n} \to a_{2n} \qquad (6\text{-}17)$$

or in general form

$$a_{k,j} + a_{k,i} \cdot a_{i,j} \to a_{k,j} \qquad (6\text{-}18)$$

After j loops the new coefficients $a_{k,j}$ for one equation or row are computed and the new constant b_k for the k'th row is determined according to

$$b_k + b_i \cdot a_{k,i} \to b_k \qquad (6\text{-}19)$$

This process is then repeated for the next equation or row, replacing $k - 1 \to k$ and resetting j to the respective initial value. The above elimination process is repeated $(n - 1)$ times, each time with the indices i, j, and k reduced by one.

The substitution process for the evaluation of the unknowns is diagrammed in two loops to make it completely general with the auxiliary quantity c introduced for ease of programming. The counting index i is set to n at the beginning of the substitution phase and it is reduced by 1 each time the solution for one unknown has been obtained. To illustrate the loop operation and indexing for the substitution phase the relations for three unknowns are given.

$$b_n / a_{nn} \to x_n \qquad (6\text{-}20)$$

$$(b_{n-1} + x_n a_{n-1,\, n}) / a_{n-1,\, n-1} \to x_{n-1} \qquad (6\text{-}21)$$

$$(b_{n-2} + x_{n-1} a_{n-2,\, n-1} + x_n a_{n-2,\, n}) / a_{n-2,\, n-2} \to x_{n-2} \qquad (6\text{-}22)$$

General loops for the evaluation of such different expressions in a set of unknowns require some considerations for the correct conduct of the program through the loops. When x_n is evaluated the location for x_j, which is addressed in the first pass by the index $n + 1$, must contain zeros, so that the c-loop has no effect. For x_{n-1} the c-computation is made once, for x_{n-2} it is made twice, etc.

Note in particular, that the transfer to the c-loop is done with the index j incremented. The indices of this subloop and the major substitution loop are interrelated in such a way that the transfer to the subloop with decremented index would be very cumbersome, requiring special settings for indices. Therefore, the instruction JIX, jump and increment, is used.

This instruction does not include the check based on which the index is increased and the jump is performed. Therefore the JIX must be preceeded by other instructions for this purpose. Here the check after the c-computation would consist of CLA j, SUB n, and JAM. This means that for negative difference $(j - n)$ the program goes to JIX and for positive difference or zero, to the next instruction. The detailed coding of the Gauss elimination problem, following the chart in Fig. 6-6, is left as an exercise for the student.

An alternate method for the solution of simultaneous linear equations is the solution by determinants. Given the simple set of equations

$$a_{11}x_1 + a_{12}x_2 = b_1 \qquad (6\text{-}23)$$

$$a_{21}x_1 + a_{22}x_2 = b_2$$

the solutions for x_1 and x_2 are

$$x_1 = \frac{\begin{vmatrix} b_1 & a_{12} \\ b_2 & a_{22} \end{vmatrix}}{\begin{vmatrix} a_{11} & a_{12} \\ a_{21} & a_{22} \end{vmatrix}} = \frac{a_{22}b_1 - a_{12}b_2}{a_{11}a_{22} - a_{12}a_{21}} \qquad (6\text{-}24)$$

$$x_2 = \frac{\begin{vmatrix} a_{11} & b_1 \\ a_{21} & b_2 \end{vmatrix}}{\begin{vmatrix} a_{11} & a_{12} \\ a_{21} & a_{22} \end{vmatrix}} = \frac{a_{11}b_2 - a_{21}b_1}{a_{11}a_{22} - a_{12}a_{21}} \qquad (6\text{-}25)$$

The solution by determinants is straightforward and it is useful when a small set of equations is to be solved by hand calculation. For the machine solution of larger sets of equations the determinant method is less suitable than the Gauss elimination method which lends itself better to the looping of the program. With these loops a completely general program can be written for any number of simultaneous linear equations as shown in Fig. 6-6.

For the solution of equations (6-24) and (6-25) it is hardly worthwhile to draw a flow diagram and the code can be written directly from the equations. Though this code is simpler than some of the previous codes, it shall be presented to illustrate the relative increase in detail and number of instructions for programs without loops.

Example 6-6. Symbolic Code for Solution of Equations by Determinants.

Loc	Op.	Addr. Index	Comments
	LDQ	a_{12}	$a_{12} \to Q$
	MPY	a_{21}	$a_{12}a_{21} \to A$
	STA	T	$(A) \to T$
	LDQ	a_{11}	$a_{11} \to Q$
	MPY	a_{22}	$a_{11}a_{22} \to A$
	SUB	T	$(a_{11}a_{22} - a_{12}a_{21}) \to A$
	STA	T	$(A) \to T$
	LDQ	a_{12}	$a_{12} \to Q$
	MPY	b_2	$a_{12}b_2 \to A$
	STA	x_1	$(A) \to x_1$
	LDQ	a_{22}	$a_{22} \to Q$
	MPY	b_1	$a_{22}b_1 \to A$
	SUB	x_1	$(a_{22}b_1 - a_{12}b_2) \to A$
	DIV	T	$(a_{22}b_1 - a_{12}b_2)/(a_{11}a_{22} - a_{12}a_{21}) \to Q$
	STQ	x_1	$(Q) \to x_1$
	LDQ	a_{21}	$a_{21} \to Q$
	MPY	b_1	$a_{21}b_1 \to A$
	STA	x_2	$(A) \to x_2$
	LDQ	a_{11}	$a_{11} \to Q$
	MPY	b_2	$a_{11}b_2 \to A$
	SUB	x_2	$(a_{11}b_2 - a_{21}b_1) \to A$
	DIV	T	$(a_{11}b_2 - a_{21}b_1)/(a_{11}a_{22} - a_{12}a_{21}) \to Q$
	STQ	x_2	$(Q) \to x_2$

In the above code some saving of storage space is achieved by placing the second term of the nominators temporarily in the locations x_1 and x_2 in which the results x_1 and x_2 are eventually stored. The coefficient determinant in the denominator is computed once and preserved in the working storage location T. The code starts with the actual computation and assumes that the coefficients and constants have already been loaded.

6-8. MATRIX OPERATIONS

For the solution of multi-variable problems extensive use is made of the systematic arrangement of the variables and their coefficients in the form of matrices. The repetitive nature of matrix operations makes them particularly amenable to the handling by machines. As a first illustration the *multiplication* of two 2-dimensional *matrices* is discussed.

The product matrix $C = AB$ is obtained by multiplying the rows of A with the columns of B. Introducing here the subscript notation of i for rows, j for columns and k as general index, each element $c_{i,j}$ of the product matrix C is the product-sum resulting from the multiplication of one row by one column.

$$c_{i,j} = a_{i,1}b_{1,j} + a_{i,2}b_{2,j} + \cdots + a_{i,k}b_{k,j} = \sum_{k=1}^{n} a_{i,k}b_{k,j} \quad (6\text{-}26)$$

for square matrices with $i_{max} = j_{max} = n$. For rectangular matrices n is determined by the number of elements in the rows of A or in the columns of B, whichever is smaller.

The index k is used with both factors a and b of the partial products, indicating for a the column position in the i'th row and for b the row position in the j'th column. In forming the product-sums $c_{i,j}$ the index k counts each time from 1 to n. The number of product sums $c_{i,j}$ of elements of the product matrix C is the product of the row number I of the A-matrix times the column number J of the B-matrix, as shown in the following example.

$$\begin{pmatrix} a_{11} & a_{12} & a_{13} & a_{14} \\ a_{21} & a_{22} & a_{23} & a_{24} \\ a_{31} & a_{32} & a_{33} & a_{34} \\ 0 & 0 & 0 & 0 \end{pmatrix} \times \begin{pmatrix} b_{11} & b_{12} & b_{13} & 0 \\ b_{21} & b_{22} & b_{23} & 0 \\ b_{31} & b_{32} & b_{33} & 0 \\ b_{41} & b_{42} & b_{43} & 0 \end{pmatrix} = \begin{pmatrix} c_{11} & c_{12} & c_{13} & 0 \\ c_{21} & c_{22} & c_{23} & 0 \\ c_{31} & c_{32} & c_{33} & 0 \\ 0 & 0 & 0 & 0 \end{pmatrix} \quad (6\text{-}27)$$

The elements of the first column in the C-matrix are obtained by

$$c_{11} = a_{11}b_{11} + a_{12}b_{21} + a_{13}b_{31} + a_{14}b_{41} \quad (6\text{-}28)$$

$$c_{21} = a_{21}b_{11} + a_{22}b_{21} + a_{23}b_{31} + a_{24}b_{41}$$

$$c_{31} = a_{31}b_{11} + a_{32}b_{21} + a_{33}b_{31} + a_{34}b_{41}$$

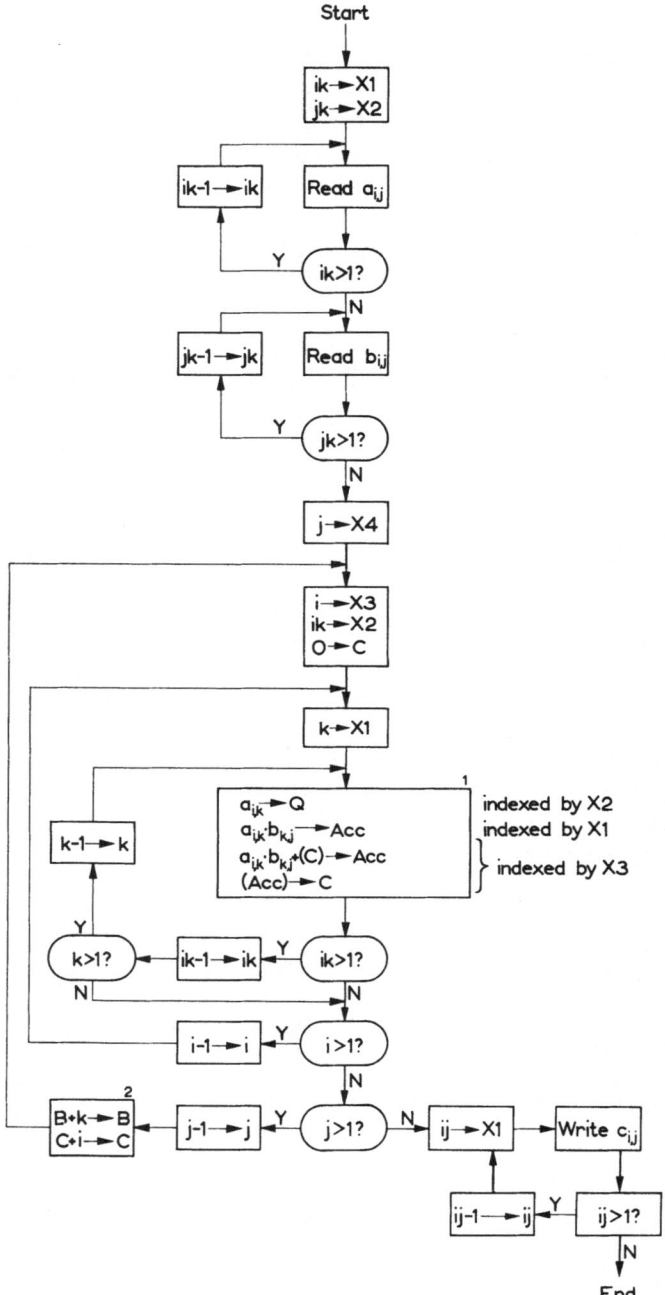

Fig. 6-7. Flow Chart for Matrix Multiplication

with $k=4$, since both the rows of A and the columns of B have 4 elements; if one had only 3 elements, k would be 3.

The flow chart Fig. 6-7 is drawn for the case where all elements ik of the A-matrix and jk of the B-matrix are read into memory at the beginning of the program. The small letters i and j are now used not only for indices but also for the row number of A and the column number of B to distinguish from I and J as the locations for these quantities.

For the computation of each element $c_{i,j}$ the program is directed k-times through operation box 1. For each $c_{i,j}$ one location $C_{i,j}$ is assigned, used for the storage of the intermediate results $c_{i,j}$ and for the final element $c_{i,j}$. After k passes the index in X3 is reduced by one for reference to the next location $C + 1$ and the counter in X1 is set again to k for the computation of the next element $c_{i,j}$.

The elements $c_{i,j}$ for one column are computed from the elements $b_{i,j}$ of one column of the B-matrix and the entire set of $a_{i,j}$ elements of the A-matrix, used in chronological order as indicated by equations (6-28). Therefore, it is expedient to set the counter in X2 to the total number of elements a and to index the instruction which addresses locations $A_{i,j}$ by this counter.

After the elements $c_{i,j}$ of the first column have been computed for i rows, the program steps to the next column. In order to use the same instructions in the operation box the addresses of the B locations have to be moved up by $B + k \to B$ and the C locations by $C + i \to C$, as indicated by modification box 2. Furthermore, the X1, X2, and X3 counters have to be reset.

The moving up of B and C at the beginning of the computation for a new column is not required when at one time only one B-column is read in and one C-column is computed and printed out. Then the same sets of storage locations can be used for successive B- and C-columns.

As previously explained, the pseudo-operation EQU assigns one storage location for the value given in the address part and BSS reserves a block of storage with the number of locations according to the number in the address part. If, for example, ik = 12, then in IK the number 12 is stored and by BBS, ik or 12 storage locations are reserved from A to $A + ik-1$.

The code for the program according to Fig. 6-7 follows.

Example 6-7. Symbolic Code for Matrix Multiplication

Loc.	*Op.*	*Addr.*		*Index*	*Comments*
1000	ENX	IK	,	1	$ik \to X1$
	ENX	JK		2	$jk \to X2$
	RDS	tape			read select tape given in Addr.
L1	CPY	A + ik	,	1	$a_{i,k} \to A_{i,k}$
	JPX	L1	,	1, 1	$f(X1) > 1$, reduce by 1, go to L1
	RDS	tape			read select tape given in Addr.
L2	CPY	B + jk	,	2	$b_{k,j} \to B_{k,j}$
	JPX	L2	,	2, 1	if $(X2) > 1$, reduce by 1, go to L2
	ENX	J	,	4	$j \to X4$
L13	ENX	I	,	3	$i \to X3$
	ENX	IK	,	2	$ik \to X2$
	STZ	C			$O \to C$
L5	ENX	K	,	1	$k \to X1$
L4	LDQ	A	,	2	$a_{i,k} \to Q$
L8	MPY	B	,	1	$a_{i,k} \cdot b_{k,j} \to Acc$
L10	ADD	C	,	3	$Acc + (C) \to Acc$
L12	STA	C	,	3	$(Acc) \to C$
	JPX	L3	,	2, 1	if $(X2) > 1$, reduce by 1, go to L3
L3	JPX	L4	,	1, 1	if $(X1) > 1$, reduce by 1, go to L4
	JPX	L5	,	3, 1	if $(X3) > 1$, reduce by 1, go to L5
	JPX	L6	,	4, 1	if $(X4) > 1$, reduce by 1, go to L6
	ENX	IJ	,	1	$ij \to X1$
	WRS	tape			write select tape given in Addr.
L7	CPY	C + ij	,	1	$c_{i,j} \to tape$
	JPX	L7	,	1, 1	if $(X1) > 1$, reduce by 1, go to L7
	HLT				end of program
L6	LDX	L8	,	1	addr. part of L8 or $B \to X1$
	JIX	L9	,	1, k	$B + k \to X1$
L9	STX	L8	,	1	$(X1) \to$ addr. part of L8
	LDX	L10	,	1	addr. part of L10 or $C \to X1$
	JIX	L11	,	1, i	$C + i \to X1$
L11	STX	L10	,	1	$(X1) \to$ addr. part of L10
	STX	L12	,	1	$(X1) \to$ addr. part of L12
	JMP	L13			go to L13
IK	EQU	ik			
JK	EQU	jk			
I	EQU	i			
J	EQU	j			
K	EQU	k			
IJ	EQU	ij			
A	BSS	ik			
B	BSS	jk			
C	BSS	ij			
	END				

Further details with regard to the actual operating program are entered under comments.

Another interesting example for the looping of programs is the matrix inversion by a variation of the Gauss elimination method. Given a coefficient matrix with n^2 elements and adding a pivot row with the elements a_{p1} through a_{pn} and an unit vector column, we have:

$$
\begin{array}{cccc}
a_{11}a_{12} \ldots a_{1n} & 1 \\
a_{21}a_{22} \ldots a_{2n} & 0 \\
\vdots \quad \vdots \qquad \vdots & \vdots \\
a_{n1}a_{n2} \ldots a_{nn} & 0 \\
\\
a_{p1}a_{p2} \ldots a_{pn} &
\end{array}
\tag{6-29}
$$

The inversion procedure is an iterative process which is repeated n times. The coefficients a'_{ij} which are obtained after the n'th repetition are the coefficients of the inverse matrix. All the coefficients obtained after the preceding repetitions are intermediate results which replace successively the previous set of coefficients.

As in the elimination process, after each step the respective first row and column disappears, but different from the elimination process, the size of the coefficient matrix must be maintained, because original and inverse matrix are of equal size. At every step row i replaces row $i - 1$, the pivot row moves up to the position of row n, column j replaces column $j - 1$, and the unit vector column becomes the n'th column.

At the beginning of a new step a new pivot row and unit vector column are added. The elements for the pivot row a_{pj} are:

$$
a_{pj} = \frac{a_{1,j+1}}{a_{11}}
\tag{6-30}
$$

and the new values for the coefficients are computed according to:

$$
a_{ij} = a_{i,j+1} - a_{i,1} \cdot a_{pj}
\tag{6-31}
$$

The computations are done at each step for the n elements of the pivot row, the n'th element always being the reciprocal of the pivot $1/a_{11}$, and for the $(n-1)n$ coefficients, from row 2 to n and column 2 to n and the unit vector column. For these repetitive operations program loops can be designed which use the same instructions and refer to the same set of address locations.

The concept of the inverse or reciprocal matrix is applicable to the solution of simultaneous linear equations. A system of equations, as given by (6-9) through (6-11) can be written in matrix form:

$$
\begin{pmatrix}
a_{11}a_{12} \ldots a_{1n} \\
a_{21}a_{22} \ldots a_{2n} \\
\vdots \quad \vdots \\
a_{n1}a_{n2} \ldots a_{nn}
\end{pmatrix}
\cdot
\begin{pmatrix}
x_1 \\
x_2 \\
\vdots \\
x_n
\end{pmatrix}
=
\begin{pmatrix}
b_1 \\
b_2 \\
\vdots \\
b_n
\end{pmatrix}
\tag{6-32}
$$

or

$$
\begin{pmatrix}
x_1 \\
x_2 \\
\vdots \\
x_n
\end{pmatrix}
=
\begin{pmatrix}
a_{11}'a_{12}' \ldots a_{1n}' \\
a_{21}'a_{22}' \ldots a_{2n}' \\
\vdots \quad \vdots \\
a_{n1}'a_{n2}' \ldots a_{nn}'
\end{pmatrix}
\cdot
\begin{pmatrix}
b_1 \\
b_2 \\
\vdots \\
b_n
\end{pmatrix}
\tag{6-33}
$$

where the prime indicates the coefficients of the reciprocal or inverse matrix. From (6-33) the unknowns x are obtained as follows:

$$
\begin{aligned}
x_1 &= b_1 a_{11}' + b_2 a_{12}' + \ldots + b_n a_{1n}' \\
&\vdots \qquad \vdots \qquad \vdots \qquad \qquad \vdots \\
x_n &= b_1 a_{n1}' + b_2 a_{n2}' + \ldots + b_n a_{nn}'
\end{aligned}
\tag{6-34}
$$

Another important property of the inverse matrix is that the product of an original matrix A with its inverse A^{-1} gives the identity matirx I, with one's in the main diagonal and zero's for the other coefficients.

$$
A \cdot A^{-1} = I \tag{6-35}
$$

If A is a diagonal matrix with values only in the main diagonal and the other elements equal to zero, the inverse A^{-1} is also a diagonal matrix with the reciprocal values of the elements of A in its main diagonal.

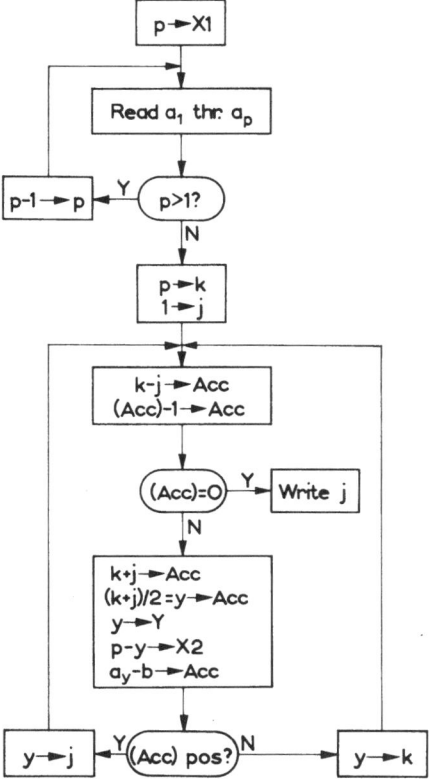

Fig. 6-8.   Flow Chart for Binary Search

6-9.   SEARCHING AND SORTING

Searching and sorting are basic operations which are widely used in many business and scientific data processing procedures. From the variety of existing techniques, an example for *searching* a binary search program is presented which is quite representative of the manner in which the machine handles search problems.

For the discussed binary search program an array of numbers $a_1, a_2 \ldots a_p$ in descending order $a_1 \geq a_2 \geq a_3$, etc., and a number b is given which falls within the range of the array, such that $a_1 \geq b > a_p$. The program determines the subscript j for which

$$a_j \geq b > a_{j+1} \tag{6-36}$$

where j and $j + 1 = k$ are successive numerical subscripts such that $k - j = 1$.

The initial settings for the subscripts are $j = 1$ and $k = p$ and the first approximation for the subscript is computed according to the relation

$$y = (k + j)/2 = (p + 1)/2 \qquad (6\text{-}37)$$

Then the approximation y replaces either j or k depending on whether the number a_y is larger or smaller than b until $k - j = 1$. The flow chart for this program is shown in Fig. 6-8.

According to this flow chart the following code is written with the assumption that the numerical values for p and b are provided at assembly time.

Example 6-8.   Symbolic Code for Binary Search.

Loc.	Op.	Addr.	Index	Comments
1000	LDX	P	, 1	$p \rightarrow X1$
	RDS	tape		read select tape given in Addr.
L1	CPY	$A + p$	, 1	$a_1 \rightarrow A$ thr. $ap \rightarrow A + p - 1$
	JPX	L1	, 1, 1	if $(X1) > 1$, reduce by 1, go to L1
	CLA	P		$p \rightarrow Acc$
	STA	K		$p \rightarrow K$
	CLA	C		$1 \rightarrow Acc$
	STA	J		$1 \rightarrow J$
L4	CLA	K		$k \rightarrow Acc$
	SUB	J		$k - j \rightarrow Acc$
	SUB	C		$k - j - 1 \rightarrow Acc$
	JAZ	L2		if $(Acc) = 0$, go to L2, otherw. next instruction
	CLA	K		$k \rightarrow Acc$
	ADD	J		$k + j \rightarrow Acc$
	ARS	1		$(k + j)/2 = y \rightarrow Acc$
	STA	Y		$y \rightarrow Y$
	CLA	P		$p \rightarrow Acc$
	SUB	Y		$p - y \rightarrow Acc$
	STA	T		$p - y \rightarrow T$
	LDX	T	2	$p - y \rightarrow X2$
	CLA	$A + p$	, 2	$a_y \rightarrow Acc$
	SUB	B		$a_y - b \rightarrow Acc$
	JAP	L3		if (Acc) pos., go to L3, otherwise next instruction

Loc.	Op.	Addr.	Index	Comments
	CLA	Y		$y \to$ Acc
	STA	K		$y \to$ K
	JMP	L4		jump to L4 for next pass
L3	CLA	Y		$y \to$ Acc
	STA	J		$y \to$ J
	JMP	L4		jump to L4 for next pass
L2	WRS	tape		write select tape given in Addr.
	CPY	J		$j \to$ tape
K				
J				
Y				
T				
A	BSS	p		reserves locations for a_1 thr. a_p
P	EQU	p		places numerical value of p into P
B	EQU	b		places numerical value of b into B
C	EQU	1		places 1 into C

Most *sorting* techniques fall into the general categories of sorting by merging and radix sorting which are described in detail by Frined[23] in "Sorting on Electronic Computer Systems". The example which is presented here may be classified under the category of sorting by merging.

In the example two records of numbers are given a_1 thr. a_n and b_1 thr. b_n which may be considered as credit and debit accounts. For each corresponding pair the difference $a_i - b_i$ shall be computed and recorded if the difference is positive, otherwise zero shall be entered for the pair, thus sorting the pairs with positive balance and recording this balance. The flow chart for the problem is shown in Fig. 6-9.

Since for the a and b files the same number n of recorded data is assumed, where some data may have the numerical value zero, the index for all loops is n. The flow chart shows the setting of four index registers at the start, but for this program with simple loops one index register would be sufficient which would have to be reset to the index n at the beginning of each loop.

For the sorting of different information which is contained in one computer word extraction procedures are employed using masks which are filled with one's for the part of the word for which the information shall be extracted and with

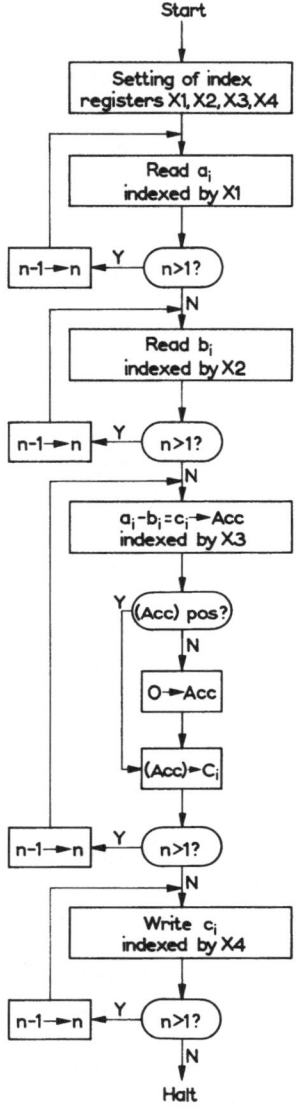

Fig. 6-9. Flow Chart for Sorting Example

zero's for the rest of the word. The logical AND operation applied to the information word and the mask then extracts the desired information part from the information word.

If, for example, one computer word contains information pertaining to department, individual worker, regular and overtime hours worked, it might be required to determine the overtime worked in the department. First the overtime is extracted for each individual worker using a mask for the overtime field and the results are stored in consecutive locations from which they can be fetched for summation with one indexed ADD instruction. The distinction between departments for which the overtime determination shall be made is best done when the properly grouped information words are read as records into the computer.

6-10. NUMERICAL SOLUTION OF DIFFERENTIAL EQUATIONS

As an example for the numerical solution of differential equations on computers the Runge-Kutta method is discussed. Here each point of the solution for a function $dy/dx = f(x,y)$ is obtained by calculating the increments Δy at equidistant values h of the independent variable x according to a definite set of formulas which are for first order equations

$$k_1 = f(x_0, y_0)h \tag{6-38}$$

$$k_2 = f\left(x_0 + \frac{h}{2}, y_0 + \frac{k_1}{2}\right)h$$

$$k_3 = f\left(x_0 + \frac{h}{2}, y_0 + \frac{k_2}{2}\right)h$$

$$k_4 = f(x_0 + h, y_0 + k_3)h$$

$$\Delta y = \frac{1}{6}\left(k_1 + 2k_2 + 2k_3 + k_4\right)$$

$$x_1 = x_0 + h, \; y_1 = y_0 + \Delta y$$

For simultaneous equations the increments are calculated for all dependent variables in the same way according to their functional relationship to the independent variable. To illustrate let us consider the set of simultaneous equations which describe the two-dimensional motion of a rocket in still air.

$$\dot{V} = \frac{T}{m} - \frac{D}{m} - g \sin \Theta \tag{6-39}$$

$$\dot{\Theta} = \frac{V}{r_0 + y} \cos \Theta - \frac{g}{V} \cos \Theta \tag{6-40}$$

$$\dot{y} = V \sin \Theta \tag{6-41}$$

$$\dot{x} = \frac{r_0}{r_0 + y} V \cos \Theta \tag{6-42}$$

where V= velocity in direction of flight, T= thrust, D= drag, m = mass, g = acceleration due to gravity at any altitude, Θ = flight path angle with horizontal, r_0 = radius of the earth, y = altitude above sea level, x = distance along sea level sphere. All derivatives of the variables are with respect to time which is the independent variable. The value $\Delta x = h$ becomes here Δt for which different values may be selected as integration steps for different phases of the trajectory.

A direct application of equations (6-38) to a single point solution, for example, for variable y would lead to the following equations in which superscript (O) is used for the values entering the integration and the superscripts (1, 2, 3) for the values developed during the integration.

$$k_1 = \dot{y}^{(0)}\Delta t = [V^{(0)} \sin \Theta^{(0)}]\Delta t \tag{6-43}$$

$$k_2 = \dot{y}^{(1)}\Delta t = [(V^{(0)} + \tfrac{1}{2}\Delta t \dot{V}^{(0)})(\sin(\Theta^{(0)} + \tfrac{1}{2}\Delta t \dot{\Theta}^{(0)}))]\Delta t$$

$$k_3 = \dot{y}^{(2)}\Delta t = [(V^{(0)} + \tfrac{1}{2}\Delta t \dot{V}^{(1)})(\sin(\Theta^{(0)} + \tfrac{1}{2}\Delta t \dot{\Theta}^{(1)}))]\Delta t$$

$$k_4 = \dot{y}^{(3)}\Delta t = [(V^{(0)} + \Delta t \dot{V}^{(2)})(\sin(\Theta^{(0)} + \Delta t \dot{\Theta}^{(2)}))]\Delta t$$

$$\Delta y = \frac{\Delta t}{6}(\dot{y}^{(0)} + 2\dot{y}^{(1)} + 2\dot{y}^{(2)} + \dot{y}^{(3)})$$

$$t_{i+1} = t_i + \Delta t, \ y_{i+1} = y_i + \Delta y$$

The practical procedure for the solution of the interrelated equations for the variables V, θ, y, and x with the Runge Kutta integration method is shown in the flow chart of Fig. 6-10.

At the entry of the integration routine a counter or index register is provided which directs the successive iterations to paths 1, 2, 3, and 4 by reducing the index each time around by one. At the fourth pass the counter is reset. The superscripts are used for the intermediate integration results to distinguish them from the solution points, and in order to keep the notation general. At each integration step, e.g., going from y_0 to y_1, y_1 to y_2, etc., the initial value at the integration is denoted by $y^{(0)}$ or $\dot{y}^{(0)}$ respectively.

At the first path the initial values which are the first terms in the summation for the increments are stored into cells

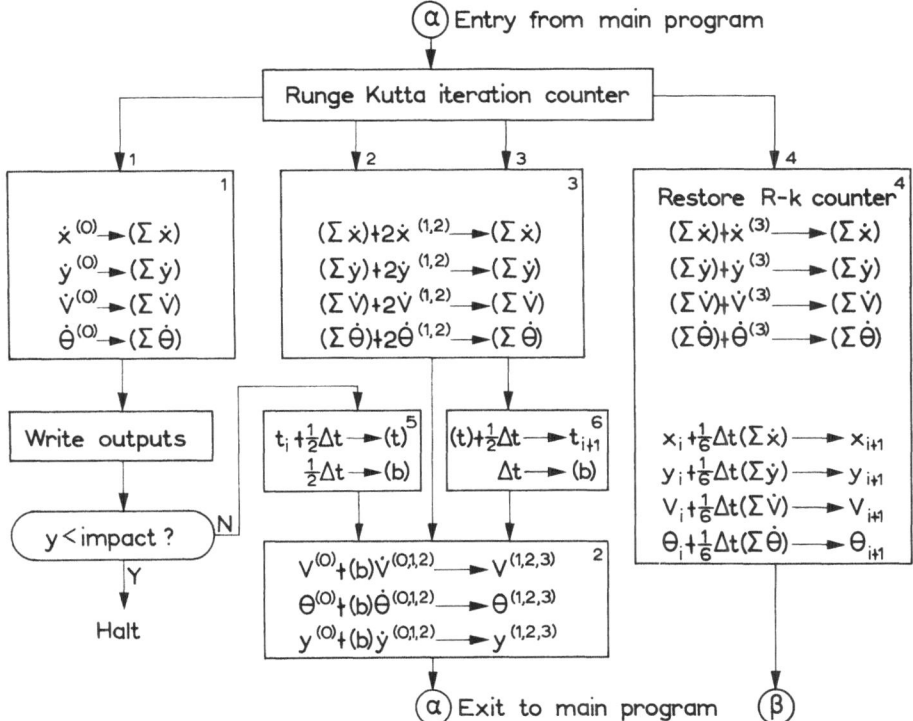

(α) Entry from main program

Runge Kutta iteration counter

1

$\dot{x}^{(0)} \rightarrow (\Sigma \dot{x})$
$\dot{y}^{(0)} \rightarrow (\Sigma \dot{y})$
$\dot{V}^{(0)} \rightarrow (\Sigma \dot{V})$
$\dot{\Theta}^{(0)} \rightarrow (\Sigma \dot{\Theta})$

3

$(\Sigma \dot{x}) + 2\dot{x}^{(1,2)} \rightarrow (\Sigma \dot{x})$
$(\Sigma \dot{y}) + 2\dot{y}^{(1,2)} \rightarrow (\Sigma \dot{y})$
$(\Sigma \dot{V}) + 2\dot{V}^{(1,2)} \rightarrow (\Sigma \dot{V})$
$(\Sigma \dot{\Theta}) + 2\dot{\Theta}^{(1,2)} \rightarrow (\Sigma \dot{\Theta})$

4

Restore R-k counter

$(\Sigma \dot{x}) + \dot{x}^{(3)} \rightarrow (\Sigma \dot{x})$
$(\Sigma \dot{y}) + \dot{y}^{(3)} \rightarrow (\Sigma \dot{y})$
$(\Sigma \dot{V}) + \dot{V}^{(3)} \rightarrow (\Sigma \dot{V})$
$(\Sigma \dot{\Theta}) + \dot{\Theta}^{(3)} \rightarrow (\Sigma \dot{\Theta})$

Write outputs

5
$t_i + \tfrac{1}{2}\Delta t \rightarrow (t)$
$\tfrac{1}{2}\Delta t \rightarrow (b)$

6
$(t) + \tfrac{1}{2}\Delta t \rightarrow t_{i+1}$
$\Delta t \rightarrow (b)$

$x_i + \tfrac{1}{6}\Delta t(\Sigma \dot{x}) \rightarrow x_{i+1}$
$y_i + \tfrac{1}{6}\Delta t(\Sigma \dot{y}) \rightarrow y_{i+1}$
$V_i + \tfrac{1}{6}\Delta t(\Sigma \dot{V}) \rightarrow V_{i+1}$
$\Theta_i + \tfrac{1}{6}\Delta t(\Sigma \dot{\Theta}) \rightarrow \Theta_{i+1}$

y < impact ? N

Y

Halt

2
$V^{(0)} + (b)\dot{V}^{(0,1,2)} \rightarrow V^{(1,2,3)}$
$\Theta^{(0)} + (b)\dot{\Theta}^{(0,1,2)} \rightarrow \Theta^{(1,2,3)}$
$y^{(0)} + (b)\dot{y}^{(0,1,2)} \rightarrow y^{(1,2,3)}$

(α) Exit to main program   (β)

Fig. 6-10. Flow Chart for Runge Kutta Integration

reserved for the increasing sums. The contents of the cells with the initial values are replaced by the derivatives with the superscripts 1, 2, and 3 which are developed in the following loops. In this way reference can be made to the same cells at each loop. It is expedient to arrange in the first path the writing of the results and the test if impact is reached because at other places in the main program which are passed through at all four loops special instructions would be required to bypass the write and impact test during three loops.

In preparation of the next path t_i is then increased by $1/2\ \Delta t$ and $1/2\ \Delta t$ is placed in some cell b. At the third path Δt is placed in the same cell, making it possible to write the next block in general terms referring to cell b with $1/2\ \Delta t$ for path 1 and 2 and Δt for path 3. In this block 2 the three intermediate values of the variables V, Θ, and y are computed consecutively which are then used in the main program to compute the corresponding derivatives of the variables according to equations 6-39 through 6-42.

The intermediate derivatives with the superscripts 1, 2, and 3 are used in the iteration paths 2, 3, and 4 respectively. In path 3 the contents of cell t which was set to $t_i + 1/2 \Delta t$ is increased by $1/2 \Delta t$ thus establishing the time for the next solution point $t_i + \Delta t = t_{i+1}$. In the first and second iteration loop the system equations (6-39 ... 42) are solved for time $t_i + 1/2 \Delta t$ and in third iteration for t_{i+1}. In the fourth path the final sums of the intermediate derivatives and with them the solutions for the $(i + 1)$th point are computed.

6-11.   A COMPLETE PROGRAM FOR A ROCKET TRAJECTORY

The composition of various parts into a complete program is shown in Fig. 6-11 for a simple two-dimensional rocket trajectory using the equations of motion (6-39 thr. 42) and the integration procedure Fig. 6-10.

At the loading of the program the following input data are read into the machine in addition to the set of instructions: Standard constants used in various subroutines; values used by all rockets in trajectory calculations, such as the coefficients of the polynomials used in the generation of atmospheric functions; values given for a particular rocket such as thrust, mass, flow rate, and diameter; values which pertain to a given problem or to a particular trajectory to be flown under standard or perturbed conditions. The last group of values is changed from run to run and it is printed out before the program starts, to identify the particular run.

The program begins with the determination of the integration intervals for the various flight phases. The intervals are smaller for the power flight, e.g., 1/8 sec., and they are increased for the ballistic free flight, e.g., to 1/4 or 1/2 sec. and they are eventually decreased again for the terminal phase. After the completion of every integration procedure the program is reentered at point β to set the interval Δt for the next point of the solution. Next the altitude is tested and according to the atmospheric zone the rocket is in, the density and temperature ratio are computed using constants from standard atmospheric tables and the momentary altitude which has been scaled down by 10^{-5} for computational reasons. The intermediate integration loops reenter the program at point γ because the altitude has changed from $y^{(0)}$ to $y^{(1, 2, 3)}$ respec-

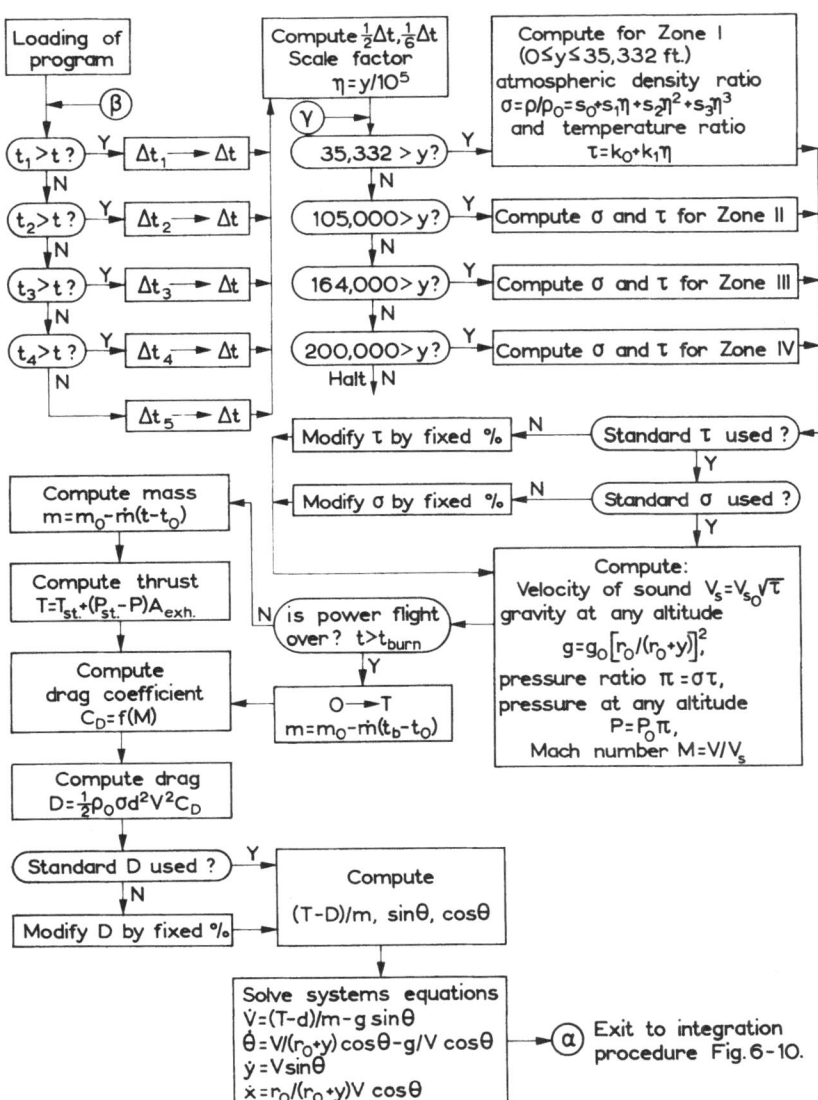

Fig. 6-11. Flow Chart for 2-D Rocket Trajectory

tively and with this change everything which follows has to be computed.

If the effect of non-standard atmospheric conditions are to be evaluated, the standard values are modified by the pre-scribed percentages. The subsequent computations determine the velocity of sound from which in turn the Mach number and the drag coefficient are developed, the pressure at any altitude, needed for the computation of the thrust gain, and the gravity at any altitude, required for the solution of the systems equations.

The next test determines whether or not the power flight is over. During the power phase, the change in mass due to the fuel flow rate $\dot{m}$ and the thrust which increases over the static thrust due to thrust gain in higher altitudes have to be computed. After this the computations are done again for both, power and free flight. The drag coefficient is developed here only as a function of Mach number, while for guided missiles it is also a function of angle of attack and fin deflection. The drag force depends not only on the dynamic pressure $1/2\rho\ V^2$ and the drag coefficient C_D but also on the dimensions of the rocket, introduced here as the diameter squared. Then provisions are made for runs with deviations of the drag from its normal value.

In the flow chart the computations for $(T–D)/m$, $\sin\theta$, and $\cos\theta$ are shown in a separate box in order to have in the following box the solution of the system equations set off distinctively by themselves. The programmer has some lati-tude in the partition of the operation boxes. Since, e.g., $\sin\theta$ and $\cos\theta$ are computed by subroutines it may be indicated to show them in separate boxes. But regardless of the break-down of operation boxes, the three distinct different program elements, the operation process, the test and decision process, and the modification or alteration process should always be shown in separate boxes.

After solving the systems equations the integration proce-dure Fig. 6-10 is entered for the four different paths as de-scribed in the preceding section. After paths 1, 2, and 3 the main program is reentered at point γ and after path 4 at point β.

The atmospheric functions and the function for the drag coefficient can be solved either by computation with the respective coefficients of the polynomials stored in the computer or by table look up. The latter method is generally faster but requires more memory cells for the storage of the tables.

To give an idea of the order of magnitude, the described two-dimensional rocket program consists of approximately 400 instructions and requires about 2250 memory cells.

Within the framework of this book it was only possible to give in the preceding sections some brief descriptions of a few programs. The books "Mathematical Methods for Digital Computers", edited by Ralston and Wilf and "Numerical Methods for Scientists and Engineers", by R. W. Hamming *(See bibliography)* are recommended as valuable guides in the selection and formulation of mathematical methods for computer solutions.

PROBLEMS

6-1. Draw flow chart and write code for solution of

    a. $z_i = x_i^2 - 6x_i y_i - y_i$;

    b. $z_i = x_i^2 y_i^2 - 3x_i + y_i$;

    c. $z = 2x^3 - x^2 y + x$.

6-2. Draw flow chart and write code with proper linkage to subroutines for square root, sin, and cos for

    a. $y_i = \dfrac{a + x_i - \sqrt{2x_i + .5}}{5a^2}$, four $i = 1, 2, \ldots 50$;

    b. $y_i = x_i + \cos 2x_i$;

    c. $y_i = a \sin \omega x_i + b \cos \omega x_i$.

6-3. Program the following problem of the difference calculus. Given two sets of data, the equidistand data $x_0, x_1 \ldots x_n$ and the data $y_0 = f(x_0)$, $y_1 = f(x_1)$, $\ldots y_n = f(x_n)$. Compute the difference table for forward differences as follows:

$$\Delta f(x_0) = f(x_1) - f(x_0), \Delta f(x_1) = f(x_2) - f(x_1), \ldots \Delta f(x_{n-1})$$
$$= f(x_n) - f(x_{n-1});$$
$$\Delta^2 f(x_0) = \Delta f(x_1) - \Delta f(_0), \ldots \Delta^2 f(x_{n-2})$$
$$= \Delta f(x_{n-1}) - \Delta f(x_{n-2}); \ldots$$
$$\Delta^n f(x_0) = \Delta^{n-1} f(x_1) - \Delta^{n-1} f(x_0).$$

6-4. Build in the preceding program checks which stop the computation when differences become zero.

6-5. Reprogram Example 6-4 for the extraction of square roots for a series of arguments a_1 through a_n.

6-6. Write program for the solution of the exponential function $y = e^x$ by series expansion

$$y = e^x = 1 + x + \frac{x^2}{2!} + \frac{x^3}{3!} + \ldots + \frac{x^n}{n!}.$$

6-7. Write code for the Gauss elimination problem following the flow chart Fig. 6-6.

6-8. Draw flow chart for matrix inversion according to the computational steps as outlined in SEC. 6-8 equations (6-29) through (6-34).

6-9. Write code for matrix inversion following the diagram as developed by problem 6-8.

6-10. Write code for the sorting problem of SEC. 6-9 following the flow chart Fig. 6-9.

CHAPTER 7

Automatic Programming

7-1. MEANING OF AUTOMATIC PROGRAMMING

In the preceding chapters it had been seen that the usefulness of digital computers is mainly based on their automatic operation. For a single instruction the computer automatically performs many steps of data moving and manipulation. The programmer can write a set of instructions in a symbolic form and the machine translates the symbols into numerical form upon which the computer can operate. What then is the distinction between an automatic program and a machine program which consists of a list of instructions? Actually the difference in automation between machine and automatic programs is only one of degree, while the decisive difference between the two kinds of programs is their orientation, the former being oriented toward the machine and the latter toward the problems to be solved. A program is machine oriented when it is written in the instruction code of a particular machine. The problem – or source-oriented program is written basically in a form which is independent of the machine on which the problem is to be solved. Therefore the different programs might be better distinguished as machine and source programs, instead of machine and automatic programs.

The trend toward source programs is very strong, being advanced by both computer users and manufacturers. The latter are faced with the problem that the increasing number of high speed computers to be marketed are kept busy and really needed; and, more important, the users are concerned with making the powerful computers accessible to a larger group of scientific and business analysts. This can be achieved when computer programs are written in a language which is oriented toward problems, eliminating to a certain extent the dependency on skilled programmers who in the past were practically indispensable for putting the problems of the systems analysts on particular machines.

Therefore, the overall objective of automatic programming is a wider and more extensive utilization of computers. The achievement of this goal requires two major developmental efforts: the specification of programming languages universal enough to serve large areas of application, say the area of scientific computations or business accounting, and the design of computer programs which will automatically develop from the symbolism of the source program the sequence of instructions and memory assignments with which the machine can work. Such automatic translation programs are called compilers. The automatic compilation of machine programs is specially referred to as automatic programming.

In a broader sense automatic programming is also concerned with the so-called operating systems which are not related to the problems or individual jobs to be done but to the entire activity of the computer. Operating systems are developed to bridge the gap between the machine and the programmer who due to the increasing complexities of machines and problems can no longer be an expert in every phase of efficient machine usage and debugging aids which have become available. The operating systems which aid the programmer in operational problems consist mainly of input-output systems to get data in and out of the machine and supervisory systems for the sequencing of jobs and the communication between programmer and operation.

The various objectives of automatic programming, as sketched in Fig. 7-1, are discussed in the following sections.

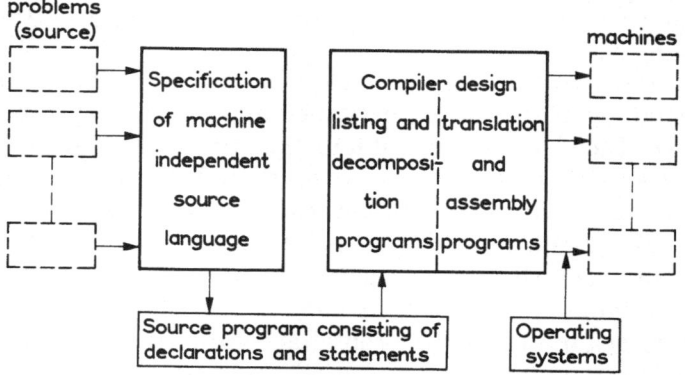

Fig. 7-1. The Objectives of Automatic Programming

7-2. PRINCIPLES OF LANGUAGE DESIGN

Languages which are designed for the use and communication with computers are called mechanical or formal languages in contradistinction to natural languages which develop in an evolutionary way. Both problem oriented and machine oriented languages are mechanical languages. The design of machine languages is a rather pragmatic process dictated by the relationship between symbols and their interpretation by a particular machine. The problem oriented languages must be designed to be independent of special machine characteristics with a great number of expressions, sufficient, and rich enough to express a large variety of problems, and at the same time, clearly definable by codes which the machine can recognize as discrete signals and uniquely analyze as to their meaning.

It is the design of this type of mechanical language which is of particular interest because it requires special considerations far more basic and difficult than for machine languages. The problem arises from the general principle that the more suitable a language is for human understanding, the more difficult it will be to translate from the language into machine code. The technical requirements for this translation make the mechanical languages appear more or less as strings of symbols and the user must learn how to arrange them according to defined conventions in order to express his problem (the terms "string" and "symbol" are used here rather loosely; they will be defined more exact later).

With regard to natural languages linguistic studies consider the units from which a language is built, the structure or syntax of the language and the semantics or meaning of language expressions. A mechanical or formal language is defined as a distinguished, usually infinite subset of all the possible finite strings (sequences of occurrences) of symbols also called characters, from a set called the alphabet. If a string belongs to a language it may be called a sentence of that language.

The language may be specified either by stating how to generate all sentences that belong to it, or by stating how to recognize whether or not any given string is a sentence of that language. The two types of specifications are referred to as grammar or recognition grammar of the language. The grammar of a language is then a finite set of rules by which the sentences of that language can be generated. These rules are also called production rules. Sometimes the grammar of a language is referred to as the specification or syntactical language for the mechanical language. In order to avoid confusion concerning the context of the word "language" the term grammar will be used exclusively when reference is made to language specifications.

Artificial or mechanical languages can be designed with different degrees of complexity and flexibility according to the set of symbols making up the alphabet and according to the rules by which symbols can be rewritten as strings. The rules may provide for simple rewriting or, in addition, for rewriting only when a symbol occurs in a specified context. Accordingly a hierarchy of languages has been established (see reference 24) in which different types of languages are ordered with increasing possibilities of expression and recognition. The lowest order language is the finite state language with a small number of symbols in its alphabet. The language class which includes most of the mechanical languages used with computers is called simple phrase structure language. It is preceded in the language hierarchy by the phrase structure language to which the natural languages belong. The difference between the simple phrase and the phrase structure is the richer grammar of the latter containing rules by which symbols may be rewritten only in a special context with specified strings as evidenced by the great variety and different expressions in word and sentence structure of natural languages.

The design of mechanical languages, at present to a certain extent still an art, will develop into a science of symbol manipulation effecting not only the activity but also the design of computers which in their present configuration are not particularly suited for the generation, recognition and translation of language sentences. The syntactic capabilities in manipulating lists or strings of symbols will determine the broader usefulness of computers in the future.

The symbol manipulation is done in the machine by automatic programs called compilers. These programs are an essential part of the mechanical language; they generate sentences according to the rules or grammar of the language structure. The source program which is presented to the computer as merely a set of strings is made into a language by the compiler.

The language design task can then be broken down into some sub-tasks, notably the formulation of grammar rules, the definition of basic symbols and expressions of the language, and precedures to form the language and its sentences from symbols and expressions according to the given grammar.

7-3. THE STRUCTURE OF ALGOL

As an example of a machine independent source language, the general structure of the international algorithmic language ALGOL will be discussed. ALGOL was worked out and agreed upon by representatives from Denmark, England, France, Germany, Holland, Switzerland, and the United States in January 1960. The concepts and agreements of the committee are presented in what is now generally referred to as the ALGOL Report[25] supplemented by the revised ALGOL Report[25a], practically the original version with some modifications.

In Figure 7-2 a graphical presentation of the hierarchy of ALGOL constituents is attempted with some connecting lines indicating the build up of elements in the hierarchy, normally from lower level elements but in some cases recursively also from higher elements.

The basic characters of a language whose codes are eventually to be uniquely recognized by the machine are letters, digits, and symbols. For symbols the broader class of delimiters has been established in ALGOL, including not only arithmetic, relational, and logical operators, but also symbols or words for sequencing, separation, bracket inclosure, declaration and specification.

From the basic symbols the ALGOL constituents are constructed according to specifications which define the syntax and semantics of the language in a progressive manner. Elements, which are specified in terms of basic symbols, are used for the specification of higher order elements of the language. A compact notation for the specification of the syntax and semantics of ALGOL is given by Backus normal form[26]. Other notations can be formulated, but the specification by Backus normal form was the first systematically developed and officially used grammar description for ALGOL.

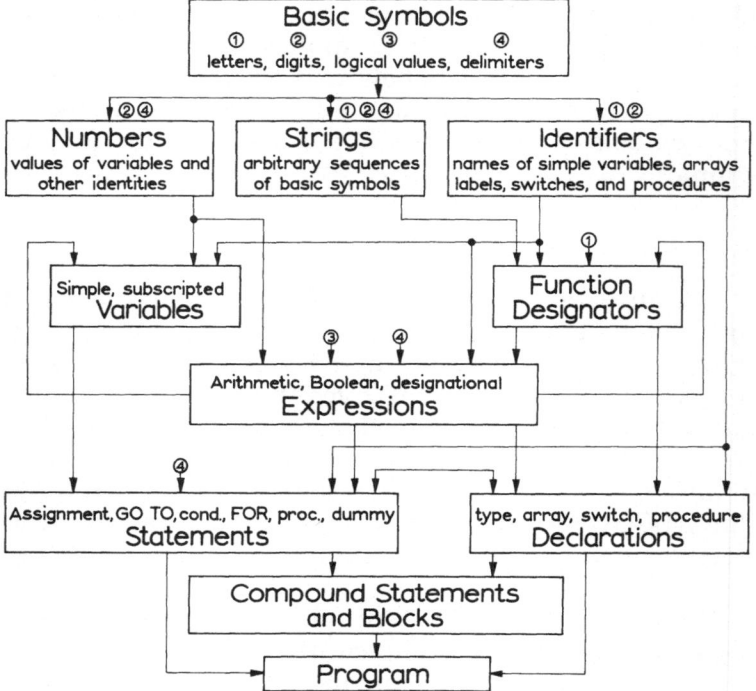

Fig. 7-2. Hierarchy of ALGOL Constituents

The production rules are stated in this description in the compact form of equations, using the production symbol ":: =" for stating that the left side of the equations can be produced by the right side. Furthermore the choice (or) symbol "|" is used when on the right side several items have to be listed which alternately can generate the left side. These items are names or symbols; when they are names they are surrounded by brackets "< · · · >" with the intent to designate the extent of the name. In the basic cases where the name is letter or digit we have the simple production rules:

$$< \text{letter} > :: = a \mid b \mid c \mid . \mid y \mid z \mid A \mid B \mid C \mid . \mid Y \mid Z$$
$$< \text{digit} > \ :: = 0 \mid 1 \mid 2 \mid 3 \mid 4 \mid 5 \mid 6 \mid 7 \mid 8 \mid 9 \tag{7.1}$$

In these relations the bracket inclosure designates a set of symbols as the extent of the name. In other cases strings of symbols or in other words, sets of strings are the designated extent of the name. Then the bracketed name may be called the name of a sublanguage which is specified by the sets of strings which can be generated according to the production rule which has the name on the left side.

The formal description of the class of delimiters in Backus normal form shows again the compactness and clarity of this notation. The description is as follows:

$<$ delimiter $>$: : $= <$ operator $>$ | $<$ separator $>$ | $<$ bracket $>$ |
          $<$ declarator $>$ | $<$ specificator $>$

$<$ operator $>$: : $= <$ arithmetic operator $>$ | $<$ relational opera-
          tor $>$ | $<$ logical operator $>$ | $<$ sequential
          operator $>$

$<$ arithmetic operator $>$: : $= + | - | \times | / | \div | \uparrow$

$<$ relational operator $>$: : $= < | \leq | = | \geq | > | \neq$

$<$ logical operator $>$: : $= \equiv | \supset | \vee | \wedge | \neg$ (7-2)

$<$ sequential operator $>$: : $= go\ to$ | if | $then$ | $else$ | for | do

$<$ separator $>$: : $= , | . |$ $_{10} | : | ; | := | \times | step | until | while |$
         $comment$

$<$ bracket $>$: : $= (|) | [|] | ‘ | ’ | begin | end$

$<$ declarator $>$: : $= own | Boolean | integer | real | array | switch |$
         $procedure$

$<$ specificator $>$: : $= string | label | value$

It will be noticed that the word delimiters are not enclosed in brackets indicating that they are not names but delimiting symbols. Symbols as any character are intended to name themselves. The side-by-side arrangement of symbol and word delimiters shows their identical syntactical meaning.

Most of the symbols in the above rules have the conventional meaning. For division the operators / and $\div$ are introduced. The operator / is commonly used for division while the operator $\div$ is defined only for two operands both of the type *integer* and yielding a result of type *integer*. The operator $\uparrow$ denotes exponentiation with the base on the left and the exponent on the right of the arrow. The symbol : =, to be considered as a single symbol, separates the left and right part in assignment statements and has the meaning to assign the value of the right to the left part. The symbol $\times$ denotes a space used within strings to space substrings which constitute words.

The punctuation symbols are used in their ordinary sense with the semicolon only applied for the separation of different statements or declarations. Square brackets enclose array declarations of subscripted variables. The apostrophes or string quotes "(" and ")" denote strings as a sequence of symbols or symbols and strings enclosed in the opening and closing quotes; e.g., ⟨abc or ⟨ab ⟨cd⟩⟩.

The word delimiter *comment* following a semicolon or *begin* introduces explanatory text without any effect on the action of the program. The sequence of symbols for the text shall not contain a semicolon because the next appearing semicolon marks the end of the text.

In ALGOL, identifiers are used for the identification of simple variables, arrays, labels, switches, and procedures. Identifiers are formed according to the following rule:

$$< \text{identifier} > : : = < \text{letter} > | < \text{identifier} >$$
$$< \text{letter} > | < \text{identifier} > < \text{digit} > \qquad (7\text{-}3)$$

The rule states that the class < identifier > can be produced as a set of symbols from the set of symbols named letter or as a set of strings by concatenation of the sets of symbols named identifier and letter or identifier and digit. In the latter concatenation letters appear before digits. Therefore an individual identifier is a single letter or a sequence of letters (lower case and capital) and digits which begin with a letter. Q, Paul, and V2 are correct identifiers, but not 2V.

Note that the concatenation or chaining of sets of symbols or strings is not specified for certain contexts of the strings what is typical for simple phrase structure languages. New sets are constructed from existing sets A and B according to two definitions, the union < A >|< B > (also written A U B, A V B, A + B) which expresses that the new set can have every string or sumbol which is either in A or in B, and the concatenation < A > < B > (also written AB) which expresses that the new set can have every string ab where a is in A and b is in B. A system of simultaneous implicit equations in unions of concatenations defines the family of sets which are the constituents of the language.

Before proceeding to the next higher level in the syntactical hierarchy consisting of variables and function designators a few words about the quantities named by identifiers are in order. Names are first given to these quantities in the form of a single letter or strings of letters and digits, to some of which values are assigned later during the execution of the program. The meaning of simple variable is clear by its distinction from subscripted variables.

An *array* is the combination of a set of data for which all elements are operated on in the same way. There is only one name for this array, and individual elements are called out by subscripts. In ALGOL subscripts cannot be written on a lowered line but they are enclosed in square brackets immediately following the name of the array. In this way subscripted variables are denoted by an array identifier followed by the subscripts enclosed in brackets. Every array requires an array declaration giving first the lower and then the upper bound for the values of the subscripts.

A set of subscripted variables a_1, a_2, ... a_n is written in ALGOL as *array* a $[1:n]$, or the elements a_{11} through a_{33} of a 3 × 3 matrix are written as *array* a$[1:3, 1:3]$.

Labels are used in ALGOL programs to mark statements for reference purposes, or more important to provide the capability of jumping to such labeled statements. The name by which the label is identified appears immediately in front of a statement, separated from the statement by a colon. The way in which the name is used implies that it denotes a label and there are no explicit declarations of labels.

The quantity *switch* is introduced as a condensed notation when reference is made to several labels to which control is transferred alternately depending on the value of a variable. A switch designator is defined as switch identifier followed by an expression in square barackets of the form s[i] where the value of the expression, evaluated during the program, designates the corresponding label of the switch.

Procedures are the subroutines of ALGOL. Procedure identifiers correspond to the name and procedure declarations to the description of subroutines. The call or application of a procedure is activated through the use of procedure statements. The procedure declaration which defines the procedure associated with a procedure identifier consists of a heading and a body. The heading contains the name (identifier), the formal parameters, and optional information about the type and kind of the formal parameters which facilitates the translation into machine code. The procedure body, the principal constituent of the procedure declaration, contains the statements describing the procedure.

Procedure identifiers are generally the names of functions which are solved by the procedures. Some standard functions for which corresponding identifier configurations are reserved are sqrt, sin, cos, arc tan, ln, exp, abs, sign. The name *sin* names the function and the function designator *sin* (E) defines the value of the function evaluated for the expression E. Function designators and procedure statements, both of which are used to initiate the execution of the procedure body, have the same syntactical structure: the procedure identifier followed by the actual parameter part. The actual parameters are identifiers, strings, or most generally expressions.

Preparatory to the execution of the procedure body the formal parameters quoted in the value part of the heading are assigned the values of the corresponding actual parameters. The procedure body, modified in this way, is then inserted in place of the procedure statement and executed.

The above replacement requires correspondence between the formal and actual parameters with regard to the number of entries and the kind and type of the parameters. Different kinds are identifier or expression, different types are *integer, real, Boolean.*

In ALGOL simple variables are declared as one of these types for clarity in the program and to facilitate the translation. Subscripted variables declared by an array declaration are understood to be of type real. If, however, the declared variables are of the type *integer* or *Boolean,* the array declaration has to be preceded by the corresponding type declarator, e.g., *integer, array* a, b[1:n]. The variables declared *real* or *integer* have values corresponding to these two types of numbers. Boolean variables assume only the values *true* and *false.*

In the preceding paragraphs quantities and types, as used in the ALGOL nomenclature, were discussed. In this connection also brief explanations were given about the syntactical structure and the semantics of variables and function designators. The next level in the hierarchy of ALGOL constituents is the all important level of *expressions.*

Particularly the *arithmetic expressions* which have been called the backbone of ALGOL provide by their construction for an efficient formulation of computational problems.

Arithmetic expressions are rules for computing numerical values. They are made up of operands, operators, and parentheses in cases which are ambiguous as to the sequence of operations. The operands which are called primaries are numbers, variables, function designators or arithmetic expressions.

With the arithmetic operators in the order of exponentiation, multiplying and adding, new expressions are formed which are called factor, term, and simple arithmetic expression. The syntax gives not only the precedence rule first " ↑ ", second "×", "/", "÷", third "+", "−", but it establishes also the rules for the general case with some or all operations missing by stating the alternate generic sequence < simple arithmetic expression > : : = < term > : : = < factor > : : = < primary >.

The < if clause > is used for Boolean and designational expressions and conditional statements. It is a concise form for stating the conditional choice from arithmetic expressions. The Boolean variables in the Boolean expression of the if clause are evaluated in sequence from left to right until one is found with the value *true*. Then the value of the simple arithmetic expression following the if clause is the value of the arithmetic expression. Otherwise the program goes to the arithmetic expression following the sequential operator *else;* this expression may have another if clause providing a chain of conditions.

Designational expressions which are primarily used in go to statements are either labels or switch designators when the label to which the program is to be switched depends on the value of a variable. Here the syntax also provides for the possibility to go to different labels depending on the condition given in the if clause.

Statements are the units of operation within ALGOL corresponding generally to instructions in machine language. They will be executed consecutively unless otherwise directed by go to and conditional statements.

Assignment statements direct the execution of computations and assign the value of an evaluated expression to one or several variables. The value which is obtained by the evaluation of the expression on the right side of the assignment statement is stored in the storage location assigned to the variable appearing on the left side.

Several variables can be linked with assignment symbols, as follows: n : =m : = n+ s means the assignment of the value of n + s to n and m; i : = i + 1 means the increase of the variable i by 1. The assignment statement V : = A ∧ B > C would give the Boolean variable V the value *true* when both A and B > C are true, otherwise the value would be *false*.

Go to statements direct the program to a statement whose

label has its value defined by a designational expression, thus interrupting the normal sequence of operations.

If statements and conditional statements make the execution of statements dependent on the running values of specified Boolean expressions.

There are two possible forms of the conditional statement, the if statement by itself and the if statement followed by the delimiter *else* defining the successor statement which can be again a conditional statement, setting up a chain of conditions. Otherwise both forms have the same operational effect as shown by the following example.

Example 7-1.   Use of If Statement
       10: *if* i > 0 *then*
       11: *begin* y $: =$ y $+ 1$; z $: =$ z $\times$ y ; *go to* 13 *end*
       12: z $: =$ y $+ 1$
       13: next statement
or: 10: *if* i > 0 *then*
       11: *begin* y $: =$ y $+ 1$; z $: =$ z $\times$ y *end*
            else
       12: z $: =$ y $+ 1$
       13: next statement

If the statement 11 is skipped due to 10 being false the program is directed to statement 12 in the first case automatically and in the second case by the delimiter *else* designating the successor. If 10 is true and 11 is executed, 12 is skipped automatically in the second case while in the first case the insertion go to 13 is required in order to skip 12.

For *statements* are a concise notation for the programming of loops or recursive processes.

The *for list* consisting of a series of arithmetic expressions is used when a statement S shall be evaluated according to an irregular sequence of expressions or numbers, e.g., as given by a table. When the set of expressions or numbers for which recursive evaluation shall be made progresses in a regular fashion the form E_1 *step* E_2 *until* E_3 is used, where E_1 is the first value in the set, E_2 is the stepping value, and E_3 is the upper or lower limit of the set which may not be a part of the set. The example 1 *step* 2 *until* 4 designates the numbers 1 and 3.

Procedure statements invoke the execution of a procedure body. They were briefly explained in the discussion of procedures.

Dummy statements execute no operations. They may be used to place a lable.

Declarations are used to define properties of identifiers. All identifiers of a program must be declared with the exemption of labels, formal parameters of procedure declarations, and some standard functions. ALGOL has type, array, switch, and procedure declarations.

Type declarations declare the type of simple variables as real or integer or Boolean.

Array declarations and procedure declarations have been explained in connection with the discussion about arrays and procedures.

Switch statements are produced by the assignment of designational expressions to switch identifiers.

Compound statements are any sequence of statements enclosed between the word delimiters *begin* and *end*. Some of the enclosed statements may already be compound, resulting in a form:

$$begin \; S; \; S; \ldots; \; S; \; begin \; S; \; S; \ldots; \; S \; end \; end$$

Two good reports by Bottenbruch[27] and Schwarz[28] are recommended to gain further insight and understanding of ALGOL.

The meaning and context of various ALGOL Constituents can be explained best by their use in some simple programming examples.

Example 7-2.   Simple Arithmetic Problem
A program for the evaluation of $Z = ay + by^2 - cy^3$ is written as follows:

```
real a, b, c, y, z;
begin read (a, b, c, y);
    z: = y × (a + y × (b − c × y));
    write (z)
end
```

The first line is a type declaration which tells that input and output parameters may assume values within the range of real numbers. The program, enclosed in the delimiters *begin* and *end*, consists of a sequence of three statements; the read, assignment and write statement.

The delimiters which enclose this sequence are also called statement parentheses.

Parentheses proper are used to determine the sequence and completion of actions. In read and write statements parentheses are required to indicate to the machine the complete set of input and output data. In expressions as on the right side of the above assignment statement the sequence of the evaluation is determined by the arrangement of parentheses and the precedence rule for arithmetic operations. The expression between a left and the matching right parenthesis is evaluated by itself first and the obtained value is used in subsequent calculations. In our case c is first multiplied by y, the obtained product is subtracted from b, the resulting value is multiplied by y, etc.

When the above function is to be evaluated in the interval i ≤ y ≤ k for values of y spaced by j the following program could be written.

```
begin read (a, b, c, i, j, k);
     y : = i;
L:    z : = y × (a + y × (b − c × y));
     write (z);
     y : = y + j;
     if y ≤ k then go to L
end
```

This program can be written in a shorter form using the for statement and combining the assignment and write statements.

```
begin read (a, b, c, i, j, k):
     for y : = i step j until k do
     begin write (y × (a + y × (b − c × y)))
     end
end
```

The delimiters *begin* and *end* may be used freely as statement parentheses in order to enhance the breakdown of a program.

Example 7-3. Summation Procedure.

For the formation of sums a general procedure can be written in the following form listing in parentheses the formal parameters l and u for the lower and upper bounds for which the sum shall be formed, f for the function to be summed, x for the argument of the function, and s for the sum.

> *procedure* sum (l, u, f, x, s);
>   *begin* s: = 0
>   *for* x: = l *step* 1 *until* u *do* s: = s + f
>   *end;*

For the summation of an array of numbers n(i) for i = 1, 2, . . . , 10 the procedure statement following the above procedure declaration would be

> *for* i : = 1 *step* 1 *until* 10 *do* read (n[i]);
> sum (1, 10, n[i], i, a);
> punch (a)

with the actual parameters corresponding to formal parameters listed behind sum.

The entire program may then be written as follows:

> 1. *begin real* a; *integer* i; *array* n[1:10];
> 2.   *procedure* sum (l, u, f, x, s);
> 3.   *begin* s : = 0
> 4.   *for* x : = l *step* 1 *until* u *do* s : = s + f
> 5.   *end;*
> 6.   *for* i : = 1 *step* 1 *until* 10 *do* read (n[i]);
> 7.   sum (1, 10, n[i], i, a);
> 8.   punch (a)
>   *end*

Lines 1 and 2 are the heading and lines 3, 4, and 5 the body of the procedure declaration; lines 6, 7, and 8 are the procedure statement or call.

Other Problem-Oriented Languages in wide use, are COBOL and FORTRAN.

COBOL, for Common Business Oriented Language, is an English Language programming system which was conceived and developed in 1959 and accepted and approved for publication and distribution in January, 1960, by the

Executive Committee of the Conference on Data Systems Languages (CODASYL). The statements in this language are not made in the formalistic way of ALGOL to which mathematicians are accustomed but in verbal form utilizing familiar business terms as applied to the processing of data for accounting, sorting, inventories, etc. COBOL programs, written in terms of everyday business, are easily comprehended and facilitate the communicating of business problems to computers. The precise meaning of the words used is extremely important and it must be defined as clearly as the symbols in ALGOL so that the machine can interpret them without ambiguity.

FORTRAN, for Formula Translation, is the IBM-version of an algorithmic language, similar to ALGOL. The FORTRAN language has been accepted not so much through some official agreement as through wide-spread, practical use. While ALGOL is machine independent the specifications for FORTRAN are influenced by the structure of the IBM general purpose scientific computers for which FORTRAN is written. As more advanced models of these computers were introduced, new versions of FORTRAN were also provided. FORTRAN I was originally written for the IBM 704, FORTRAN II is in use with the IBM 704 and IBM 709/7090 and FORTRAN IV for the IBM 7044 and 7094. A certain machine dependency of the source language simplifies the translation to the language of the corresponding machine but in order to keep this advantage the source language b ecomes subject to alterations with changes of the machines.

7-4. BASIC CONSIDERATIONS FOR COMPILERS

In the previous sections, source languages and programs were discussed with which the computer can be addressed in terms related to problems and independent of machines. For such languages, a computer program, called *compiler* or translator, is required to translate the source language into the machine language of a particular computer. The source program consists of words and symbols which have to be manipulated in such a way that the computer can work upon them according to its given operation code. Under the direction of the program called compiler the computer performs this symbol manipulation automatically. This process, specifically, is referred to as automatic programming, because the resulting machine program according to which the computer ultimately solves the problem is compiled or written automatically.

The compiler is written in a language different from both, source and machine languages. The language used for compilers is sometimes called language for symbol manipulation or *information* processing language[29,30].

The latter language has been developed for problems which are not defined in the sense of computational or accounting problems with reasonably deterministic solutions. Information processing languages are conceived for the handling of problems in the area of the so-called artificial intelligence such as game playing and heuristic approaches in the solving of problems or the proving of theorems. Formal algebraic procedures do not postulate intervening processes or incomplete knowledge at any step of the solution, while the heuristic method in problem solving, so characteristic of human behavior, is subject to these conditions.

Information processing languages, designed as programming systems for this type of problems, involve extensive manipulation of symbols, changes in storage requirement and data structure, and modification of procedures at various levels according to information which has been developed during the course of the problem. Many of these characteristics are also present in the process of compiling a program and compilers are utilizing concepts of information processing languages which are gaining rapidly in importance through their dual usage for "intelligence" problems and compilers. We are concerned here with the features of information processing languages which are applied to the design of compilers.

Some of these features are list structures, symbol arrays, recursive function definitions, flexible memory structure, and nesting of subroutines to permit the composition of programs of complex functions from more simple functions. A treatment of compilers as a major subject would require a detailed discussion of these and other features which are presently in a fluid state of development. The question of how to compile efficiently can only be answered after a thorough study and comparison of the various available processes. This text gives a brief description of the major compiler functions and the examples of translation processes have been selected for their simplicity, even though some sophistication in the schemes might give higher translation efficiency.

It must also be recognized that compiler and program running efficiency present conflicting requirements. Fast translation may be achieved at the expense of running efficiency while the later will be obtained only when the translator makes full use of the machine's properties in the translated code. The user will have to decide where to place the emphasis, depending on the type of his programs which might be either often changing programs with short running times, or extended and complex programs which are run many times.

The compiler functions can be broken down in a natural way following the steps from the listing of the input information in tables, through the decomposition of statements and the development of an intermediate or pseudo code, to the final assembly into a set of specific machine instructions.

These activities can be performed fastest by translating in one pass from the source into the machine language assuming correctly tested programs for which the intermediate assembly language is not needed as checkout tool. In many cases the two-pass translation is preferred going first from the source to the intermediate language and then to the machine language, allowing the user to see and eventually to correct his program in assembly language before it is translated into machine language. Most compilers have provisions to be run optionally either in the one-or two-pass mode. The following sections will deal mainly with the first phase of the two-pass system because this phase is to a large extent independent of particular machines.

Before going into the discussion of these compiler functions a word concerning the definition of the terms *translator* and *compiler* is in order. The term *translator* is used for programs which translate from one language to another, it may be from one machine language to another, or from source to assembly to machine language. A program connecting parameters into previously written subroutines is called a compiler; translation is usually a part of this. A useful way to classify and name the various types of programs is to consider a hierarchy in which each program is assigned to a level according to the scope of its activity. Compilers would be on a higher level in the programming hierarchy than translators because they perform the function of the latter and in addition the manipulation and integration of building blocks of already prepared programs.

Since compiler developments are manifold and in no way uniform it is indicated to consider first some basic principles and ideas which have evolved from original considerations concerning the design of compilers.

7-5. THE IT COMPILER

The first fully described and widely accepted automatic programming system was the IT Compiler, standing for Internal Translator, which was developed by A. J. Perlis[31] and associates for the IBM 650. In the introduction of Reference 31, characteristics of computable algorithms are described relevant to their automatic compilation and solution. A computable algorithm is defined as a finite collection of arithmetic operations or distinguishable processes tied together by a control function which unambiguously determines a successor for each process from a finite set of one or more possible successors. The first and final processes are designed by special values of the control function while otherwise the successor to each process is selected from among meaningful successors by a rule or a sequence of rules, each of which is reduced to a binary decision process. The automatic processing and compilation of information in digital computers makes extensive use of binary decisions which in computer terms basically compare the magnitude of two quantities. The selection of one of the two possible successors in the binary process depends on whether or not one quantity is greater than or equal to the other. Ultimately computers recognize symbols by their assigned and encoded values.

The flow charts described in Chapter 6 are graphs with the nodes representing the processes and with directed connections giving the structure of the control function. The compilation process starts from a problem formulation very similar to a verbal description of the flow chart as indicated by the previously shown ALGOL programs. For the IT compiler a particular formal language was specified to express the types of processes and control functions found in the flow charts by statements in the language in such a form that translation may be achieved uniquely.

Since the IBM 650 recognizes only the digits 0 through 9 and the Roman capital letters A through Z, delimiters such as arithmetic and logical operators, parenthesis, quotation and punctuation marks are represented by single alphabetical characters, e.g., S for plus, M for minus, L and R for left and right parenthesis. Each single alphabetical character has only one meaning in this language, except when it occurs in an English word. Special combinations of characters are defined for admissible variables and constants both of which are operands which form expressions when combined with an admissible operator character. The description of flow chart processes and linkages naturally leads to essentially the same types of statements for all compilers. For the IT compiler language the following statements are defined: substitution, conditional and unconditional linkage, halt, input, output, and iteration statement, the latter quite similar to the FOR statement in ALGOL.

There is also an extension statement in the IT language to tie subroutines as building blocks into the program thus extending the range of the language beyond the originally defined algebraic operations. The ability to piece together building blocks of existing programs makes the IT translator into a compiler.

The compilation process itself is determined by the manner in which the processed characters are examined. The IT compiler uses a symbol pair technique whereby successive pairs which are admissible according to the rules of the language are examined. The basic question as to which direction in the scanning process is more efficient is discussed in section 7-7. The IT compiler scans from right to left. Each admissible symbol pair has a unique effect on the compilation and is associated with a sub-program, called generator. Upon recognition of a meaningful symbol pair the respective sub-program is entered through a table. Each sub-program may consist of one or more instructions in assembly or machine language according to whether the compiler works in the two or one pass mode.

Binary and relational operations are compiled in the order in which the leftmost character of their left operands are found. For example, in the expression

$$(I1 + 2/I2) + Y1 \tag{7-4}$$

the parenthesis are required when the quotient is to be computed before adding to Y1. Otherwise the I of the variable I2 would be through examination of the pair/I the first leftmost character of a left operand to be found and the instructions for adding I2 and Y1 would be generated. With the parentheses the operations are completed in the order: first $I1 + 2$, then $I1 + 2/I2$, and finally $(I1 + 2/I2) + Y1$. Unary operations are compiled as they occur.

The overall working of the IT compiler in the two-pass mode is shown in Figure 7-3.

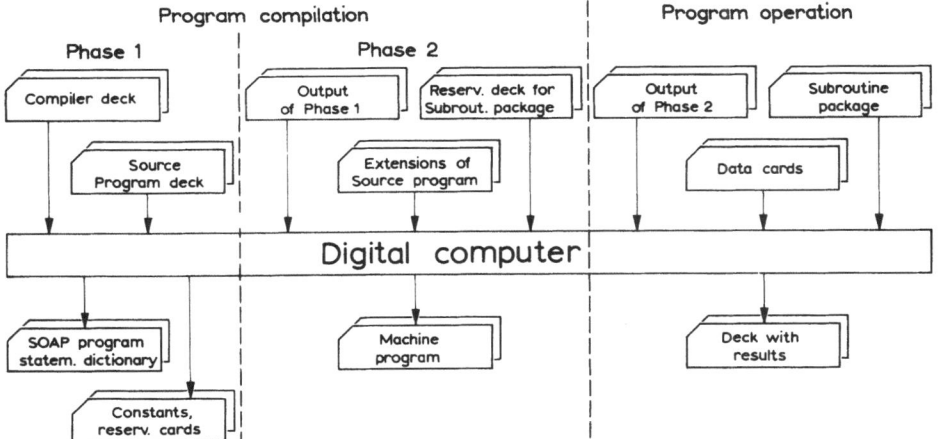

Fig. 7-3. Working of IT Compiler in Two-Pass Mode

In the two-pass mode the program compilation proceeds in two phases, the phase 1 translating the source program into a symbolic program and phase 2 performing the assembly into a specific machine code. During both phases compilation of building blocks takes place. The symbolic or assembly code of the IBM 650 for which the IT compiler was developed is called SOAP, for Symbolic Optimum Assembly Program. SOAP is a mnemonic code with each operation code containing exactly three letters which suggest the operations implied.

The input to the first compilation phase consists of the compiler deck and the complete program deck with the source language statements. The compiler deck is entered first, loading into the machine the program under the control of which the processed symbol pairs are examind and the associated sub-programs are called upon. This program which is called compiler is the real heart of the automatic compilation process.

The source program deck has a header card which provides information about the maximum subscript numbers of the variables, the maximum statement number, and the total number of locations required by extensions and the selected standard subroutine package. This information is necessary to determine the overall storage requirement and the allocation to the various program parts. If the available storage is exceeded, segmentation of the problem becomes necessary. The subsequent cards contain the source program statements with particular columns assigned to statement number and characters. Only one statement is permitted on a card, but longer statements can be punched on several cards with the statement number repeated on each card.

The output of the first phase consists of the symbolic program in SOAP code, a statement dictionary which is the first card punched for each statement providing linkages for transfer statements, a list of constants, and reservation cards to reserve space for the constants, problem variables, and the statement dictionary. During the first phase symbolic, specially lettered locations are assigned to all entities such as instructions, variables, constants, temporary storage required by parentheses, and entries to extensions. The symbolic locations of the variables are their names. The contiguous blocks of storage assigned to the various entries are indicated on the reservation cards.

The input to the second or assembly phase is the complete output of the first phase and additional decks with reservation cards for the selected subroutine package and any extensions in symbolic SOAP form which are called for by extension statements in the original source program. The augmentation by subroutines is an essential feature of any program, whether compiled automatically or by hand. The IT compiler provides subroutines in the form of specially used extensions and in the form of standard subroutine packages from which selection can be made dependent on whether or not exponentiation is used in the program. In the latter case three different packages are available for exponents in fixed point, floating point or mixed and undetermined arithmetic. During the second phase all symbolic addresses are assigned machine addresses and the output of this phase becomes the desired machine program.

For the operation or production run of the program the

selected subroutine package, the machine program of phase 2, and the deck with the problem data are entered. If the original program had more than one READ statement or uses such statement more than once, the data cards must be loaded in the order that they are required.

The described working steps of the IT compiler can be considered as typical for automatic programming systems. In the following sections some compiler functions are discussed in more detail.

7-6. THE LISTING PROCESS

When the string of symbols in which the source program is expressed is presented to the computer the individual symbols have to be distinguished, collected and ordered according to their meaning. This process, referred to as listing, is executed under the control of a program which is a part of the compiler. Details of this program vary with the different source languages to be processed. Since the structure of ALGOL has been introduced previously, as an example, the listing of ALGOL symbols will be discussed. The flow chart, presented in Figure 7-4, is a somewhat relabeled and simplified version of a program described by Robert W. Floyd.[32]

It may here be well to direct attention back to Figure 7-2, Hierarchy of ALGOL Constituents, and to the given production rules for some constituents, in particular rule 7-3 for identifiers. The compiler must be able to recognize and order all constituents which are formed according to the rules.

In order to keep explanation simple the presented program distinguishes only between identifiers and numbers which are problem constants. In the general case variables, arrays, labels, and procedures are listed on separate identifier tables under the control of the word delimiters *array, procedure,* and *label* which the machine recognizes as specially coded symbols. Furthermore, each block which has local identifiers must have its own tables. Identifiers which are listed, as in Fig. 7-4, without preceding declarator or specificator symbols are to be considered as variables.

Entities set in quotation mark, such as 'I1', N1', 'N2', or '.', '$_{10}$', '—' have assigned values which do not change during the program. The latter are the specified delimiters for forming numbers. Entities which are assigned changing values are I for identifier, N for numbers, CTR for counter, INCREM for

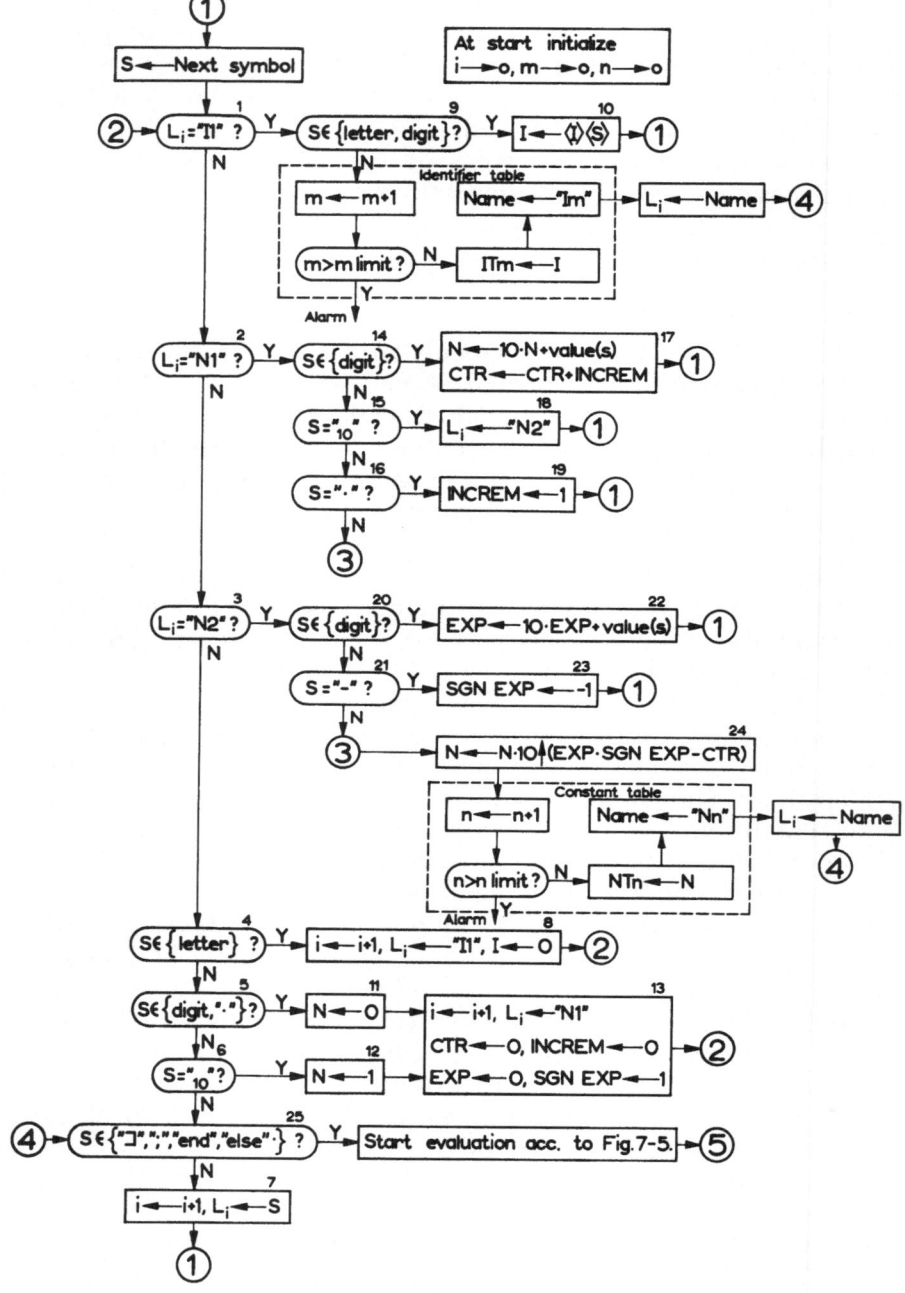

Fig. 7-4. Listing of ALGOL Symbols

increment, EXP for exponent, SGNEXP for sign exponent. Se
{digit, '.'} means that S is either the symbol '.' or one of the
symbols which belong to the set with the name digit.

The simplified program Fig. 7-4 assumes the successive
moving of symbols, one symbol at a time, into a station S
where they are examined. Groups of symbols which form
identifiers or numbers are first collected and then placed into
subsequent locations of the respective tables and assigned
names identifying the table and their location in the table
which is a block of memory set aside for the table. These
symbolic names of identifiers and numbers which refer to
their address location as well as the symbols which have not
been placed into tables, such as operator symbols, are entered
in a special storage L_i, called push-down list or stack. The
push-down list is particularly useful in the decomposition
process and will be discussed in the next section.

After these general remarks the working of the program will
be traced in more detail. At the beginning the location L_0 of
the push-down list contains a terminator symbol, therefore the
three checks 1, 2, and 3 are negative and the symbol in S is
examined by checks 4, 5, and 6. If all checks are negative the
stack is pushed down one position, the symbol in S is transferred into the stack and the next symbol is moved to S.

If the symbol is a letter, always the first character of an
identifier, the stack is pushed down and in the new high
position of the stack the fixed code word 'I1' is placed making
the program ready for the identifier processing through check
9 and box 10. If the identifier consists of one letter, such as
many variables, box 10 is passed only once, while otherwise
multi-character identifiers are concatenated in location I
through the process in box 10 after I has been cleared at the
beginning of each identifier processing. When check 9 indicates the end of the identifier string the content of I is
transferred into the moved up position IT_m of the identifier
table, and given the symbolic name 'I_m' expressing in one
word the position m in the table IT which was assigned to the
processed identifier. The name is placed in the stack replacing
the code word 'I1' and the program goes to check 25.

If S is a terminator symbol, indicating that all symbols of a
subscript array or a statement have been listed, the program
is directed to the evaluation or decomposition part of the
compiler. Otherwise, in block 7 the stack is pushed down and

the symbol in S is transferred into the new high position of the stack.

The number listing starts after the symbol S has been determined, through checks 5 and 6, to be either a digit or decimal point '.', or base '$_{10}$', the latter being the first symbol of a number representing an exponent. Boxes 11, 12, and 13 initialize the number processing, as box 8 does for identifiers, by placing the code word 'N1' in the pushed down stack and clearing the positions N for numbers, EXP for exponent, SGNEXP for sign exponent and a counter for the counting of fractional digits. The need for setting N to 1 when the number is only an exponent will be seen later.

After initializing, the symbol S is checked by 14, 15 and 16. Number digits are collected in N according to process 17 with the counter inactive as long as the increment is 0. For exponents a new code word 'N2' is placed in the stack by 18 and for fractions the counter is activated by 19. The setting of 'N2' must be made subsequent to 'N1' to avoid entering into the constant table an incomplete number with the exponent part missing. Exponent digits are collected in location EXP by 22, and 23 takes care of an eventual change in the sign exponent. Before entering the number in the constant table the values obtained for N, EXP, SGNEXP, and CTR are combined according to 24 with the correction-CTR on the exponent to account for the fractional digits. Here it can be seen that N must be set to 1 if only an exponent is processed. The process of listing and naming in the constant table is the same as for the identifier table.

The program described will process numbers correctly even if they are not normalized but presented to the computer in any common form such as $2.998 \cdot 10^8$ m/sec for the speed of light or $1.256 \cdot 10^{-6}$ volt·sec/Amp·m for the constant of induction. The numbers have only to be wrewritten according to the ALGOL notation as $2.998_{10}8$ or $1.256_{10}-6$.

The checks 1, 2, and 3 are arranged before checks 4, 5, and 6 to facilitate and speed up the collection of multi-character identifiers and numbers. The somewhat irregular numbering of checks and boxes was made solely as an aid to the verbal description in the sequence in which these parts are covered. As an example of the described procedure the listing of the following formula is given.

$$\text{begin } u := vl + 100 \times w \text{ end} \tag{7-5}$$

S ← 'begin' : L_1 ← 'begin'
S ← 'u'   : L_2 ← 'l1'; I ← 0; I ← 'u'
S ← ':='   : IT_1 ← 'u'; Name ← 'I_1'; L_2 ← 'I_1'; L_3 ← ':='
S ← 'v'   : L_4 ← 'l1'; I ← 0; I ← 'v'
S ← '1'   : I ← 'v1'
S ← '+'   : IT_2 ← 'v1'; Name ← 'I_2'; L_4 ← 'I_2'; L_5 ← '+'
S ← '1'   : L_6 ← 'N1'; N ← 0; N ← '1'
S ← '0'   : N ← '10'
S ← '0'   : N ← '100'
S ← '×'   : NT_1 ← '100'; Name ← 'N_1'; L_6 ← 'N_1'; L_7 ← '×'
S ← 'w'   : L_8 ← 'l1'; I ← 0; I ← 'w'
S ← 'end'   : IT_3 ← 'w'; Name ← "I_3'; L_8 ← 'I_3'

After the listing the push-down list has the following contents in its cells L_1 through L_8:

L_1	L_2	L_3	L_4	L_5	L_6	L_7	L_8
begin	I_1	:=	I_2	+	N_1	×	I_3

The *end* symbol causes the symbols placed in the push-down list to be evaluated, meaning to be transformed into machine operations. The evaluation is done in succession for each symbol from right to left until *begin* appears which cancels out against the *end* symbol. The evaluation or decomposition process is discussed in the following section.

7-7.   THE DECOMPOSITION PROCESS

As long as a string of symbols is processed only for listing purposes the direction of the process makes no difference. However, if the symbols of a formula are scanned for translation into a code, the direction of the scan effects the encoding process. Generally the right-to-left scan is more efficient for the coding of arithmetic operations on one-address machines with accumulators.

The symbolic coding for the formula

$$x := (a\omega_1 b)/(c\omega_2 d) \tag{7-6}$$

with the ω's expressing arbitrary arithmetic operators, leads for the two types of scan to the following sets of instructions:

Left-to-right	Right-to-left
CLA a	CLA c
ω_1 b	ω_2 d
STR L_1	STR L_1
CLA c	CLA a
ω_2 d	ω_1 b
STR L_2	DIV L_1
CLA L_1	STR x
DIV L_2	
STR x	

The presented compiler processes left-to-right during the listing and naming of simple variables and constants and from right-to-left during the decomposition or evaluation of formulae, as described in this section. For subscripted variables the subscripts, which may be either a list or an expression, are evaluated as they occur in order to have them available at the formula evaluation time in coded form. This evaluation is also done from right-to-left.

The listing and decomposition algorithms, shown in Fig. 7-4 and Fig. 7-5, are integral parts of the compiler. Whenever a right bracket ']' indicates the end of a processed subscript array or ';', 'end', or 'else' indicate the end of a processed statement or program part, the compiler starts to evaluate what has been processed so far until upon arrival of a left bracket '[' or 'begin' the program is returned to the listing. Box 25 in Fig. 7-4 gives the connection to the decomposition algorithm Fig. 7-5.

This type of information processing and manipulating is greatly facilitated by a concept which is now generally known as push-down list, stack or cellar. Some preliminary ideas leading to this concept were contributed by Rutishauser[33]. Push-down lists have the "last-in-first-out" principle which is very useful in the processing of symbol structures with bracketing character.

When the sequence of symbols includes operating rules according to the syntax of the processed language, such as parentheses prescribing an ordering of operations or precedence rules, as those defined in ALGOL for arithmetic operators, a simple sequential transformation into machine instructions is not possible. During translation, symbols which can not be evaluated immediately have to be passed by temporar-

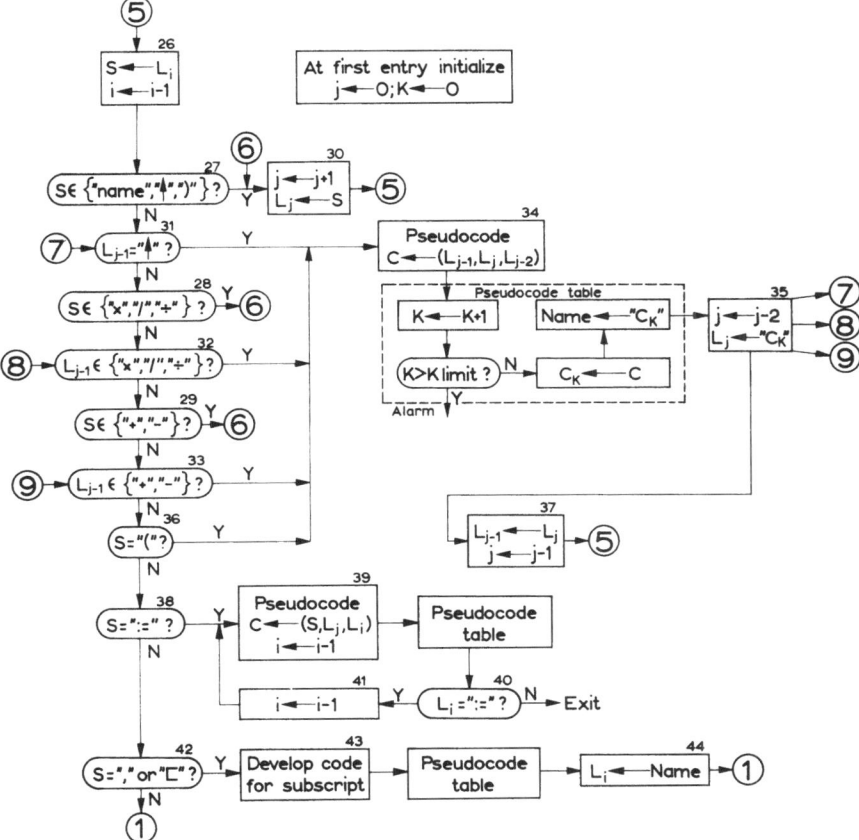

Fig. 7-5. Arithmetic Decomposition Algorithm

ily but they must be available at the time when their evaluation is called for by subsequent symbols.

The symbols passed by are temporarily stored and pushed down in the stack whose highest position contains always the last symbol introduced and makes it available for comparison with the next symbol. Based on the comparison the new symbol is either transferred to the stack pushing down the symbol it was compared with, or a sub-program is started generating a pseudo code for the evaluation of symbols which have been temporarily introduced in the stack. In the process the evaluated symbols are removed from the stack in reversed order and the name of the generated code is placed in the new high position of the stack.

For many machines it is convenient for further translation into machine instructions to have the pseudo code include the operator symbol and the addresses of the operands. One bit in the code may be used to distinguish between fixed and floating point mode with one or zero in the designated bit position. For codes, other than for binary operations, e.g., for subscripts, the second address portion in the code may be filled with zeros.

Push-down storage is implemented on existing machines, mostly by programmed address modification and it is expected that it will be realized in future machines by an appropriate logic and circuit design.

The arithmetic decomposition algorithm Fig. 7-5 uses a push-down storage with the locations L_j in the above described manner, while in the stack L_i of Fig. 7-4 the symbols, processed during listing, are pushed down ($i \leftarrow i + 1$) left-to-right and they are pushed up ($i \leftarrow i - 1$) right-to-left during evaluation.

In the following the arithmetic decomposition algorithm Fig. 7-5 is explained in more detail. The algorithm is based on syntax rules of ALGOL.

At entry to the decomposition process in box 26 the symbol in the highest position of stack L_i is moved in the "last-in first-out" fashion for examination and comparison purposes to station S which may or may not be the same as in Fig. 7-4. Stack L_i is pushed up to make the next symbol in the stack available at the high position. Positive checks 27, 28, and 29 cause a temporary storage of the processed symbol into stack L_j which is pushed down every time a symbol is entered (box 30).

Checks 31, 32, and 33 determine if the coding of arithmetic operations is indicated. The checks are performed on the symbol in the next to the highest position L_{j-1}, in order to have the next symbol already in L_j in case that the pseudocode shall be formed according to box 34. The pseudocode places the arithmetic operator, found in L_{j-1}, in the first portion of the code and the name or addresses of the symbols in L_j and L_{j-2}, notably operands, in the remaining part of the code. The sequence of checks 31, 32, and 33 is arranged according to the ALGOL precedence rule: exponentiation first, multiplication and division next, addition and subtraction last. After placing the generated code on the pseudocode table and giving the code the name 'C_k' the stack is pushed up two positions and the name of the code is placed in the new high position L_j (box 35).

A left parenthesis directs the program directly to the coding of the preceding symbols. If for this the general program in boxes 34 and 35 is used, the program entering from 36 has to exit to box 37 where corrections with regard to the previously processed right parenthesis are made.

For example, the evaluation of the expression

$$(a+b)/(c+d) \tag{7-7}$$

proceeds from right to left in the following way:

$S \leftarrow$ ')' ; $L_1 \leftarrow$ ')'
$S \leftarrow$ 'd' ; $L_2 \leftarrow$ 'd'
$S \leftarrow$ '+' ; $L_3 \leftarrow$ '+'
$S \leftarrow$ 'c' ; $L_4 \leftarrow$ 'c'
$S \leftarrow$ '(' ; Code $\leftarrow$ ('+', 'c', 'd'); $C_1 \leftarrow$ Code; Name $\leftarrow$ 'C_1';
$\quad L_2 \leftarrow$ "C_1'

At this stage, after execution of box 35, the correction in box 37 eliminates the right parenthesis in L_1 by $L_1 \leftarrow L_2$ and compensates the push down, caused by this transfer, by $j \leftarrow j - 1$. Then the evaluation continues:

$S \leftarrow$ '/' ; $L_2 \leftarrow$ '/'
$S \leftarrow$ ')' ; $L_3 \leftarrow$ ')'
$S \leftarrow$ 'b' ; $L_4 \leftarrow$ 'b'
$S \leftarrow$ '+' ; $L_5 \leftarrow$ '+'
$S \leftarrow$ 'a' ; $L_6 \leftarrow$ 'a'
$S \leftarrow$ '(' ; Code $\leftarrow$ ('+', 'a', 'b'); $C_2 \leftarrow$ Code; Name $\leftarrow$ 'C_2';
$\quad L_4 \leftarrow$ 'C_2'

After the evaluation the pseudocode table contains the following codes:

$$'C_1' : \text{'+', 'c', 'd'}$$
$$'C_2' : \text{'+', 'a', 'b'}$$
$$'C_3' : \text{'/', 'C_2', 'C_1'}$$

From the pseudocodes the following symbolic coding might be generated:

CLA   c
ADD   d
STR t_1 (temporary storage 1)
CLA   a
ADD   b
STR t_2
CLA t_2
DIV t_1
STR   T   (storage assigned to result)

Continuing with the description of Fig. 7-5, the positive check 38 directs the program to the generation of the code in box 39 which assigns the coded result in L_j to the variable in L_i. Stack L_i is then pushed up and interrogated by 40 if there is another assignment symbol, in which case the next variable is pushed up in L_i and an additional assignment code is generated. The arrangement takes care of serial assignments which are possible in ALGOL, such as a : = b : = expression.

The encoding of subscripts is done under control of check 42 and the name of the code is placed back in the listing stack L_i. Therefore, during listing of statements with subscripted variables the program moves back and forth between Fig. 7-4 and Fig. 7-5, whereby the closing bracket of a subscript array ']' directs the program to the coding part. After the name of the subscript code has been placed in the high position of L_i the program goes back to the listing part.

For further illustration, the statement (7-5) is evaluated with the described decomposition algorithm. The statement has been listed in the preceding section and is stored after listing, with names for variables and constants referring to their assigned addresses, in stack L_i in the following form:

$$begin\ I_1 := I_2 + N_1 \times I_3 \tag{7-8}$$

The evaluation can now be shown in a more realistic form than that of the previous example (7-7) because at evaluation time variables and constants generally have been replaced by their addresses. The evaluation proceeds as follows, with the locations L now referring to stack L_j:

$S \leftarrow \text{`}I_3\text{'}$ ; $L_1 \leftarrow \text{`}I_3\text{'}$

$S \leftarrow \text{`}\times\text{'}$ ; $L_2 \leftarrow \text{`}\times\text{'}$

$S \leftarrow \text{`}N_1\text{'}$ ; $L_3 \leftarrow \text{`}N_1\text{'}$

$S \leftarrow \text{`}+\text{'}$ ; Code $\leftarrow$ (`$\times$', `$N_1$', `$I_3$'); $C_1 \leftarrow$ Code; Name $\leftarrow$ `C_1';
  $L_1 \leftarrow \text{`}C_1\text{'}$; $L_2 \leftarrow \text{`}+\text{'}$

$S \leftarrow \text{`}I_2\text{'}$ ; $L_3 \leftarrow \text{`}I_2\text{'}$

$S \leftarrow \text{`}:=\text{'}$ ; Code $\leftarrow$ (`+', "I_2', `$C_1$'); $C_2 \leftarrow$ Code; Name $\leftarrow$ `C_2';
  $L_1 \leftarrow \text{`}C_2\text{'}$

  Code $\leftarrow$ (`:=', `I_1', `$C_2$'); $C_3 \leftarrow$ Code; Name $\leftarrow$ `C_3'

From the codes, placed on the pseudocode table, the compiler then develops the symbolic and the machine code.

The important compiler functions of listing and decomposition can be treated in a rather general, machine-independent way, while the subsequent translation into symbolic code and the assembly of the machine code are dependent on the command structure of particular machines.

7-8. COMPILER SUMMARY

In the preceding sections some basic compiler functions were discussed and explained in detail by means of practical and simple algorithms, but it must be understood that the overall functioning of a compiler is much more complicated. The complication stems not only from the variety but also from the intermixing of the functions performed.

The macroscopic structure of a compiler can be divided into sections in different ways. One quite common division is into storage allocation and listing algorithm, decomposition or evaluation algorithm, and translation and assembly algorithm. Some functions such as listing and storage allocation are not confined to one part of the program, but are performed throughout as e.g., the listing of the codes generated by the decomposition algorithm. The latter generates, in general, not only the code for the evaluation of expressions but also the code for control according to transfer, conditional, and reiteration statements.

The translation algorithm translates each line of the pseudocode array into symbolic machine code. It would be possible to produce machine code from the original scan which already takes care of storage allocation. But the generation of the pseudocode array is generally preferred because the translation from the array form to machine code can be done with a relatively simple algorithm, avoiding redundancies and facilitating optimizations, such as reusing of temporary locations and elimination of common subexpressions. If the compiler translates first into symbolic code, the remaining final assembly is a symbolic assembly program which is also used in machine dependent programming. The direct assembly from the array form requires a combination of translation and assembly algorithms.

For the description of some compiler functions different terms are used which mean practically the same. The terms evaluation, decomposition, and coding are all used for the translation of formulas or subscript arrays into pseudocodes. The process of going from pseudo to symbolic code is usually referred to as translation while going from symbolic to object machine code is called assembly. The symbolic code from which the latter process starts is also called assembly code.

The decomposition process is the most important function of the compiler and handles the essential problem of translation from a language with bracket structure, such as ALGOL, to the bracket-free and sequential machine language. Despite the great variety of existing decomposition algorithms, it may be stated that there are basically two different approaches to the problem.

One is shown in the preceding algorithm in section 7-7, which recognized operators and parentheses and with them the syntactical groups that are to be produced as output. This algorithm is the so-called "jiggling scan" expression scanner.

The other approach encodes syntactical elements, such as single variables and operators or expressions and connective operations, and places each definition for syntactical groups using the same code on a separate row of a so-called syntax table, which may be made general enough to be used for the processing of different statements. The table is read into the computer as data, and at each step of the processing of an encoded statement the table is searched to identify the syntactical elements. Prior identification of the components of statements, such as variables, constants, and operators will greatly help to increase the efficiency of the search. But for the decomposition, particularly at the level of expressions, the jiggling scan is usually more efficient.

As an example, the compiler PSYCO for ALGOL 60 on the CDC 1604 requires a complete syntax table of the source language for the translation. If such a table is developed for other source languages, the same compiler could be used for the other languages, merely by changing the tables.

Many constituents of ALGOL and other source languages are defined in a recursive manner, which means, for example, a constituent of an arithmetic expression may be another arithmetic expression. The recursive nature of language entities requires dealing with a nesting of structures. Syntactical states must be defined as controlling elements for the processing of symbols, similar to the states I1, N1, N2 in Fig. 7-4. In this simple example the controlling states are placed temporarily in the same push-down list L_i which is used for the listing of symbols. To accomodate the processing of recursive subroutines which can slave itself without loss of information on the former level, the controlling states must be placed in a separate control stack. The state controlling the work on an inner structure pushes down the state for the containing structure which is pushed up again when work on the latter structure is resumed.

In a very general way a switch matrix can be developed with column designations according to the controlling syntactical states and rows according to the processed syntactical elements. For the possible coincidences of states and processed elements the corresponding subroutines are entered to which the program shall be switched. A fully developed switch matrix for ALGOL is shown in "Recursive Processes and ALGOL Translation" by Grau[34]. The complete compiler algorithm can be expressed in a very concise form by such a matrix and a set of subprograms for the subroutines which have to be executed according to the matrix.

This brings us back in an interesting way to the statement which was made at the beginning of the book, that computer action and output is determined by the present state and the momentary input of the computer.

APPENDIX A

Summary of Instructions by Alphabetic Code

INSTRUCTION	CODE	DESCRIPTION OF OPERATION
Add	**ADD**	(L) + (A) → A; (L) unchanged
AND logical	**ADL**	(A-numeric) AND (L) → A-numeric; (L) unchanged
A left shift	**ALS**	Shift (A); left bits lost; sign unchanged
A right shift	**ARS**	Shift (A); right bits lost; sign unchanged
Clear A and add	**CLA**	(L) → A; (L) unchanged
Clear A and subtract	**CLS**	−(L) → A; (L) unchanged
Complement magnitude	**COM**	Complement (A); sign unchanged
Copy	**CPY**	Copy to or from locations specified by L
Divide	**DIV**	(A) or (AQ) ÷ (L) → Q; remainder → A
Enter index	**ENX**	(Address part of ENX) or index → X
Halt and jump	**HJP**	Stop computer and jump to address in HJP after pressing start key
Halt	**HLT**	Stop computer
Halt and procede	**HPR**	Stop computer and procede to next instruction after pressing start key
Jump when A is minus	**JAM**	If (A) neg., go to address in JAM, otherwise to next instruction
Jump when A is non-zero	**JAN**	If (A) ≠ 0, go to address in JAN, otherwise to next instruction
Jump when A is plus	**JAP**	If (A) pos., go to address in JAP, otherwise to next instruction
Jump when A is zero	**JAZ**	If (A) = 0, go to address in JAZ, otherwise to next instruction
Jump and increment	**JIX**	(X) + D → X, go to address in JIX
Unconditional jump	**JMP**	Go to instruction in address part of JMP
Jump on index	**JPX**	If (X) > D, (X) − D → X, go to address in JPX otherwise to next instruction
Jump when Q is minus	**JQM**	If (Q) neg., go to address in JQM, otherwise to next instruction
Jump when Q is plus	**JQP**	If (Q) pos., go to address in JQP, otherwise to next instruction
Load logical	**LDL**	(L) → A-numeric; (L) unchanged
Load Q-register	**LDQ**	(L) → Q; (L) unchanged
Load address into X	**LDX**	(Address part of L) → X; (L) unchanged
Long AQ left shift	**LLS**	Shift (AQ); Q_1 → A_{35}; sign Q → sign A
Long AQ right shift	**LRS**	Shift (AQ); A_{35} → Q_1; sign A → sign Q
Multiply	**MPY**	(L) × (Q) → A or AQ; (L) unchanged
No operation	**NOP**	Machine takes next instruction in sequence
OR logical	**ORL**	(A-numeric) OR (L) → A-numeric; (L) unchanged
Q left shift	**QLS**	Shift (Q); left bits lost; sign unchanged
Q right shift	**QRS**	Shift (Q); right bits lost; sign unchanged
Read select	**RDS**	Select for reading component specified by L

Store A	**STA**	$(A) \rightarrow L$; (A) unchanged
Store logical	**STL**	$(A\text{-numeric}) \rightarrow L$; $(A\text{-numeric})$ unchanged
Store Q	**STQ**	$(Q) \rightarrow L$; (Q) unchanged
Store X	**STX**	$(X) \rightarrow$ address part of L; (X) unchanged
Store zero	**STZ**	(L) replaced by zeros; sign of L plus
Subtract	**SUB**	$(A) - (L) \rightarrow A$; (L) unchanged
Write select	**WRS**	Select for writing component specified by L

APPENDIX B
Powers of Two

2^n	n	2^{-n}
1	0	1.0
2	1	0.5
4	2	0.25
8	3	0.125
16	4	0.062 5
32	5	0.031 25
64	6	0.015 625
128	7	0.007 812 5
256	8	0.003 906 25
512	9	0.001 953 125
1 024	10	0.000 976 562 5
2 048	11	0.000 488 281 25
4 096	12	0.000 244 140 625
8 192	13	0.000 122 070 312 5
16 384	14	0.000 061 035 156 25
32 768	15	0.000 030 517 578 125
65 536	16	0.000 015 258 789 062 5
131 072	17	0.000 007 629 394 531 25
262 144	18	0.000 003 814 697 265 625
524 288	19	0.000 001 907 348 632 812 5
1 048 576	20	0.000 000 953 674 316 406 25
2 097 152	21	0.000 000 476 837 158 203 125
4 194 304	22	0.000 000 238 418 579 101 562 5
8 388 608	23	0.000 000 119 209 289 550 781 25
16 777 216	24	0.000 000 059 604 644 775 390 625
33 554 432	25	0.000 000 029 802 322 387 695 312 5
67 108 864	26	0.000 000 014 901 161 193 847 656 25
134 217 728	27	0.000 000 007 450 580 596 923 828 125
268 435 456	28	0.000 000 003 725 290 298 461 914 062 5
536 870 912	29	0.000 000 001 862 645 149 230 957 031 25
1 073 741 824	30	0.000 000 000 931 322 574 615 478 515 625
2 147 483 648	31	0.000 000 000 465 661 287 307 739 257 812 5
4 294 967 296	32	0.000 000 000 232 830 643 653 869 628 906 25
8 589 934 592	33	0.000 000 000 116 415 321 826 934 814 453 125
17 179 869 184	34	0.000 000 000 058 207 660 913 467 407 226 562 5
34 359 738 368	35	0.000 000 000 029 103 830 456 733 703 613 281 25

REFERENCES

1. A. W. Burks, H. H. Goldstine, and J. von Neumann, *Preliminary Discussion of the Logical Design of an Electronic Computing Instrument.* PRINCETON, N.J.: Institute for Advanced Study, 1st ed., June 28, 1946.
2. W. H. Ware (ed.), *Soviet Computer Technology – 1959.* Comm. of Ass. for Comp. Mach., March 1960.
3. George Boole, *Investigation of the Laws of Thought.* NEW YORK: Dover Publications, 1854, reprint in 1951.
4. D. Hilbert and W. Ackerman, *Principles of Mathematical Logic.* 1928 in German; reprinted in English translation. NEW YORK: Chelsea Publishing Company, 1950.
5. Claude E. Shannon, *A Symbolic Analysis of Relay and Switching Circuits.* Trans. NEW YORK: AIEE, 1938, 57, pp. 713-723.
6. E. W. Veitch, *A Chart Method for Simplifying Truth Functions.* Proc. ACM Meeting, May 1952, pp. 127-133.
7. M. Karnaugh, *The Map Method for Synthesis of Combinational Logic Circuits,* Trans, NEW YORK: AIEE, Nov. 1953, 72, pp. 593-599.
8. W. V. Quine, *The Problem of Simplifying Truth Functions,* Am. Math. Monthly, Oct. 1952, 59, No. 8, pp. 521-531.
9. D. A. Huffman, *The Synthesis of Sequential Switching Circuits,* PHILADELPHIA: Journal of the Franklin Institute, 1954, 257, Nos. 3 and 4, pp. 161-190, and 275-303.
10. George H. Mealy, *A Method for Synthesizing Sequential Circuits.* NEW YORK: Bell System Technical Journal, September 1955, 34, pp. 1045-1079.
11. E. F. Moore, *Gedanken Experiments on Sequential Machines.* PRINCETON, N.J.: Princeton University Press, Automata Studies, 1956, pp. 129-153.
12. Morris Rubinoff, *Remarks on the Design Sequential Circuits.* University of Pennsylvania, The Moore School of Electrical Engineering, March 15, 1957.
13. A. M. Turing, *On Computable Numbers with an Application to the Entscheidungs Problem.* Proc. of the London Math. Soc., Ser. 2, Vol 42, 1936, pp. 230-265; Correction, Ibid., Vol 43, 1937, pp. 544-546.
14. N. Wiener, *Cybernetics,* CAMBRIDGE, MASS.: The Technology Press, 1948, and reprints.
15. A. Church, *The Calculi of Lambda-Conversion,* PRINCETON: Princeton University Press, 1941, Annals of Mathematics Studies, No. 6.
16. A. A. Markov, *Theory of Algorithms* (Russian), Moscow: USSR Academy of Sciences, Steklov Mathematical Institute, 1954.

17. S. C. Kleene, *Representation of Events in Nerve Nets and Finite Automata*, PRINCETON: Princeton University Press, Automata Studies, edited by C. E. Shannon and J. McCarthy, 1956, pp. 3-41.

18. A. A. Liapunov, *Mathematical Investigations Related to the Use of Electronic Computing Machines*, Mathematik USSR 2a Sorok Let 1917-57, Moscow, 1959, pp. 857-877; translated by Friedman, Comm. of Ass. for Comp. Mach., February 1960, pp. 107-118.

19. J. McCarthy, *A Basis for a Mathematical Theory of Computation*, Prel. Rpt., Proc. of Western Joint Comp. Conf., May 1961, pp. 225-238.

20. H. H. Goldstine and von Neumann, *Planning and Coding of Problems for an Electronic Computing Instrument*, PRINCETON, N.J.: Inst. for Adv. Study, 1947.

21. S. Gorn, *Standardized Programming Methods and Universal Coding*, Journal of the Ass. for Comp. Mach., July 1957.

22. United Aircraft Corporation, *SHARE Assembler, UA SAP 1 and 2*, HARTFORD, CONN., March 1956 and following additions.

23. Edward H. Friend, *Sorting on Electronic Computer Systems*, Journal of the Ass. for Comp. Mach., Vol 3, July 1956.

24. R. D. Elbourn and W. H. Ware, *The Evolution of Concepts and Languages of Computing*, Proc. of the IRE, May 1962, pp. 1059-1066.

25. P. Naur (ed.), et al., *Report on the Algorithmic Language ALGOL 60*, Comm. of the Ass. for Comp. Mach., Vol 3, May 1960, pp. 299-314; or Numer. Math. 2, 1960, pp. 106-136.

25a. P. Naur (ed.), et al., *Revised Report on the Algorithmic Language ALGOL 60*, Comm. of the Ass. for Comp. Mach., Vol 6, January 1963, pp. 1-17.

26. J. W. Backus, *The Syntax and Semantics of the proposed International Algebraic Language of the Zurich ACM-GAMM Conference*, Proc. of International Conference on Information Processing, 1959, MUNICH: Oldenbourg, 1960, pp. 125-131.

27. H. Bottenbruch, *Structure and Use of ALGOL 60*. Journal of the Ass. for Comp. Mach., Vol 9, No. 2, April 1962, pp. 161-221.

28. H. R. Schwarz, *An Introduction to ALGOL*. Comm. of the Ass. for Comp. Mach., Vol. 5, No. 2, February 1962, pp. 82-95.

29. A. Newell, J. C. Shaw, and H. A. Simon, *Empirical Explorations of the Logic Theory Machine: A Case Study in Heuristic*. Proc. of Western Joint Comp. Conf., February 1957, pp. 218-239.

30. A. Newell and F. M. Tonge, *An Introduction to Information Processing Language V*, Comm. of the Ass. for Comp. Mach., April 1960, pp. 205-211.

31. A. J. Perlis, J. W. Smith, and H. R. Van Zoeren, *Internal Translator IT, A Compiler for the 650*. PITTSBURGH, PA.: Carnegie Institute of Technology, Computation Center, June 1958.

32. Robert W. Floyd, *An Algorithm for Coding Efficient Arithmetic Operations*, Comm. of the Ass. for Comp. Mach., January 1961, pp. 42-51.

33. H. Rutishauser, *Automatische Rechenplan-fertigung bei programgesteuerten Rechenmaschinen*. ZURICH: Mitt. f. Angew. Math. der ETH No. 3, 1952.

34. A. A. Grau, *Recursive Processes and ALGOL Translation*. Comm. of the Ass. for Comp. Mach., January 1961, pp. 10-15.

BIBLIOGRAPHY

Aiken, *Synthesis of Electronic Computing and Control Circuits.* CAMBRIDGE, MASS.: Harvard Press

Caldwell, *Switching Circuits and Logical Design.* NEW YORK & LONDON: Wiley

Eng. Res. Ass., *High-Speed Computing Devices.* NEW YORK: McGraw-Hill

Hamming, *Numerical Methods for Scientists and Engineers.* NEW YORK: McGraw-Hill

Hildebrand, *Introduction to Numerical Analysis.* NEW YORK: McGraw-Hill

Householder, *Principles of Numerical Analysis.* NEW YORK: McGraw-Hill

Keister, Ritchie, Washburn, *The Design of Switching Circuits.* PRINCETON, N.J.: D. Van Nostrand

Larrivee and Stibitz, *Mathematics and Computers.* NEW YORK: McGraw-Hill

McCracken, *Digital Computer Programming,* NEW YORK: Wiley

Pfister, *Logical Design of Digital Computers.* NEW YORK: Wiley

Ralston and Wilf, *Mathematical Methods for Digital Computers.* NEW YORK: Wiley

Richards, *Arithmetic Operations in Digital Computers.* PRINCETON, N.J.: D. Van Nostrand

Scarborough, *Numerical Mathematical Analysis,* BALTIMORE: John Hopkins Press

Scott, *Analog and Digital Computer Technology.* NEW YORK: McGraw-Hill

Shannon and McCarthy, *Automata Studies.* PRINCETON: Princeton University Press

Wilkes, *Automatic Digital Computers.* NEW YORK: Wiley

Handbook of Automation, Computation and Control. Vol. 2 Computers and Data Processing, NEW YORK: Wiley

INDEX